In the Front Door

D0145500

In the Front Door

Creating a College-Going Culture of Learning

Hugh Mehan

with
Gordon C. Chang, Makeba Jones, and Season S. Mussey

Paradigm Publishers
Boulder • London

All rights reserved. No part of this publication may be transmitted or reproduced in any media or form, including electronic, mechanical, photocopy, recording, or informational storage and retrieval systems, without the express written consent of the publisher.

Copyright © 2012 Paradigm Publishers

Published in the United States by Paradigm Publishers, 5589 Arapahoe Avenue, Boulder, CO 80303 USA.

Paradigm Publishers is the trade name of Birkenkamp & Company, LLC, Dean Birkenkamp, President and Publisher.

Library of Congress Cataloging-in-Publication Data

Mehan, Hugh, 1941-
  In the front door : creating a college-going culture of learning / Hugh Mehan ; with Gordon C. Chang, Makeba Jones, and Season S. Mussey.
    p. cm.
  Includes bibliographical references and index.
  ISBN 978-1-61205-103-1 (hardcover : alk. paper) — ISBN 978-1-61205-104-8 (pbk. : alk. paper)
  1. College preparation programs—United States. 2. Educational equalization—United States. 3. Children with social disabilities—Education (Secondary)—United States.
4. Charter schools—United States. I. Chang, Gordon C. II. Jones, Makeba. III. Mussey, Season S. IV. Title.
  LB2351.2.M44 2012
  379.2'6—dc23

                                                                        2012017941

Printed and bound in the United States of America on acid-free paper that meets the standards of the American National Standard for Permanence of Paper for Printed Library Materials.

Designed and Typeset by Straight Creek Bookmakers.

16 15 14 13   2 3 4 5

Contents

Acknowledgments

Cecil Lytle prodded and cajoled me for years to help him build a college-prep school for low-income students. His dream is being realized on our campus and on others he has inspired. This book extends the trajectory of CREATE, The Preuss School, and our other partnership schools begun in *The Burden of Excellence* (Lytle 2007). I am deeply grateful for Cecil's compelling vision and inspiring leadership.

I am also deeply grateful for the financial support provided by the Spencer Foundation. The generosity of the foundation enabled me to form a robust research group within CREATE composed of committed scholars and powerful educators. Indeed, perhaps the most gratifying aspect of the entire experience has been the opportunity to interact with the innovative and dedicated educators and parents at Preuss, Gompers, and Lincoln.

Kathy Mooney provided incisive and provocative suggestions that improved the quality of the manuscript.

I am especially grateful to Margaret Riel for constant support and conversations in which she challenged my inchoate thoughts. When I was faced with technical meltdowns, she always restored the natural order.

—*Hugh Mehan*

Chapter 1

Introduction

The children of ethnic minorities and recent immigrants, and those from low-income families, have always received inferior education in the United States. In colonial times, Native Americans, blacks, and Catholics were denied access to public schools attended by whites and Protestants. The US Supreme Court legitimated the doctrine of "separate but equal" education in the 1896 *Plessey v. Ferguson* decision. Black and other minority students were relegated to schoolhouses that were separate, certainly. But because these schools were allocated fewer educational resources and assigned less-qualified teachers, they were hardly equal.

Minority adults have suffered many similar indignities. Even after slavery was abolished, when black soldiers returned from war, they were denied service in restaurants and hospitals. Black women working as domestic servants always came and went by the back door. Black and "Latin" athletes and entertainers who were cheered on the playing field and applauded on the stage stayed in run-down boarding houses while their white colleagues stayed in fancy hotels. If they could get work at all, minorities were paid less than their white counterparts for the same job. Or they labored in jobs no others wanted. In the Jim Crow era of racial discrimination, virtually all black Americans traveling across the United States searched cautiously for a place where they could eat, sleep, buy gas, or go out at night without the threat of humiliation or violence (Green 1964). Churches, schools, theaters, bars, swimming pools, seats on buses and trains, and even water fountains were segregated—some designated for "coloreds," others for "whites."

These kinds of entrenched, long-standing, society-wide practices, notably glass ceilings and institutionalized discrimination in schools, everyday life, and the workplace, produced *structured* inequalities. That is, these inequalities were built into the very fabric of schools and other institutions in US society. Civil rights legislation enacted in the 1960s was crafted to strike down these injustices. In educational arenas, affirmative action policies were supposed to level the playing field across racial and ethnic groups by taking into account the history of past abuses suffered by minorities. These policies, however, engendered backlash from opponents and self-doubt from presumed beneficiaries. Blacks and Latinos were accused of benefiting from special privileges—"set asides"—that enabled them to enter college through the back door (i.e., gain admission by meeting different, sometimes less rigorous criteria) and get jobs intended for "more deserving" whites. In the face of such accusations, minority students have reported coming to doubt their own credentials and academic worth (Steele 1997).

Near the end of the twentieth century, some states—first among them California—began banning the use of race and ethnicity in public college and university admissions decisions. To meet the challenge of increasing the diversity of their campuses without running afoul of anti-affirmative action laws, many public colleges and universities have mounted extensive outreach efforts (Orfield and Miller 1998). Expanded programs that enable parents and students to interact with campus representatives who are knowledgeable about admissions, financial aid, and college life are notable in this regard.

OVERVIEW

Structural inequality is the bias that is built into the composition of organizations or institutions that provides advantages for some members and marginalizes or produces disadvantages for other members. Structural inequality can involve unequal access to resources such as health care, housing, and education. The practices of the public school system contribute to structured educational inequality by stratifying students' access to educational resources. The tracking of students by race or class, the assignment of teachers with fewer qualifications to schools with a majority of minority or low-income students, and the allocation of fewer tax dollars to schools in low-income neighborhoods are some of the practices that contribute to maintaining the existing structure of educational inequality.

In this book, we describe and assess educational policies and practices that seek to rectify structured inequality without using the techniques of affirmative action. The approach we discuss here does not involve special concessions to minorities on college or job applications, nor is it limited to traditional informational outreach efforts that advise students about which courses and tests to take. The practices we focus on were developed and implemented through collaborative efforts, including those of university researchers, local educators, parents, and community members. The approach we describe in the chapters to come enables underrepresented minorities (URM) to enter four-year colleges and universities through the front door (i.e., gain admission by meeting the same criteria as every other student) and pursue a degree in a field of their choosing.

The Regents of the University of California eliminated affirmative action in undergraduate admissions decisions in 1995. In 1997, our campus—the University of California San Diego (UCSD)—responded to the challenge of providing more post–high school life choices to underrepresented minority students by laying the groundwork for two new interrelated facilities: the Center for Research in Educational

Equity, Access, and Teaching Excellence (CREATE) and The Preuss School, a grades 6–12 charter school for URM students, located on the UCSD campus (see Chapters 2 and 4 for details). CREATE scholars conduct basic and design research on a wide range of educational equity issues, and they engage local schools in efforts to improve their teachers' professional effectiveness and their students' academic preparation. CREATE staff and affiliates assist schools that are struggling to improve students' learning and inform university researchers about how they can respond to the expressed needs of educators on the ground. The tools of design research are employed to study the educational practices inherent in these models and to assist educators in adapting the lessons learned by selected schools in areas with a high concentration of underrepresented minority populations.

The Preuss School, which admits only students from low-income families in which the parents or guardians have not graduated from a four-year college or university, welcomed its first cohort in 1999. The school's guiding principles are derived from current thinking about cognitive development and the social organization of schooling. Research suggests that all normally functioning humans have the capacity to complete a rigorous course of study in high school—one that prepares them for college—provided that course of study is accompanied by a system of social and academic supports (Cicourel and Mehan 1985; Bruner 1986; Meier 1995; Mehan et al. 1996; Cole 1999; Oakes 2003). In most US high schools, conventional practice holds instructional time constant for all students but varies the curriculum offered. This typically results in tracking—meaning that some students are placed in classes in which they receive instruction intended to propel them toward college while other students are placed in vocational education or general courses in which they receive instruction aimed at preparing them for the world of work after high school.

Tracking has significant negative consequences. Research shows it to be biased and inequitable (Cicourel and Mehan 1985; Lucas 1999; Oakes 2005). The distribution of students to college-prep, general, and vocational education tracks is often disproportionately related to ethnicity and socioeconomic status. Children from low-income or one-parent households, or from families with an unemployed worker, or from linguistic and ethnic minority groups, are more likely to be assigned to general or vocational education tracks. Students from middle- and upper-income families are more likely to be assigned to college-prep tracks. Furthermore, low-income students of color are consistently overrepresented in special education programs and continuation schools, and they are underrepresented in programs for the "gifted and talented."

Detracking instructional models (Oakes et al. 1997; Alvarez and Mehan 2006; Rubin 2006; Burris et al. 2008; Burris, Welner, and Bezoza 2009) deliberately reverse the conventional time-curriculum equation. The higher students' academic performance, the fewer scaffolds needed; likewise, the greater students' academic needs, the more academic and social supports provided. The Preuss School implements a detracking model that recognizes the importance of dynamic support for academic development. Every student is enrolled in a college-prep course of study, and Preuss educators have instituted a variety of academic and social supports to assist students with meeting the challenges of the rigorous curriculum required for entering four-year colleges and universities. (See, especially, Chapters 2 and 4 for more on academic and social scaffolds.) Most notably, the school extends its year by eighteen days, which gives students more *time* to meet the academic demands of college-prep courses. Preuss students also are offered more *opportunities* to strengthen their academic skills. UCSD students serve as tutors in class and after school. Students still in need of additional help are required to participate in tutoring sessions on nonschool days ("Saturday Academies"). Academic support is complemented by social supports. Counselors as well as other Preuss staff address the complexities facing students who attend this academically demanding school from impoverished neighborhoods that are unsafe, gang infested, and offer far too few economic opportunities.

A commitment to providing a pathway to college for low-income students of color led to our involvement in the restructuring of Lincoln High School, a San Diego public school serving a low-income minority population, and the formation of Gompers Preparatory Academy. Charter schools are celebrated uncritically in some venues (e.g., the documentary *Waiting for Superman*) and demonized in others (Ravitch 2010b; Dutro 2011). Assessments from large-scale research on charter schools are considerably more nuanced, although also mixed. One line of research finds charter schools to be more effective than comparable public schools; another line of research reports opposite conclusions. We contribute to this debate by offering an on-the-ground look at the two charter schools we helped form and continue to assist. In Chapters 2, 3, and 4 we describe the tangle of state, community, and university politics that threatened the formation of these schools, and we examine the strategies and maneuvers the schools' network of supporters deployed and continue to use in ongoing efforts to support college-bound underrepresented minority students.

Separate from the question of their academic effectiveness, charter schools frequently are strongly criticized for pushing public schools down the slippery slope toward privatization. Our experience has been much different. In the Preuss case, UCSD faculty members, bolstered by community leaders and an engaged press, convinced university administrators to open an on-campus charter school; in the Gompers case, activist parents, dismayed by perceived neglect from a recalcitrant district administration and school board, energized the local community, found common cause with the outgoing school superintendent, and convinced our university to assist them in forming a charter school independent of the local school district. These two schools' formation and development provide a counter example to the privatization narrative.

Our work with Preuss, Gompers, and Lincoln High School also sheds light on the development of public policy, showing it to be more often a co-constructed process than a top-down one. Large bureaucracies such as school districts attempt to retain their power and authority by consolidating power centrally and by issuing directives from the top. Gompers educators and community supporters have continued to challenge district attempts to dismantle their charter by complying with some directives, resisting others, and frequently recommending alternatives. In so doing, Gompers educators demonstrate that grassroots political action can thwart, or at least slow down, the power-preserving tendencies of entrenched bureaucracies (see Chapter 3). Looking closely at Preuss, Gompers, and Lincoln reveals that school change unfolds in unpredictable and nonlinear ways as individuals in different settings interact under conditions of uncertainty, diversity, and instability. In addition, by highlighting the ways power and perspective influence the dynamics of change, we are able to draw attention to power as a central feature of the educational policy process, both in development and in implementation (Berliner and Biddle 1995; Hargreaves and Fullan 1998).

The schools we partner with have demonstrated success in preparing low-income students of color for college and university enrollment. Nevertheless, questions remain about the long-term effects of the interventions in place at these schools. Much of the research on educational inequality emphasizes the permanence of inequality. Preuss and Gompers graduates, however, express changes in their outlook for the future, and they credit those changes in part to the strategic use of extra resources. They now feel they "can be somebody." Inasmuch as these students are on a trajectory to complete college, their material conditions are changing along with their worldview (see Chapter 5 for details). These changes in dispositions and prospects for upward mobility suggest that robust institutional arrangements in schools can put a dent in the reproduction of educational inequality. Before we become overly exuberant, however, we must ensure that these enhanced prospects for upward mobility will not be suppressed by the privilege-preserving practices of people in positions of power. As we discuss in Chapters 5 and 6, educational change can be derailed if individuals in authority choose, for example, to raise credential requirements or suppress access to change-producing mechanisms, including cutting funding to effective programs.

A final issue we address throughout this book, but especially in Chapter 6 and Appendix 1, is the problem of educational disparities. This issue is more commonly formulated as the "achievement gap." Low-income African American and Latino students are described as performing poorly on a wide range of educational measures, including standardized tests, course grades, and rates of high school completion and college enrollment, compared with their more well-to-do white and Asian contemporaries. The achievement gap formulation focuses attention on the actions (or inactions) of underperforming students, their teachers, and their parents. We employ a different way of representing the problem, calling attention to educational disparities, not achievement gaps. Some prominent educators have suggested behavioristic measures to reduce these disparities, including rewarding "successful" teachers with merit pay and punishing ineffective teachers by removing them (Duncan 2010). These suggestions miss the point. Teachers—from kindergarten to college—want realistic salaries to be sure, but they are motivated more by the desire for professional work conditions—including time and space to collaborate with colleagues, reasonable facilities, sufficient teaching equipment, and sensible class sizes—than by merit pay (Darling-Hammond 1997, 2010).

Representing inequality in terms of educational disparities does not blame underachieving students, their teachers, or their families. Instead, it brings attention

to differences in the distribution of resources among schools in well-to-do neighborhoods compared to the distribution of resources among schools in neighborhoods
where families are less well off. Schools in low-income neighborhoods lack material
resources such as lab equipment, computers, and athletic facilities. They also lack
human resources such as effective teachers. The uneven distribution of resources
extends to neighborhoods as well. The 25 percent of children in the United States
who live below the poverty line are concentrated in urban neighborhoods. Compared
to their middle-income contemporaries, the urban poor experience poor nutrition,
substandard health care, few job opportunities, neighborhood violence, and environmental toxins—all of which have a strong negative effect on school success. Blaming
teachers and parents will not significantly improve achievement. If, though, we can
protect our children from the effects of poverty by making neighborhoods safe,
improving access to health care, and raising employment prospects, then we have a
better chance of improving students' educational opportunities.

THEORETICAL ORIENTATION

As we explain in this section (and in greater detail in Appendix 1), our formulation
of ways to assist students of color from low-income backgrounds to walk in the
front door of colleges and universities is grounded in a specific theoretical perspective regarding the reproduction of inequality. The theory orienting our work draws
on the ideas of Pierre Bourdieu (and his interpreters). In Bourdieu's formulation
(1977, 1985; see also Bourdieu and Passeron 1990; Bourdieu and Waquant 1992),
the school contributes significantly to the reproduction of inequality because the
cultural knowledge and skills acquired in middle- and upper-income families and
neighborhoods are accorded greater value in schools than are the knowledge and
skills of other social classes. Bourdieu and his colleagues propose that the families
of each social class develop distinctive cultural knowledge ("cultural capital") and
transmit this to their children. The class-specific cultural knowledge, skills, manners,
norms, dress, style of interaction, and linguistic facility children inherit form what
Bourdieu calls their *habitus.* This term refers to a system of lasting, transposable
dispositions that guides individuals' actions in social space (Bourdieu 1977: 82). The
children of middle- and upper-middle-class parents tend to read "good books," visit
museums, attend symphonies, and go to the theater, actions through which they
acquire an ease and familiarity with the dominant culture. This cultural fluency is,
in turn, valued and rewarded by the educational system.

Middle- and upper-middle-class children also benefit from their families' connections to resource-rich social networks that provide what Bourdieu (1985) calls
"social capital" (see also Bourdieu and Passeron 1990). Much the way money can
be exchanged for valued goods and services, social relationships can be converted
into valued outcomes, such as getting into college or landing a good job. Participation in highly valued cultural activities (e.g., attending Ivy League schools, being
members of exclusive social clubs) also connects members of the upper classes to each

other, creating more and stronger network ties. Thus, social capital, like money, can produce profits or benefits in the social world, can be converted into other forms of capital, can accumulate, and can reproduce itself in identical or in expanded form (Bourdieu 1985). Because the cultural and social capital of individuals from low-income backgrounds is neither valorized in educational institutions nor sought after in the workplace, students from working-class and poor families are at a disadvantage in both arenas. Lacking the "right" kind of social and cultural capital limits these students' chances to learn from the educational material they encounter in school and restricts their ability to interact profitably with teachers. This makes it less likely they will attend college, which in turn closes off entry into high-paying professional jobs.

Our approach to reducing educational disparities and expanding post–high school choices for underserved students begins with the premise that all human social activity—including social theorizing, public policy discourse, and people's sense-making—both expresses *and* constructs meanings that define the social world. The question of the degree to which individuals are free to choose any course of action versus the degree to which free choice is constrained by forces outside an individual's control has been a topic of intense debate for centuries. In the sociological domain, this debate is most often phrased in terms of *structure* and *agency.* Theorists who hold that people have the will to act freely emphasize people's agency, whereas those who assert that people's actions are determined by external forces emphasize the constraining forces of social structures. In our view, the supposed dichotomy between structure and agency is misleading. We see culture, structure, and agency as mutually constitutive properties of social life. We reject the assertion that social structures, or economic systems, or human biology, determine social action. We also reject the assertion that social actors are free to make any and all choices, unfettered by social constraints. Instead, we argue that social structure shapes social action and that it, in turn, is shaped by social structure. These reciprocal relations often occur at the same time, as the experiences we detail in this book clearly show.

Relations between social structures and social actions are shaped by cultural processes, which include taken-for-granted beliefs, values, and understandings. Because cultural arrangements impact both structure and agency, we treat the cultural sphere as an object of critical inquiry in its own right. The conception of culture we employ recognizes that people—regardless of their social class position—draw from a range of assets and resources that are distributed across the socioeconomic spectrum (Sewell 1992; Young 2010). Social actors sometimes compete, exerting various forms of power or authority in order to impose a particular definition or meaning on a given situation; other times, they cooperate, making bargains and compromises that incorporate multiple interests in the construction of meanings (Gusfield 1981, 1996; Holquist 1984; Shapiro 1988; Mehan, Nathanson, and Skelly 1990; Mehan 1997; Rosen and Mehan 2003; Chang and Mehan 2006, 2008). Understanding social action this way avoids the error of reducing people—students, teachers, parents, workers, employers—to passive role-players who are shaped exclusively by structural forces such as the demands of capital (MacLeod 1995; Mehan 2009).

Finally, recognizing that structure and agency are mutually constitutive directs attention away from determinism and toward the possibility of social change. Provided they have some access to material and symbolic cultural resources, social actors can apply these resources in creative ways and thereby modify social structures. When applied specifically to education and policymaking, this perspective highlights the ways in which policy arises from the interactions of real people in concrete social settings, such as classrooms, school board meetings, courts of law, and state legislatures. In these everyday contexts, social actors, including teachers, principals, students, and administrators, respond in a variety of ways to the structural and cultural features of school and society. With respect to policy directives, they may initiate alternatives, advance or sustain directives, or resist or actively subvert them. The important point here is that people can and do shape structure even as they are being shaped by it.

METHODS AND MEASUREMENTS IN THE SOCIAL SCIENCES

Using sociology's time-honored device of the fourfold table, Michael Burawoy et al. (2004) distinguish between professional sociology, public sociology, policy sociology, and critical sociology. The distinction turns on the intersection between instrumental knowledge and reflexive knowledge. *Instrumental knowledge* is cast in means-ends terms; it entails solving the puzzles of a discipline employing the rules, canons, and practices of (social) science. *Reflexive knowledge* holds up instrumental knowledge for examination in terms of its presuppositions, often challenging those presuppositions as arbitrary, or as not meeting the moral presuppositions of the discipline.

Burawoy (2005) advocates a return to public sociology—which he defines as a discipline that brings sociology to publics beyond the academy—and which places the values to which we adhere under critical scrutiny. He reminds us that sociology originated with a moral imperative. Each in his own way, Karl Marx, Max Weber, and Emile Durkheim (the "founding fathers" or "holy trinity" of sociology) were driven by an appraisal of and attempt to remedy the malaise engendered by modernity: alienation, inequality, hyper-rationality, domination, and anomie. In more recent times, C. Wright Mills (1959) and Alvin Gouldner (1970) called on sociologists to make sociology relevant for issues of social justice. Dell Hymes (1972) and Peggy Sanday (1976) led an equivalent resurgence in anthropology; Douglas Foley and Angela Valenzuela (2006) and Jean Schensul (2010) have added their voices to that appeal in recent years.

Critical researchers offer cultural critiques by writing about ruling groups, ruling ideologies, and institutions. Writing a critical ethnography is a political statement (Foley and Valenzuela 2006). When researchers aim "to use their scholarship to assist various decolonizations" (Wood 1999: 3), they give voice to the voiceless and challenge the taken-for-granted assumptions and actions of the privileged. No longer content with addressing an academic audience, some critical researchers have abandoned research entirely. Instead, they appear as expert witnesses, as commentators on radio or TV shows, or as authors of op-ed pieces and blogs, informing the public about how to challenge questionable legal, medical, media, and corporate practices.

In calling for a public sociology over either a critical sociology or simple policy statements, Burawoy et al. (2004) seek to restore a balance between basic research and a commitment to social justice. It is not enough for researchers to write op-ed articles for newspapers or appear on television talk shows because these are often analytically thin efforts aimed at passive audiences. Researchers also have to be careful about writing policy statements. If these statements are not well substantiated by basic research, researchers can be victimized by a client or become beholden to a patron.

By contrast, public sociologists challenge basic researchers, policy sociologists, and critical researchers to engage in dialogue about issues of social concern, drawing on bodies of theoretical knowledge and peer-reviewed empirical findings. Social critiques require a solid theoretical and empirical foundation. Without this grounding, sociological and anthropological claims can evaporate into shrill and empty commentaries. On the other hand, without a commitment to social justice, even well-crafted empirical studies will not necessarily further the public interest.

It is our intention to create and describe equitable educational environments, not just document educational inequality. We envision CREATE as an "educational field station" (Duster et al. 1990; Lytle 2007; Mehan et al. 2010) in which we simultaneously provide technical, cultural, and structural resources to schools with high proportions of underrepresented minority students; conduct basic and design research at our partner schools and other public schools; and make the lessons we collaboratively learn about how to build a college-going pathway available to researchers, educators, and policy makers in the educational field.

Public Sociology and Design Research

While we certainly applaud Burawoy's clarion call to sociologists to make research relevant to audiences beyond the academy, we engage a variation on that call. Borrowing an expression from the cognitive sciences, we call this variation *design research*. Design research differs from public sociology primarily in terms of the relationship that the researcher has to the "subjects" of in-process research and the "audience" of completed research. Public sociology, as articulated by Burawoy, is aimed at audiences outside of the academy.

That implies that the public sociologist conducts research in much the way a professional sociologist would, but the report at the end of the study (or studies) is aimed at a different audience. So, too, the sociologist who conducts public sociology is like the sociologist who conducts professional sociology in terms of his or her relationship to the research "subjects": in both cases, the study is done upon the subjects.

By contrast, the researcher engaged in design research has a much different relationship to his or her "subjects" and "audience." Researchers and practitioners work together to frame research problems and to seek their solutions. Design research is primarily committed to improving complex systems; this implies a long-term engagement. Committed to theory and explanation as well as to improving complex systems, practitioners and researchers work together to develop articulate explanations regarding how and why programs, designs, or ideas do or do not work.

Our experience with design research in the service of a public sociology suggests general implications for researcher/practitioner collaborations. The challenge for such collaborations is, on the one hand, to respect the local needs of practitioners and, on the other hand, to develop more useable and generative knowledge for the field. Design research demands that investigation and the development of an end product or innovation occur in cycles of design, enactment, analysis, and redesign. The skills, goals, and knowledge of the participants, as well as the relationships that exist between the actors involved in the work, significantly affect the ability to build and transfer theoretical understandings. Design-research projects, sometimes followed by the joint authorship of a publication, illustrate the advantages of collaboration around problems of practice. These intimate collaborations illustrate how a researcher can become an actor who is instrumental in changing practice, and how practitioners can acquire a new language that guides their work.

Ethnographic Description and Design Research

The commitment to long-term engagement in design research brings ethnography into the picture. In its broadest sense, ethnography has been defined as *a description of a culture, community, or society.* Whether a self-contained culture, a community, or a cultural setting such as a school is being studied, ethnographic investigations share certain methodological tenets in common. First, a cultural description requires a long period of intimate study and residence among members of the community being studied. Second, cultural description is comparative or contrastive. A cultural system, a community, or a cultural setting is not studied in isolation but in relation to other known and comparable systems of organization. Third, ethnography is vigorously naturalistic. From its earliest formulations (e.g., Malinowski 1922), the goal has been a richly detailed and fine-grained description of everyday life that captures the point of view of the natives, rather than employing the names, categories, scripts, or schemas derived from either "objective science" or the researcher's own culture.

We incorporate the injunction from critical ethnographers to document oppression in its many forms and to make this information accessible to the public. But we feel we need to do more; we cannot be only critics. We must aid in the reconstruction of educational environments. And we must resist dividing the labor between ethnographers and practitioners such that researchers conduct "basic research" while practitioners implement research findings. We strive to sustain an approach in which practitioners and researchers co-construct basic knowledge and simultaneously attempt to build progressive policy.

Our stance has epistemological as well as methodological implications. "The knowable world is incomplete if seen from any one point of view, incoherent if seen from all points of view at once, and empty if seen from nowhere in particular" (Shweder 2006: 3). Given the choice among incompleteness, incoherence, and emptiness, Richard Shweder opts for incompleteness, a stance we and "critical researchers" support. This approach replaces the grand objectivist vision of speaking from a universalist, presumably neutral, standpoint with the more valid one of speaking from a historically and culturally situated standpoint (Foley and Valenzuela 2006). It also rejects the incoherence, intellectual chaos, and nihilism that can arise when one privileges no view at all—the stance of some radical postmodern skeptics (Shweder 2006).

While still remaining faithful to anthropologists' "emic" perspective, some ethnographers have also become somewhat critical of the power dynamics inherent in the relationships between observer and participant. They recognize that "we [researchers] see the lives of others through the lenses of our own grinding and that they look back on ours through ones of their own" (Geertz, quoted in N. González 2004: 17). In at least some corners of ethnographically informed educational research, this critical self-reflection has led to a reformulation of researcher roles. One such role shift involves the move from "being a so-called participant observer to becoming an especially observant participant. This means paying close attention to not only one's point of view as an observer, but to one's relations with others (who one is studying and working with) and one's relations with oneself" (Erickson 1996: 7).

This concern about "one's relations with others," along with the conviction that ethnography—or any scientific investigation, for that matter—is not politically neutral, has led critical ethnographers to make explicit the political, cultural, and ideological assumptions that guide their analyses. Researchers cannot avoid using analytic terms and categories that are politically loaded. Thus, we agree with critical ethnographers who assert that all analytic statements must be subjected to scrutiny to determine whose interests are being served—and whose are being suppressed.

METHODS AND MATERIALS USED IN THIS INVESTIGATION

This book reports findings from a design research study. From early 1997 to mid-2010, we participated in a wide range of activities associated with the formation of CREATE, The Preuss School, Gompers, and Lincoln High School. Although our involvement continues, for the purposes of analyzing and reporting our findings here, we felt compelled to circumscribe the duration of the study. We helped shape the organizations we describe. As we participated in events, we also observed and reported (and continue to report) on them. The descriptions and analyses we present here are based on our experiences. Chapters 2–5 draw on information obtained through participant observation, interviews, questionnaires, focus groups, media reports, and official documents (see specific chapters for more detail regarding these data sources).

The activity of conducting research is never value neutral. Researchers, especially those engaged in design research, shape research by their selection of topics to investigate, materials to analyze, and instances of data to interpret (Cicourel 1964; Peshkin 1991). Researchers, including us, do not simply observe and report "brute facts." By our very engagement with individuals and artifacts in research settings, we shape materials into interpretations. The inevitable reflexive relation between researchers and objects of study was made even more complicated in our research because of the special relationship we have to the settings and because of our commitment to documenting inequality while also creating equitable educational environments.

Author Hugh Mehan's access to Preuss and Gompers is facilitated because he helped design the schools, is a member of their boards of directors, and directs CREATE, the research center responsible for developing academically rigorous schools for low-income students of color and documenting the change process associated with those schools. Mehan's position with CREATE has enabled him to participate in, observe, and report on planning meetings, university meetings, and school board meetings; and to participate in the preparation of both Preuss's and Gompers's charter documents and presentations to the San Diego Unified School District (SDUSD) school board.

Coauthor Makeba Jones's position is similar. Along with Susan Yonezawa, she has conducted studies that examine the consequences of restructuring large comprehensive high schools into smaller theme-based ones (Jones and Yonezawa 2008, 2009). District administrators' positive reaction to these studies that give students voice on topics important to them facilitated her involvement in the development and description of the refurbished Lincoln High School. Coauthor Gordon Chang's involvement is less direct. He joined the research team in 2008, conducted background research on charter schools, participated in and observed several events and meetings at Gompers, and interviewed educators about teacher retention and the expansion of Gompers to a grades 6–12 school. Coauthor Season Mussey is an insider; she was a science and advisory teacher at The Preuss School for six years. Her advisory role connected her with a cohort of students from sixth grade through their graduation in twelfth grade. She took advantage of this role to ask her advisees to reflect on their experience in college after they had graduated from Preuss. She has reported on some of her findings elsewhere (Mussey 2008).

In Chapter 5 of this book, we reanalyze Mussey's materials, along with results from Mehan, Khalil, and Morales's 2010 report on the attitudes of 182 Preuss School students regarding the challenges they faced as they adapted to their new school's college-going culture. The findings of Mehan, Khalil, and Morales (2010) are derived from the work of two other Preuss insiders, Nadia Khalil (who was a tutor at the school from 2004 through 2005) and Jose César Morales (who collaborated on an evaluation of Preuss students' progress; see McClure and Morales 2004). Our reanalysis brings together data from all three of these sources and explicitly employs Bourdieu's key concepts to evaluate the findings. We juxtapose information obtained from surveys with more intimate conversations that emerged during interviews, resulting in a richer depiction of students' views on their life possibilities than is possible from a presentation of survey results alone (see Chapter 5).

Throughout our study, we tried to keep notes during classroom visits and meetings with university and school district administrators, board members, students, parents, teachers, community groups, and UCSD faculty; but frankly, because of the emotional intensity that characterized many of these encounters, our participant role often overshadowed our observer role. When we became engrossed in the heat of the moment, our practice was to write up notes as soon after such encounters as possible (usually within twenty-four hours). Where contemporaneous information is available, we augment our recollection of events with direct quotes from other participants—some gathered from transcripts of videotaped public meetings, others from news reports of events.

The multi-dimensional roles associated with design research produce complications. A particularly vexing one has to do with unwittingly gaining access to insider information. Many parents, community members, and SDUSD educators know CREATE members only as practitioners who share their desire to enable disadvantaged students to obtain better opportunities to learn, not as members of a research team studying school improvement. As a result, sometimes we are privy to information that is significant to the research project but that has not been explicitly obtained as such. For example, a visit to Gompers to introduce to the faculty a professional development team might generate a conversation about the uneven status of the school's literacy program—an observation that school staff might not make during a formal research interview.

The question that arises in such situations is, what should we do with the information? Is it permissible to use it in our descriptions? Or is this information out of bounds? We borrowed a strategy from journalists to try to resolve the ambiguity presented by access to insider knowledge. Like reporters who distinguish between "on the record" and "off the record" comments, we treat any information we acquire in a situation not formally designated as a research encounter as off the record. Only information that has been acquired through official audio or video tape-recorded interviews, public presentations, or published documents is used as grounds for the interpretations and conclusions we present here. Sometimes we have found it productive to introduce into a formal interview questions about information we initially received off the record. If the interviewee is willing to discuss the issue, then we feel comfortable putting that information on the record.

In design research, the special relations developed between researchers and practitioners cut two ways. On the one hand, they facilitate entrée because some degree of trust has been established; on the other hand, readers may worry that our objectivity has been compromised. Rather than ignore or downplay these close relations, we acknowledge and make them visible in the analysis that follows. Therefore, our findings should not be viewed as a disinterested representation of the "truth." Instead, they are our most thorough and informed representations of our interpretations, gathered from interviews, focus groups, and hours of participation in schools and communities.

Chapter 2

The Context of the Study

Hugh Mehan and Gordon C. Chang

As we explained in Chapter 1, we view the social world as arising from an ongoing interplay among structure, culture, and agency. Our perspective recognizes that in the everyday settings of real life, people's actions are shaped by many different factors and forces, some of which they have a great deal of control over and some, very little or no control. Even under conditions of limited agency, though, people respond in a variety of ways, bringing individual and organizational interpretations of cultural norms, values, beliefs, and meanings to bear on the situation at hand. In so doing, social actors reshape the structures that constrain them. Analytically, this ongoing cycle of relations between social structures, culture, and social actions makes a thorough understanding of the *context* in which action, particularly contested and negotiated action, occurs critically important to any valid explanation of it.

With respect to public higher education and diversity goals, legal and political developments over the past forty years have dominated the context of action. Facing declining enrollments of underrepresented minorities, and limited by state bans on affirmative action strategies, many universities have responded with technical solutions (e.g., creating new procedures for increasing the numbers of underrepresented students on their campuses) and with symbolic and political solutions (e.g., constructing a new set of meanings to justify changes in procedure and exerting their authority to try to resolve conflicts over the legitimacy of new policies).

In this chapter, we examine some key aspects of this response in relation to the three secondary schools—The Preuss School on the UCSD campus, Gompers Preparatory Academy, and Lincoln High School in southeastern San Diego—that are the primary focus of our study. Specifically, we look closely at actions taken by the University of California system and by the UC San Diego campus to increase diversity and improve students' life chances in the face of significant demographic shifts, fiscal uncertainties, and political realignments. We find that the sometimes surprising resistance and frequently creative maneuvers of people on the ground brought about important changes. Because so much of our work involves charter schools, at the end of the chapter we incorporate a discussion of the scholarly literature on this educational innovation. That body of work is another dimension of the broader context that has influenced our collaborative contribution to the development of a new pathway to college for students of color from low-income backgrounds.

A PRESSING PUBLIC POLICY PROBLEM: MINORITY STUDENTS ARE UNDERREPRESENTED IN COLLEGES AND UNIVERSITIES

Recent demographic shifts, government policies, and political actions in our society have made efforts to achieve a diverse student body especially daunting for many public universities. At the beginning of the twentieth century, so-called Anglos constituted the vast majority of the population. Across the nation, Latinos and Latinas, African Americans, and Asian Americans were in the minority. Now, at the beginning of the twenty-first century, California, Texas, Hawaii, and New Mexico are becoming "majority minority" states; that is, no ethnic group constitutes a majority of the population in these states. By 2020, the white population in California is projected to be 30 percent, and the sum of all so-called minority populations, 70 percent (the projection for Hispanics is 48 percent, Asian/Pacific Islanders 15 percent, and African Americans 5 percent). Other states are undergoing similar transformations (Grodsky and Kurlaender 2010).

Black and Latino/Latina students are not enrolled in colleges and universities in proportion to their percentages in high school or the general population. In 2008, 41 percent of white students ages 18–24 enrolled in college, compared with only 32 percent of African American and 26 percent of Latino/Latina students (Pew 2009). College graduation rates unfortunately reflect this same pattern: 38 percent of African Americans, 46 percent of Hispanics, and 59 percent of whites ages 25–29 completed BA degrees in Division I colleges in 2000 (Harvey 2002).

The problem of underrepresentation is especially evident in major public universities. For example, as of 2011, the student population of the Florida State University was 72 percent white, 10 percent African American, 4 percent Asian/Pacific Islander, and 13 percent Latino/Latina (Petersons 2009), whereas the Florida high school population was 52 percent white, 20 percent African American, and 23.5 percent Latino/Latina. Similarly, of the 50,000 undergraduates enrolled at the University of Texas at Austin in 2009, 4.9 percent were African American, 18.2 percent were of Asian ancestry, 53.5 percent were white, and 18.5 percent were Latino/Latina (Grodsky and Kurlaender 2010). By contrast, 42.8 percent of the high school population in Texas was white, 12.8 percent African American, and 39.8 percent Latino/Latina. In California in 2009, 25.1 percent of the incoming freshmen on UC campuses were from underrepresented minority (URM) backgrounds while 48.4 percent of the state's public high school graduates were URM (UCOP

2009). The gap persists through college graduation. Whereas 59.5 percent of white students graduate from public colleges and universities within six years, 43.3 percent of African American students and 47.6 percent of Latinos/Latinas graduate within that same period of time (Lynch and Engle 2010a, 2010b).

How to ensure that college campuses reflect the increasing ethnic, cultural, and socioeconomic diversity of our society is a question for public debate. But, more important, we think that determining how to achieve diverse college campuses is a *research* question that universities, especially public universities, have the obligation to confront seriously. To bring this issue closer to home: the University of California systemwide has met previous social and economic challenges in agriculture, water distribution, national defense, and earthquake protection, generating innovative research, teaching, and service initiatives. In the current context, it is imperative that UC campuses develop model educational programs that both serve underrepresented minority students and help campuses reflect the changing population of the state.

THE UNIVERSITY'S AMBIVALENT RESPONSE TO THE UNDERREPRESENTATION PROBLEM

In many states, the efforts of public universities to achieve a diverse student body have been severely hampered since the 1970s, when the number of legal challenges to affirmative action policies mounted and court decisions weakened or outlawed the policies. In California such challenges culminated in 1995, when the Regents of the University of California officially banned the practice of explicitly using race, ethnicity, and gender as factors in university undergraduate admissions decisions. The ban on affirmative action in undergraduate admissions had been preceded by the *Bakke* case (*Regents of the University of California v. Bakke*, 438 US 265 1978), in which the US Supreme Court ruled in favor of a white student who had sued the state of California after being denied admission to the UC Davis medical school, despite having higher grades and board scores than minority applicants who were admitted under affirmative action. The Regents' 1995 decision was expanded in 1996 when California voters endorsed Proposition 209, which mandated abolishing race- and gender-based affirmative action in all state government actions (Orfield and Miller 1998).

When they banned affirmative action, the UC Regents instructed each campus in the system to develop plans to achieve a diverse student body without taking students' race and gender into account. To assist UC campuses in achieving this goal, the legislature added $33.5 million to the university's 1998–1999 budget, bringing a projected total of $135 million in outreach funding for the eight UC campuses with undergraduates. This injection of state funding was intended to support a new approach to "outreach," in which campuses would work more closely with the K–12 sector and with community colleges to prepare more underrepresented minority students to be eligible for UC admission. In exchange for these state monies, the university promised to "double the number of under represented minority students eligible for the University" and to "double the number of under represented minority students who are competitively eligible for the University" within five years (University of California Outreach Task Force 1997).[1]

Led by Cecil Lytle, then-provost of UCSD's Thurgood Marshall College, the campus responded to the challenge of developing a diverse student body in the absence of affirmative action by establishing the Center for Research in Educational Equity, Access, and Teaching Excellence (CREATE) and The Preuss School (see Chapter 1; also http://create.UCSD.edu and http://preuss.UCSD.edu, respectively). Although the idea of an on-campus college-prep school for low-income youth had been discussed for many years (Lytle 2007), it took the elimination of affirmative action, first by the UC Regents and then by the voters of California, to propel the idea out of limbo and into the realm of real possibility.

An initial 1997 proposal for a model school on campus drafted by Lytle and an ad hoc committee composed of UCSD faculty, staff, and community members was rejected when it failed to garner the full support of either the faculty or the new chancellor, Robert Dynes (Lytle 2007). Later the same year, however, spurred by a public outcry, negative press (notably from the *San Diego Union Tribune,* the *Los Angeles Times,* and the *Sacramento Bee*), and pressure from the UC Regents, the campus administration reconsidered its position. In the summer of 1997 it hosted public hearings to gauge the reaction to the possibility of the campus sponsoring a charter school. During those hearings, the UCSD Task Force on K–12 Outreach appointed by Chancellor Dynes listened to community members who strongly insisted that the school be located on the UCSD campus, and not in "some abandoned warehouse in a dilapidated neighborhood" (Kadumu 1997).[2]

CREATE and The Preuss School emerged as part of a reformulated, more comprehensive outreach plan that also emphasized university-school partnerships. Both the research center and the charter school owe their existence, in part, to the positive outcome of a lengthy and contentious public debate in which not only the concept of the charter school but also tacit definitions of community, equality, and the university itself became the object of contest and struggle (Rosen and Mehan 2003; Lytle 2007). In November 1997, the chancellor and the academic senate formally approved the new, more comprehensive outreach plan recommended by the UCSD Outreach Task Force. CREATE and Preuss opened in fall 1999.

Creating a Model System at UCSD for Expanding Diversity and Improving Students' Life Choices

The Center for Research on Educational Equity, Access, and Teaching Excellence was funded initially with an allocation of approximately $1.5 million from the special funds the state legislature added to UC's systemwide budget for 1998–1999. Chancellor Dynes and the academic senate charged CREATE with coordinating outreach efforts across the campus, establishing and implementing partnerships with struggling K–12 schools, stimulating and conducting basic and design research on educational equity issues, and assisting schools in adapting principles developed at The Preuss School to their local circumstances. The on-campus charter school was instructed to meet the goal of providing URM students with a wider range of options when they complete high school—most notably to be prepared to walk in the front door of four-year colleges and universities—without invoking "racial preferences." Accordingly, admissions policies at The Preuss School were carefully crafted to conform to state laws. The school accepts applications only from low-income (household earnings are less than twice the federal level for free- and reduced-cost lunch eligibility) students whose parents or guardians are not graduates of four-year colleges. Students who meet these basic criteria are further screened by a committee composed of Preuss staff, UCSD faculty, and community members and then selected randomly, by lottery.

CREATE's Research and Outreach Responsibilities

CREATE assumed responsibility for coordinating California state-sponsored K–12 outreach for the campus, and for developing a theoretical and research-based understanding of how school-university partnerships can increase the life choices of low-income students in general, and enlarge the pool of college-eligible students in particular. CREATE engaged eighteen San Diego County schools (four high schools, four of their feeder middle schools, and ten of their feeder elementary schools) in collaborative partnerships to achieve these goals. All of the schools were "low-performing" as defined by the California Department of Education. All served a majority of low-income students in underrepresented communities; eight were located in the San Diego Unified School District (SDUSD), and the remaining ten were located across three other districts. Collectively, the partnership schools enrolled 19,762 students.

The model guiding CREATE's construction of university-school partnerships is the agricultural field station (Duster et al. 1990; Lytle 2007). The Morrill Act of 1862 established land grant colleges, designed to propel social progress by educating the nation's youth for the farm, factories, and professions. Under the provisions of the Second Organic Act of 1868, the State of California sanctioned forming a new institution that enabled the state to claim the land granted by the Morrill Act (Douglass 2000). That new institution was the University of California.

The idea of propelling the university in the direction of agricultural and mechanical arts and applied sciences was met with considerable opposition by those who preferred a more classical educational approach. Undeterred, faculty on the Berkeley campus developed major agricultural research programs accompanied by programs of instruction designed to inform practitioners how they could improve their products. They implemented a model in which the research, service, and teaching missions of the university both inform and are informed by the practical challenges confronted by women and men working in real-world settings. Begun under the auspices of the university's Cooperative Extension program (inaugurated in 1913), UC agricultural field stations developed and disseminated research that has made agriculture one of the major industries in California. Based on the logic of the UC agricultural field station, other UC research programs—including those in space and ocean exploration, structural engineering, health care, and computer technology—have been developed. All contribute to economic development and the public good under the aegis of the university's broader public mission.

Researchers associated with CREATE apply the logic of the agricultural field station to "educational field stations." Colleagues from UCLA, UC Berkeley, and elsewhere (e.g., University of Chicago, University of Pennsylvania, Stanford University, and University of Arizona) have adopted similar strategies. In these partnerships, researchers conduct basic and design research at university partnership schools and other public schools and make the lessons learned about how to build a college-going future for URM students available to educators and educational policy makers. University partnership schools are not the same as the "lab schools" established more than a century ago by several universities, most notably the University of Chicago and UCLA. Lab schools and university partnership schools both seek to construct and study innovative learning environments for students and teachers; historically, though, lab schools have not been embedded in public systems of education. University partnership schools, in contrast, are part of the public school system. Innovations at these schools are designed to leverage change from the inside out.

Some university-school partnerships are controversial. Stanford New School, a charter school created and overseen by the Stanford University School of Education, was denied an extension of its charter in April 2010, when the City of Ravenswood School Board deemed it a failure because it did not meet federal goals, as measured on standardized tests (Pogash 2010; Goldman 2010). The school, like Preuss, Gompers, and Lincoln, attracts students whose parents have not finished high school. More than 70 percent of New School students are Latino/a, and a majority are English learners. The school is informed by distinguished educational researchers such as Shelley Goldman and Linda Darling-Hammond, provides an additional $3,000 per pupil per year, and enriches the curriculum with Stanford-trained teaching interns, engaging speakers, and field trips. The school board was unmoved by Stanford's assertions that students were learning in a variety of ways not measured easily by standardized tests. Board members based their decision on the fact that, using No Child Left Behind (NCLB) criteria, the school ranks among the state's lowest 20 percent of schools. This nationally publicized episode (Pogash 2010) vividly depicts the depth of challenges facing educators—even those assisted by input from thoughtful university researchers—as they attempt to overcome the debilitating effects of poverty on the academic outcomes of urban youth.

Strategies for Engaging Partnership Schools

Despite its national reputation as a top-notch research university, UCSD has not had a strong history of supporting San Diego's low-income communities of color. From the start, the campus engaged in various types of outreach activities to K–12 schools and communities, but these efforts were neither well-focused at the school sites nor well-funded. Traditional programs of financial aid counseling, presentations to parents of prospective students, academic summer camps, and classroom presentations to high school students had not proven sufficient to increase the number of students of color on campus. The Teacher Education Program initiated in 1972, although justifiably celebrated, was small, and therefore touched few schools.

UCSD's uneven history of engaging underserved schools made the campus's late-1990s foray into the world of preparing more underrepresented minorities for higher education especially challenging. CREATE had to convince local educators of the sincerity of our commitment to them when we proposed forming partnership schools. Establishing CREATE as a center devoted to school improvement was a helpful, tangible step in this process. Forging trusting and supportive relationships with schools is vital for the success of any reform efforts that aim to go beyond providing technical support (Bryk and Schneider 2003). Establishing trust is even more important when the schools involved serve predominantly underperforming and underrepresented student populations. These schools often face complex problems but receive limited guidance from their districts and uneven support from their communities. To establish trust with our colleagues in K–12 education, we promised them that we would be in this for the long haul.

To build trust with fledgling partnership schools, we often began by providing technical resources. We offered tutoring programs, after-school computer clubs, professional development activities, and college counseling, for example, to establish our good intentions and demonstrate our long-term commitment. More important, fulfilling technical demands opened key windows of opportunity to discuss structural, cultural, and political factors that restrict underrepresented students' access to high-quality educational opportunities. Once the partnership schools saw that we genuinely wanted to co-construct support for educators and students, CREATE and our partnership schools were able to negotiate other kinds of equitable actions to improve URM students' educational experiences and increase their opportunities to attend colleges and universities (Yonezawa, Jones, and Mehan 2001; Jones et al. 2002). The principles being developed and implemented at The Preuss School (described later in this chapter) informed CREATE's partnership work.

THE BROKEN PROMISE OF UC OUTREACH

The California State Legislature's commitment to an expanded outreach program did not last long. As early as 2001, legislators on both sides of the aisle expressed concern that the number and percentage of underrepresented students was not increasing fast enough. Moreover, the increase, such as it was, was not evenly distributed across campuses. In 1997, the year before the ban on affirmative action in admissions decisions was to take effect, 18.8 percent of the students on the eight campuses with undergraduates were from underrepresented minority backgrounds. In fall 1999 the percentage of underrepresented minorities dipped to 16.9 percent. By fall 2001, this figure increased to 18.6 percent, but underrepresented students were not evenly distributed across the campuses. They were concentrated in a few "nonselective" campuses, which led many legislators and campus officials to worry that the UC system was becoming segregated. For example, 40 percent of the 2008 freshman class at UC Riverside was composed of underrepresented minorities whereas only 12 percent of the 2008 freshman class at UC Berkeley was from underrepresented minority backgrounds. The situation at UCSD was dire as well. In 1998 only 11.5 percent of the freshman class was from underrepresented minority backgrounds—down from 15.3 percent during the pre–Proposition 209 years. By 2008, the freshman class percentage had risen, but only to 15 percent. The specter of segregated campuses became spectacularly apparent when the percentage change of URM enrollments was considered. While UC Riverside had increased its enrollment of URM students by 87 percent from 1995 to 2000, over that same period UCLA saw its enrollments of URM students decline by 45 percent and Berkeley experienced a 42 percent decline (Grodsky and Kurlaender 2010).

Furthermore, the enrollment of underrepresented minority students on UC campuses is well below their proportion in the state's high schools. Whereas Latino/Latina students comprised 40.96 percent of California public high school graduates in 2009, they comprised only 14.49 percent of new UC freshmen in that year—a startling gap of 26.47 percent. The pattern for African American students is similar: they comprised 6.78 percent of California public high school graduates in 2009, but only 3.26 percent of new UC freshmen in that year—a gap of 3.52 percent (CPEC 2009).

The university, which was required to report on the progress of its outreach efforts to the state legislature annually starting in 1999, argued that campus admissions and enrollment numbers were forming a U-shaped curve. When affirmative action had been the university's primary tool for trying to achieve diversity, at most 21 percent of campus enrollments were URM students. When that device was removed from the tool kit, URM admissions and enrollments plummeted. As soon as the university started using new tools, notably an enhanced Early Academic Outreach Program (EAOP), student-based efforts such as the Puente Project (an academic preparation program for underrepresented students, cosponsored by the UC Office of the President and the California Community College Chancellors' Office), Mathematics, Engineering, Science Achievement (MESA) (another academic program, aimed at preparing "educationally disadvantaged students" to excel in fields related to science, technology, engineering, or math), and school-based partnerships, the numbers started going up—almost reaching previous levels.

To some UC supporters, this U-shaped curve implied that the new tools were working—they were at least bringing the university's percentages of underrepresented minorities back to their previous pre–affirmative action ban levels. But, as members of the Latino Caucus pointed out, those numbers are *not* adequate if we use a different measuring stick—namely, the relationship between high school graduates and students eligible for admission to a UC campus. Legislators were not convinced by the university's argument. Starting in 2001, they took two decisive actions that crippled the "new outreach" paradigm's emphasis on school-university partnerships. One action was to change the rules of the game. No longer was students' eligibility for college to be the measure of success for outreach programs; henceforth, success was to be measured in terms of the actual enrollment of URM students on UC campuses. The legislature's other decisive action was to reduce funding. Regardless of the political party in power, state support for outreach dropped year by year, from the original allocation of $135 million to $29 million in 2001. At UCSD, support for CREATE dropped from a high of $1.5 million to its 2010 level of $250,000 annually.

The state legislature's approach brings to mind a scene in the movie *Monty Python and the Holy Grail*. Two knights are engaged in a sword fight. One knight lands ferocious blows on the other—cutting off first one arm, then the other arm, then a leg, until his adversary is just a stump. But at each cut, the stricken knight continues to fight. He simply refuses to give up. As changes in state policy and practice have whacked away at campus outreach efforts, we all feel more and more like Monty Python's disarmed knight. When we went into battle against privilege, racism, and inequities in the social system, our enemies took away one weapon (affirmative action), and then another (sufficient funding to sustain outreach), then another (scholarships designed for minority students). Like the losing knight, we find ourselves increasingly disarmed. Yet we, too, fight on. Our temerity and persistence has surprised and perplexed our enemies. Still, as the last of our tools and weapons are ripped away, we have to ask ourselves, how can we succeed? How can we even *proceed*?

Willie Brown, formerly a University of California Regent and the powerful Speaker of the California Assembly, maintained at the time that the university was making a devil's bargain by promising to "double the number of underrepresented minority students in five years" in return for augmented funding. It would have only itself to blame for a decline in state support of outreach (Galligani 2000). The UC system, working in concert with the lowest-performing high schools, could never prepare that many college-eligible students in such a short period of time. Brown's prediction is supported by the evidence. Students in urban schools often did not have access to college-prep courses, were taught by underprepared teachers, lacked academic and social supports, and lived in impoverished economic conditions (Oakes 2003). Although $135 million is a large sum, it was not sufficient to accomplish the enormous task of making significant improvements in the broad spectrum of underserved urban schools in the five years mandated by the state government.

As if fulfilling Willie Brown's prophecy, each year the state has exacted a greater and greater price for fewer and fewer outreach dollars. Historically, the university's relationship with the state had involved legislators providing general guidelines, such as "educate the top 12.5%," and the university doing so. In today's relationship, the state dictates the university's goals *and* the means for achieving them. This budget situation reached crisis proportions between 2009 and 2011. The university suffered a 19 percent cut in state funding in 2009–2010, and an additional 16 percent cut in 2010–2011, which led to hiring freezes, furloughs, reductions in services, pay reductions for faculty and staff, and fee increases for students.

The systemwide reduction in outreach funding that began in earnest in 2001 has had dire consequences for UCSD's original collaborations. We had to curtail our commitments to our eighteen partner schools and reduce the CRE-ATE staff by half and then half again. As a result, thousands of underrepresented minority students no longer receive services from our campus. Perhaps more important, the funding reductions have led UCSD to break its promise to the community to stay the course. Once again, detractors have cause to charge that the big white university on the hill does not meet its obligations, thereby confirming many people's view that the university has little regard for its neighbors in low-income communities.

CREATE'S PARTNERSHIP SCHOOLS

This breach in expectations and reduction in university commitment occurred just as San Diego educational leaders were considering restructuring options for Gompers Secondary School (which, when restructured, was also renamed—first as Gompers Charter Middle School and later, Gompers Preparatory Academy) and for Lincoln High School. This timing coincidence contributed to CREATE's funding-induced decision to redefine and refine its partnership efforts. The center's original theory of action involved directing services to a large number of partnership schools. This strategy often led to an uneven distribution of resources, especially in schools that resisted making college-prep courses available to underrepresented minority students or accepting college-prep-oriented professional development activities. Invitations from the Gompers and Lincoln planning teams to join them enabled us to focus our technical, cultural, and political resources more systematically, using The Preuss School as the model it was originally intended to be.

Preuss as a Model School

The Preuss School, as Chapter 1 explained, is a grades 6–12 public charter school that offers a single college-preparatory curriculum to all its students—and all are from low-income backgrounds. The school's mission is twofold: to increase the students' life chances by preparing them for college, and to serve as a model for public school improvement. Preuss educators, assisted by UCSD faculty and community members, narrow the large pool of applicants who meet the basic eligibility requirements to students they judge to have high academic potential but underdeveloped skills and then select through a lottery students to whom admittance offers are extended. In the 2010–2011 school year, there were 826 students enrolled in the school. The ethnic and racial composition of the student body was as follows: 59 percent Latino/Latina, 12 percent African American, 23 percent Asian, and 6 percent white.

To better prepare students from underrepresented minority backgrounds to have more choices after high school—especially the opportunity to walk in the front door of four-year colleges and universities—educators at Preuss concentrate on building "a college-going culture of learning" (Oakes 2003) by establishing rigorous academic courses that are taught by highly qualified teachers, and by providing academic and social scaffolds to support high achievement (see Chapter 1). Most notably, the school's extended academic year (eighteen days longer than the state standard) gives students more opportunities to meet the high academic demands. A student who joins Preuss in the sixth grade will graduate with nearly a year's extra instruction time.

Preuss students take only what are known in California as the "UC/CSU A-G" courses. This detracked college-prep curriculum makes available a complete liberal arts roster, including fine and performing arts and foreign languages— offerings that stand in stark contrast to the "back to basics" curricula adopted in many urban schools in response to NCLB accountability demands. The Preuss School's detracking principles (Alvarez and Mehan 2006) are derived from current research on cognitive development and from the literature on the social organization of schooling (Cicourel and Mehan 1985; Bruner 1986; Meier 1995; Mehan et al. 1996; Cole 1999). Detracking has been applied in district schools as well as in charter schools (Rubin 2006; Burris et al. 2008; Burris, Welner, and Bezoza 2009) in order to overcome the deleterious effects of educational stratification and give all students better access to a high-quality curriculum.

At the high school level, the Preuss curriculum includes several Advanced Placement courses, such as AP US History, AP European History, AP Calculus, and AP Statistics; extracurricular activities, such as robotics, Model United Nations, ecology club, school newspaper, and yearbook; sports, such as soccer, lacrosse, softball, and basketball; and a senior "wheel" of three trimester-long courses involving independent study (often in UCSD biology and engineering labs, theater, or music departments), service learning, internships, and research. At the end of twelfth grade, students undertake a "presentation of learning"—a senior exhibition—in which they describe orally their research project, intern experience, and service learning contributions to a panel typically composed of Preuss teachers, UCSD faculty, and community members. At all grade levels, UCSD students serve as tutors in classrooms and after school. They assist Preuss students with their academic work and serve as role models for the students they tutor. Additional instructional sessions ("Saturday enrichment academies") are provided during nonschool hours. To better engage parents in the college-going culture of the school, parents are required to devote thirty hours a year to school activities, such as the PTA, phone trees, fund-raising, and supervising student activities.

The Preuss School has accumulated an impressive list of accolades, most notably the 2011 and 2012 Number One Transformative High School in the US by *Newsweek* and the 2010 National Blue Ribbon School Award, awarded to twenty-five schools in California for superior academic performance serving economically disadvantaged students (www.cde.ca.gov/nr/ne/yr10/yr10rel101.asp). Other awards the school has garnered include the Best High School in California Serving Low Income Youth (*Business Week*, January 2009), Eighth Best High School in the United States (*US News and World Report*, December 4, 2008), and a US Top Twenty High School award for a fourth straight year, the only California school to be so honored (*Newsweek*, June 2010).

Preuss also achieved the highest Academic Performance Index (API) score among San Diego County high schools with an enrollment of at least 500 students in 2009, though it dropped to second place in 2010 and 2011 (see Table 2.1). This achievement is significant because in all three years Preuss outpaced high schools with a much lower percentage of Title 1 (i.e., low-income) students.

Table 2.1 API Scores of the Top Ten Scoring High Schools in San Diego County, 2010–2011

School Name	2010 API	2011 API	Percent Title 1
Canyon Crest Academy	894	910	2
Preuss School	885	899	100
Scripps Ranch	877	883	19
Torrey Pines	871	882	6
Coronado	865	872	5
Del Norte	856	864	9
Westview	851	860	7
San Marcos	830	859	42
San Dieguito	845	854	15
Poway	857	854	15

Further, as Table 2.2 shows, Preuss students outscore students who attend high schools in the neighborhoods where Preuss students live (i.e., the high schools Preuss students would be attending if they were not at Preuss).

Table 2.2 API Scores of High Schools in Southeastern San Diego, 2011

School Name	Student Population	2011 API Score	Percent Title 1
Preuss	704	899	100
SD Intl. Studies	423	873	98
Morse	1,488	700	64
Hoover	1,364	686	98
SD Business	302	664	100
Crawford MVA	200	657	98
Crawford IDEA	198	636	100
SD MVP Arts	256	629	100
Lincoln	1,220	617	95
Crawford Bus./Law	158	574	99
SD Comm.	150	544	100

These indices of success are further bolstered by the results of analyses that compare the educational trajectories of students who "win the lottery" and attend Preuss to (1) students who do not win a place in the school through the lottery (the "comparison group") and (2) students from similar backgrounds who did not apply to the school at all (McClure et al. 2005; Bohren and McClure 2009). Preuss students outscore comparison group students on state-mandated tests and the SAT. They take more A-G and AP courses and more standardized AP tests. Most important, they apply to and are accepted at colleges at a higher rate. As the data in Table 2.3 show, an average of 84 percent of the 685 students from the first eight graduating classes signaled their intent in their senior year to enroll in four-year colleges (Bohren and McClure 2010). This rate is about twice the national average for URM students (Pew 2009).

The eight-year average of Preuss graduates attending community college is 16 percent. It should be noted that for the past two years, more Preuss students have said they intend to enroll in community colleges (an average of 22 percent) than in the school's first six years (an average of 10.5 percent)—even though they have been accepted at a four-year college. This shift seems to be a result of the rising costs of attending colleges and universities.

To get a sense of how successful The Preuss School has been with respect to its graduates' actual enrollment in four-year colleges, Betsy Strick (2009) examined the experiences of members of the graduating classes of 2005 and 2006 in comparison to the experiences of otherwise similar non-Preuss graduates. (Students who applied to The Preuss School in 1999 and 2000, but who were not selected by lottery, form the comparison group for the graduating classes of 2005 and 2006.) Using admittedly incomplete information available from the National Student Clearinghouse, Strick estimates that between 70 percent and 91 percent of students in the 2005 and 2006 Preuss graduating classes enrolled in four-year colleges, and that between 58 percent and 78 percent of students in the comparison group did so. The Preuss graduates' college enrollment record also compares favorably to the national average of 40 percent college enrollment among low-income students (College Board 2010).

Because the Preuss and comparison groups consist of students whose records were similar when they applied to the school, the school attended represents the most significant difference between Preuss and the comparison groups. Strick's contrast thus suggests that the detracking practices implemented at Preuss have a positive influence on students who attend the school. Widening the analytical lens to include students who never applied to Preuss shows that both Preuss students *and* comparison group students outperform students who did not apply to the school. Students who applied to Preuss and were accepted and students who applied to Preuss but were not accepted outscore SDUSD students on the full range of state-mandated standardized tests: sixth-grade reading, sixth-grade mathematics, algebra 1 and 2, geometry, physics, chemistry, and biology (Bohren and McClure 2009).

This finding leads us to speculate that parents' actions are influential. The parents whose children applied to but were not accepted at Preuss do not stop trying to improve the educational opportunities of their children. Some try to enroll their children in schools considered superior to their neighborhood schools; others contribute time and energy to the local schools their children attend. Thus, the appropriate inference to make from these data is that parental commitment, combined with the Preuss detracking model, contributes to the success of the students. It is a special parent who perseveres in filling out the school's complex application form, accepts the inconvenience to the family of the 45- to 60-minute bus ride required

Table 2.3 The Preuss School Senior Class Members' College Enrollment Plans, 2004–2011

	2004		2005		2006		2007		2008		2009		2010		2011	
	N	%	N	%	N	%	N	%	N	%	N	%	N	%	N	%
Four-year colleges	44	80	64	87	68	78	68	87	86	89	93	96	72	73	80	82
Community colleges*	11	20	9	13	19	22	9	12	11	11	4	4	27	23	18	18
Other							1†	1								
Totals	55	100	75	100	87	100	78	100	97	100	97	100	99	100	97	100

* Students attending California community colleges (CCC) were offered dual admission or guaranteed transfer status, in which students enter UC as juniors after completing two years of community college course work.
† One student planned to enter the US Marines.

28

for children to get to and from the school each day, endorses children's school attendance for an extra eighteen days a year, and volunteers time at the school. That commitment certainly signals strong support for the demanding academic program instantiated at The Preuss School.

Recent History: Challenges to the Integrity of The Preuss School

By its eighth year of operation, The Preuss School had achieved a level of organizational stability. Its founding principal continued to lead the school to ever more impressive measures of success; the physical facilities were fully occupied, with kinks and quirks ironed out; the teaching staff remained stable; the innovative master schedule was settled. Events occurring in 2007–2010 conspired to disrupt the school's organizational equanimity, however. A purported grade-tampering incident precipitated a full-blown scandal and led to the removal of the principal; and the state's fiscal crisis grew, bringing unprecedented levels of cutbacks that now threaten the continuance of the school's expansive academic plan.

The tension between "facts" and "frames of reference" frequently results in alternative understandings of reality. In important moments of public political discourse, it is not necessarily the facts that matter; it is the representation of the facts that matters. As George Lakoff (2004: 17) points out, "To be accepted as truth, information must fit people's frames. If the 'facts' don't fit the frame then the frame will stay intact, and the 'facts' will bounce off." Lakoff's observations are consistent with the constitutive view that we adopt throughout this book: language is not a passive medium through which ideas flow smoothly from one person to another. Instead, the constitutive view asserts that language has the power to influence the way people think and act. Alleged grade discrepancies at The Preuss School in 2007 provide an instructive example of how different frames of reference can lead to vastly different conclusions about "facts." One of those conclusions led to a course of action that resulted in negative consequences for the school, its students, parents, and educators.

An internal audit of computer transcripts and teachers' grades in 2007—initiated by the UCSD administration in response to an anonymous tip—revealed "discrepancies in 75.8% [144/190] of transcripts reviewed" and concluded that "71.7% [of the discrepancies] had a positive impact on students' grades and academic standing" (Buchanan, Perkins, and Mannie 2007: 5). The university administration, accepting the auditors' conclusion that the principal and former counselor likely had knowledge of and/or directed inappropriate grade changes, asked the principal to resign (Fox and Drake 2008).

These actions by high-level administrators were interpreted by the media and by much of the public as evidence that intentional deception—that is, cheating—had taken place at The Preuss School. A separate contemporaneous examination of the same materials by university faculty using an alternative computation metric (grades entered rather than transcripts as the unit of analysis) computed a discrepancy rate of less than 1 percent (Mehan, Betts, and Gourevitch 2008). We used grades entered as the unit of analysis because teachers enter grades for courses one at a time. Preuss students take eight courses each trimester. Therefore each student has twenty-four grades entered on his or her transcript each year. The auditors examined 190 transcripts. That means 36,480 grades were entered. Assuming that all 144 discrepancies were errors, less than 1 percent of the entries were problematic. Some of the discrepancies were not errors; others did not take organizational contingencies into account. For example, some courses were offered at times different than reported in the audit, the principal was on leave when some grades were purportedly changed, and the school was in the process of aligning district and university policy on trimester versus quarter courses. Citing research findings that describe the challenges of making decisions in fast-paced, uncertain, and ambiguous organizational contexts that include incomplete or conflicting administrative policies and procedures, Mehan, Betts, and Gourevitch (2008) concluded that the discrepancies were the result of understandable, but regrettable, unintentional human error. They were not the result of intentional deception.

Accepting the grade-tampering representation led the UCSD administration to place The Preuss School's award-winning founding principal on leave. Accepting the discrepancies between teachers' grades and the school's computer records as the products of understandable and predictable—even if still unfortunate and unacceptable—organizational behavior, rather than as grade tampering, could have entailed different organizational consequences. For instance, rather than removing the school's distinguished leader, changes in administrative record-keeping procedures might have been initiated.

In addition to demonstrating how language shapes the way people think and thus influences the way they act, this incident also shows that when a particular representation is repeated frequently enough, it takes on a life of its own. Both the local and national media covered the grade discrepancy issue. Mehan, Betts, and Gourevitch (2008) found twenty-seven reports published between September 13, 2007, and June 2, 2008. Representations of the incident ranged from the inflammatory ("grade-tampering scandal") to the cautious ("problem with grades," "inaccurate recording" of grades, "problems with how grades were recorded"). Most of the stories treated the alleged grade changes as fact. Only one *San Diego Union Tribune* article framed the issue as an allegation ("possible grade tampering"). Only one letter to the editor of the *Union Tribune,* written by UCSD faculty not associated with the school (Sejnowski et al. 2008), raised the possibility that the discrepancies were the result of "unintentional random mistakes."

The swift and generally negative representation of the incident in the news media was intensified by public response. Bloggers reacting to the *Union Tribune* articles unleashed scathing criticism of the school and its students. Blog writers typically asserted their own long-standing skepticism that students of color from low-income backgrounds were capable of the kind of academic excellence that had been reported over the years for Preuss students. The "grade-tampering scandal" provided "evidence" that the students' success was not real after all, but only the result of cheating.

At the same time as the Preuss story broke, another area high school—one that serves primarily middle-income students—reported grading errors of its own. Both the media coverage of this problem and public reaction to it differed considerably from that surrounding the Preuss incident. Under the headline "Helix High School Mistakenly Gives A's to 36 Students," the *San Diego Union Tribune* noted that "Helix officials rejected any comparison with The Preuss School of the University of California San Diego, where an audit this week revealed evidence of *widespread grade tampering*" (Sanchez 2007; emphasis added). The choice of wording here is important. The newspaper article describes the Helix incident as a "mistake," which implies no intent to deceive, whereas the Preuss incident is depicted as "tampering," which does imply an intent to deceive.

Another incident involving grades at a San Diego area high school occurred in May 2009, when fifty-six students at Canyon Crest Academy, a school serving mostly well-to-do students in north San Diego County, were accused of cheating on homework and on tests (Sutton 2009a). The students allegedly copied homework assignments, some word-for-word, and used "cheat sheets" on exams. Marsha Sutton, the reporter who uncovered the story, expressed dismay at the blasé response from district administrators and parents (Sutton 2009a). "What's the big deal?" "It goes on everywhere," and "Why are you picking on our school?" are comments she reported hearing from parents and school administrators about the events. Digging deeper, she found that district educators and students believed cheating to be rampant, and not just among C and D students struggling to pass a course. High-achieving students who vie for good grades and acceptance in elite colleges cheat with some regularity, Sutton reported. Administrators seem to condone this behavior. A high-ranking Canyon Crest official said he was "concerned" about cheating, but added, "I don't think it's that big a deal. I don't want to downplay it, because it is a big number of kids, but cheating happens every day … especially with AP kids" (Sutton 2009a).

The response to Canyon Crest and Preuss incidents is revealing. An alleged grade-changing incident at a school devoted exclusively to the academic enrichment of low-income students of color was the subject of twenty-seven media reports and the venom of dozens of angry bloggers, whereas the media devoted only one or two reports to an incident at a school serving middle-income and upper-income students. And the journalist covering the Canyon Crest story reported that she felt pressure to simply "bury" the story. A double standard based on race and class seems to be at work here. On the one hand, students of color from low-income families who are by and large making impressive gains in academic achievement and the school they attend are excoriated for alleged administrative improprieties. On the other hand, white, well-to-do students seem to be exempt from norms of honesty, and parents, educators, and "the public" seem inclined to ignore or downplay, if not actively condone, this "white privilege."

Media reports of the UCSD audit (Buchanan, Perkins, and Mannie 2007), with its claim that 75 percent of students' transcripts had errors, has haunted Preuss students. Despite disclaimers in the audit itself that no students tampered with grades, some students have reported being denounced as "cheaters" at athletic contests and debate tournaments and in their neighborhoods. Students attending The Preuss School already face challenges from peers who question their willingness to leave the neighborhood in order to study hard and attend college (see Chapter 5). Faulty reporting only adds to the burden of pursuing academic excellence in a local context in which that kind of commitment is rare.

In sum, we have two contested representations of the Preuss incident accompanied by courses of action that flow from these competing representations. On the one hand, we have the UCSD audit version that concludes that the principal and former counselor probably were aware of and/or directed inappropriate grade changes. Based on that interpretation, the school principal was removed. On the other hand, the Mehan, Betts, and Gourevitch (2008) analysis concludes that the discrepancies were the function of human error generated in an ambiguous decision-making environment that included many incomplete or conflicting administrative policies and procedures. Had that interpretation been acted upon, we expect it would likely have led to a less severe administrative response.

The presence of the alternative accounts of the grade discrepancies at Preuss leads us back to Lakoff's injunction about the power of preconceptions: we need to be careful not to take action based on faulty assumptions. Likewise, we must avoid providing the public with information that reinforces a view that low-income students who are sought out by The Preuss School cannot succeed academically. We worry that people who frame low-income students—many of whom are students of color—as unable to achieve at the highest academic levels will seize upon the 75 percent "error rate" in the audit report as evidence to support their negative opinions.

Embedded in the misrepresentation of the grade discrepancy situation at Preuss are many of the criticisms that are routinely aimed at the school. Some are contradictory: for example, critics doubt that low-income students of color are capable of academic success, yet Preuss is accused of achieving success by "skimming the cream" of urban schools. Though the school's location on the UC San Diego campus is cited as the reason for the students' high achievement, as in "any kid can be successful if they go to school on a college campus," its location far removed from the students' neighborhoods is cited as undercutting the development of their ethnic identity. The school is also accused of being a "boutique operation"; its small size and university affiliation make replicating its features in more conventional settings difficult, critics claim.

The record of Gompers Preparatory Academy, which is modeled in large part on Preuss, addresses many of these criticisms. As we explain in the next section, Gompers is not situated on a university campus; it is a neighborhood school, populated by the same kinds of students who attend Preuss. Therefore, the academic performance of Gompers students compared with Preuss students and other comparable students offers some evidence with which to evaluate the influence of university location.

Converting Gompers Secondary School to Gompers Charter Middle School

Gompers Secondary School, located in southeastern San Diego, began as a conventional urban secondary school. By the time it was reconfigured as a charter middle school in 2005, Gompers had operated for over fifty years in a community with a high crime rate and a lengthy history of gang-related violence. The school has been redesigned several times in order to deal with educational and social challenges. It was identified as a racially isolated school in 1968. In response to court-mandated desegregation orders issued in 1977 ("the Carlin Case"), Gompers was designated a grades 7–12 math-science magnet in 1978–1979. It offered many unique and rigorous courses in computer programming and the sciences.

This experiment was abandoned in 2001 for three interconnected reasons (SDUSD 2008). First, community members complained that the math-science magnet was segregated. Students bussed in from other parts of the city attended the magnet, while neighborhood students were for the most part confined to traditional classrooms on the other side of a chain-link fence. Second, when the school board ordered the magnet school to integrate neighborhood students into its classrooms in 1985, the curriculum was not modified to address their academic needs. Third, the school did not make the transition from mainframe computing to personal computer technology. Faced with these complications, many math and science teachers left the magnet school for more suburban assignments. The quality of instruction in math and science courses disintegrated. The school continued in its grades 7–12 configuration until 2004–2005, when it was divided into a grades 6–8 middle school and a grades 9–12 high school. By that time, according to teachers and administrators who are still at Gompers, the school culture was utterly "chaotic" and "unsafe," with visible "gang colors" and frequent breakouts of fights (Mesdaq 2008; Kenda 2008). The grades 9–12 high school component of Gompers was expected to close in 2006, when the newly constructed campus of nearby Lincoln High School was scheduled to open. The school's grades 6–8 middle school component, meanwhile, was required to restructure because it had been unable to meet its NCLB performance targets for six consecutive years.

Parents, teachers, administrators, and community leaders (including representatives from the San Diego Chicano Federation, the United Front, the San Diego Organizing Project, and the San Diego Urban League) formed a working group to consider the five options approved by NCLB for restructuring the middle school: contract with an effective external organization to run the school; reopen the school as a charter school; replace all or most of the school staff who were employed during the years the school had failed to attain annual yearly progress goals; turn operation of the school over to the state; or "undertake any other major restructuring of the school's governance that would engender fundamental reform."

Michelle Evans, an activist parent, and Dora Mahar, a Gompers librarian, explain why they felt drastic change was needed:

> **MICHELLE EVANS:** So many people want to see change at Gompers. Not just parents. Not just teachers, but the administrators, the community. They all want to change. And this [restructuring the school] was our opportunity to invest in our kids' future. (Evans 2005b)
>
> **DORA MAHAR:** These parents want more. The parents don't just want their children to work at menial jobs, working in hotels, cleaning bathrooms. That's not what they want. They want their children to go to college, go to medical school, law school, engineering school, to become teachers. That's their dream. That's the dream my parents had for me. We were immigrants too. (Mahar 2005)

Restructuring options quickly became limited. The State of California declined to "take over" failing schools. Charter management organizations, such as Edison, ASPIRE, and Green Dot, did not submit bids to manage any of the San Diego schools then considering the charter option. Given its narrowed alternatives, the Gompers working group decided to consider charter status. Gompers Middle School Principal Vincent Riveroll convened meetings on Tuesday and Thursday evenings starting in September 2004. These meetings were attended by many of the school's educators and a wide spectrum of parents. Mahar (2005) and Evans (2005b) explain why parents preferred the charter option:

> **DORA MAHAR:** There are a lot of good things about going charter. You get to select the teachers.
> **MICHELLE EVANS:** It's about local control. If we can control the teachers, the parents hold the teachers accountable, and the teachers hold the parents accountable.

It was at this point that UCSD was invited into the conversation. Because of the success of The Preuss School in educating students from the Gompers neighborhood, both then-superintendent Alan Bersin and community leader John Johnson (who was leading a parallel Lincoln-Gompers high school task force) asked Professors Lytle and Mehan to consider whether UCSD could "take over" Gompers' middle school component and form a UCSD-sponsored charter school, similar to The Preuss School but located off campus. Citing the reluctance of the new UCSD administration to manage another charter school, Lytle and Mehan agreed to participate in the formation of an independent (501c3) charter school but not a UCSD-sponsored charter school.

Through their affiliation with CREATE, Lytle and Mehan were able to pledge material resources, including UCSD students to serve as tutors, expertise in teacher professional development, research and evaluation, and parent education. Perhaps more important than these material resources was the intellectual capital the university provided (Lytle 2007). CREATE offered the newly forming charter middle school a theory of action, a model for the new Gompers: a college-prep school. (See Chapter 4 for a detailed discussion of the school's reform plans.) This idea resonated with Gompers parents, more than seventy of whom had one child at Preuss and another child in neighborhood schools at the time the working group was seeking community support for a charter petition. Because these Gompers parents knew firsthand that their children could be academically successful in a rigorous academic environment, they were motivated to support the idea of reforming Gompers into a college-prep charter school:

> **MICHELLE EVANS:** We went door to door. We went in teams of two and three. And we walked this neighborhood. We're talking hours. We asked our teachers that were on the working group: can you come and walk with us and meet your students. And they did. And that gave the charter validity because the teachers walked at night. They got off at 2:00 and they stayed until 5:00, 6:00. (Evans 2005b)

These parents spoke with conviction based on their personal experience, first addressing the Gompers working group at Tuesday and Thursday meetings, and later, making their case to individual school board members, the superintendent, and the press, as well as to audiences and the school board as a whole at board meetings.

Gompers educators instituted a restructuring and reculturing plan that included a rigorous college-preparatory curriculum, supported by a range of academic and social supports. These include a longer school day and school week (e.g., a "Saturday Academy" like the one offered at The Preuss School); uniforms for all students; a comprehensive teacher professional development plan (including on-the-job training and a two-week "Academic and Culture Camp" held before school opens each year in which teachers are expected to develop a common way of organizing instruction, handling student infractions of school rules, and encouraging student excellence); a UCSD partnership that brings research, evaluation, and governance expertise; and college-student tutors to provide assistance in classrooms. (See Chapter 4 for a detailed discussion of the development of these innovations and their ongoing effects.) In the years since the school, restructured and renamed as Gompers Charter Middle School, greeted its first cohort of sixth–eighth graders in 2005, truancy, suspension, and expulsion rates have dropped while attendance rates, GPAs, and test scores have improved. Moreover, beginning with the 2008–2009 academic year, the school added a ninth-grade level; the school expanded to grades 6–12 in 2012. To signal its college-prep orientation, Gompers Charter Middle School has been renamed Gompers Preparatory Academy. Even with improvements and expansion, however, Gompers continues to face daunting challenges. Despite posting the largest gain in API scores among middle and high schools from 2009–2010 to 2010–2011 (see Table 2.4), the school remains in jeopardy, as defined by NCLB standards.

Table 2.4 Gompers API Scores, 2005–2011

	GMS* 04–05	09–10	10–11	Gain†
Schoolwide	540	569	657	88
African American	547	565	674	109
Hispanic	514	573	645	72
Socio-economically disadvantaged	530	566	657	101
English-language learner	520	522	621	99

* Gompers Middle School (GMS) scores (2004–2005) are displayed for comparison purposes only.
† "Gain" scores compare results from 2009–2010 to 2010–2011.

Restructuring Lincoln High School: Theme-Based Small Schools

Like Gompers, Lincoln High School is located in southeastern San Diego and has a lengthy history in the community. Although begun as a public middle school in 1949, by 1955 it had changed to a high school. During the 1990s, gang activity and violence undermined the school's reputation; it had not been successful either as a conventional high school or as a magnet school.

Well aware of Lincoln's troubled history when he became superintendent of the San Diego Unified School District in 1998, Alan Bersin received permission from the school board to form a planning team to propose a new vision for the school. The planning team, composed of community leaders, parents, and school district representatives, proposed demolishing the school and reopening it with new buildings, new leadership, new teachers, and a sharpened academic focus. On September 25, 2001, the school board approved the planning committee's recommendation to create smaller schools on the former school site. Each small school would have a separate principal, teachers, and student body. The small schools would come together to form sports teams and would share common resources such as a library and auditorium.

Bolstered by this extensive district-community planning process, Superintendent Bersin obtained substantial funding from the Bill & Melinda Gates Foundation to reconfigure Lincoln as four small schools, each with a distinctive theme. The grant to reconfigure Lincoln extended previous grants that funded reconstituting three other district schools (Kearney, Crawford, and San Diego High) as small schools.

Soon after Carl Cohn replaced Alan Bersin as superintendent in 2006, he formed a Lincoln "advisory steering committee" composed of community-based representatives led by Mel Collins, the newly appointed executive principal of Lincoln (Collins, like Cohn, formerly was with Long Beach Unified School District), and Libia Gil, director of the San Diego branch of the American Institutes of Research (AIR), which had fiduciary responsibility over the Gates grants. Cohn, Collins, and other members of Cohn's leadership team met with members of CREATE and The Preuss School to determine if practices developed at Preuss could be adapted to Lincoln. Cohn also asked representatives from CREATE to join educators from Lincoln, community leaders, and parents on the Lincoln advisory steering committee. When the four administrators were hired for each of Lincoln's small schools, they joined the planning group.

The advisory steering committee helped compose the school's mission statement and criteria for hiring and assessing teachers and other employees, and assisted in designing teacher professional development activities. For reasons we describe in Chapter 4, Lincoln has not been able to obtain the flexibility in making personnel, teacher professional development, or master scheduling decisions enjoyed by charter schools. Despite constraints imposed on the reconstitution of Lincoln by forces external to the school, since the formation of the Lincoln-UCSD partnership the university has been able to assign approximately forty UCSD students each academic quarter to provide tutoring assistance to Lincoln students; counseling and information about college preparation, financial aid, and visits to college campuses for both parents and students; professional development activities to support the social justice curriculum, writing across the curriculum in social studies and English, and support for administrators; assistance in developing a health center on the Lincoln campus; and assistance for teachers and students interested in learning how to conduct survey research on a range of adolescent health issues.

The reconstituted Lincoln opened in 2007 with four "centers of choice": the Center for Social Justice, the Center for Public Safety, the Center for Science and Engineering, and the Center for the Arts. The racial and ethnic composition of the approximately 2,300 students enrolled at Lincoln during the 2007–2008 academic year was 54 percent Latino/Latina, 36.5 percent African American, 7 percent Asian, and 2 percent white. Approximately 30 percent of students were Limited English Proficient (LEP), and 100 percent qualified for free or reduced-priced lunches.

In 2007–2008, Lincoln's first year as a renewed, redesigned school, it met neither its state API nor its federal "adequate yearly progress" (AYP) accountability targets. During year two, after diligently working on standards-based teacher professional development and providing increased academic supports for students, Lincoln met all of its API targets, jumping forty-seven points above the previous year's score. Similar successes were achieved with the AYP targets: in year two, Lincoln met twenty-one of its twenty-two identified targets. Across all subgroups of students disaggregated by race, socioeconomic status, and English-language proficiency, students more than doubled, and in some cases tripled, their target scores compared to the previous year. Across all high schools in the San Diego Unified School District (which is the second-largest district in the state and the eighth largest in the nation), Lincoln was one of eight schools that met most of their accountability targets in 2008–2009.

DEBATES OVER THE VALUE OF CHARTER SCHOOLS

Charter schools play a significant part in this study. Our research has been shaped by and has contributed to the literature on these increasingly popular educational alternatives. Thus, it seems appropriate to review the current state of knowledge about charter schools. We do so with a caveat: the following summary will certainly be obsolete by the time this book appears, because new studies of charter schools, especially in comparison with conventional public schools, seem to appear daily. Even with that unavoidable limitation, though, a review of current work offers a useful introduction to the flavor of the topics covered and conclusions derived from the research on charter schools as of this writing.

Charter schools are elementary, middle, or secondary schools that receive public money but have been freed from certain rules, regulations, and statutes in exchange for some level of accountability for producing specific results in student achievement. According to a National Charter School Research Project survey, 3,403 charter schools served over 900,000 students during the 2004–2005 school year. As of January 2006, forty states and the District of Columbia have passed charter school legislation (quoted in Ziebarth et al. 2005: 3). By 2008 there were thirty-five charter schools in the San Diego district, with enrollment of 13,000 students—almost 10 percent of the district's students. Thirty of the thirty-five charters were "south of 8"—the symbolic and material highway boundary separating the well-to-do neighborhoods and the less-well-off neighborhoods of San Diego (*Voice of San Diego* 2008).

The most full-throated and uncritical portrait of charter schools appears in films. *Waiting for Superman, The Lottery,* and *The Cartel* celebrate charter schools as the saviors of US public education (a system that is portrayed as failing miserably) and at the same time depict bad teachers (supported by overly zealous unions) as villains. Diane Ravitch (2010b) offers a sobering critique of these three films and, by extension, of rabid supporters of the charter school movement. Harshly critical of suggestions to fire bad teachers and privatize troubled schools, Ravitch invites policy makers to emulate the policies practiced by nations with successful school systems—Japan, Finland, Singapore, and South Korea among them. Finland, notably, has achieved eminence by patiently building up the expertise of its teaching corps, expanding social welfare programs, and reducing poverty levels—not by firing teachers or privatizing schools.

Many reasons have been offered for the emergence of charter schools. Some critics of public education have claimed that public schools are failing so badly that radical restructuring in the form of voucher plans is necessary (Freidman 1963; Chubb and Moe 1990). Thoughtful legislators see charters as a less radical and more viable alternative than public funding of private schools and voucher plans (Hart and Burr 1996). The stimulating effect of competition is also invoked as a rationale for charter schools. If parents vote with their feet by enrolling their children in charter schools, then, according to the logic of the power-of-competition argument, educators in regular public schools will be motivated to be more effective in order not to lose students to charter schools. Failing public schools will either improve or close.

Charter schools are also seen as an antidote to overly bureaucratic public school systems that stifle creativity. Propelled by an "anti-bureaucracy" rationale, charter school proponents claim that school district offices, state capitols, and/or the federal government are too distant from local schools to adequately understand or respond to needs expressed at the local level. Liberating educators from remote bureaucratic regulations, then, can foster experimentation of novel approaches that may produce improved student achievement.

Assessments of the outcomes of charter schools compared to traditional public schools reveal a mixed record (Hubbard and Kulkarni 2009). There is not much evidence that public schools learn from charter schools (Wells 1998; Carnoy et al. 2005; Zimmer et al. 2009). With full-frontal teaching, standard-length periods for instruction, and textbook-based learning, many charter schools look like conventional schools. Carnoy et al. (2005) find no evidence to support the claim that charter schools foster competition among regular public schools. A more recent study (Zimmer et al. 2009) also failed to discern any competitive impact between charter schools and nearby public schools. These critics of charter schools contend that the benefit of increased choice to parents and flexibility to administrators comes at the cost of reduced job security to school personnel. They worry that the high turnover of staff associated with charter schools undermines school performance more than it enhances it.

Drawing on interview data from 225 charter schools in ten states, the US Department of Education concluded in 1997 that charters tend to be new and small (fewer than 200 students). They are more often located in urban than in rural areas. More recent research reports that many of the schools described in studies of charter schools serve primarily middle-class populations (Deal and Hentschke 2004). While they tend to be more racially diverse, charter schools also tend to enroll fewer special needs and LEP students than do typical public schools in their respective states (US DOE 1997). Such findings lead some scholars to worry that charter schools contribute to more—not less—segregation by social class and race (Wells 1998; Carnoy et al. 2005; Renzulli and Roscigno 2007; Frankenberg and Siegel-Hawley 2009; Frankenberg, Siegel-Hawley, and Wang 2010; Miron et al. 2010). Based on a multistate study, Ron Zimmer et al. (2009) concluded that charter schools *in the aggregate* do not seem to cause dramatic racial or achievement segregation within neighborhoods. However, in some sites and in some states, charter institutions *do* significantly enroll students with different academic and/or racial profiles than nearby traditional public schools (Frankenberg, Siegel-Hawley, and Wang 2010). But such patterns are not uniform. For example, charter schools enroll more higher-achieving students in some sites and more lower-achieving ones in others. The number of black students in urban charter schools is similar to their number in nearby traditional public schools. Therefore, the available evidence seems to show that aggregate differences in racial distribution are minimal and not necessarily meaningful.

Assessments of the performance of charter schools compared to regular public schools also reveal mixed results. A meta-analysis of twenty-six studies of students' academic performance reports that twelve studies found that students' gains in charter schools were larger than those in other public schools; four found charter schools' gains higher in elementary schools, high schools, or schools serving at-risk students; six found comparable gains in charter and traditional public schools; and four found that charter schools' overall gains lagged behind those of public schools. The meta-analysis also reports that five of seven studies found that charter schools improve as they achieve organizational stability (Hassel and Terrell 2006). CREDO (2009) found variation in performance among students attending charter schools and students attending traditional public schools in sixteen states. Overall, 17 percent of charter schools provide "superior" educational opportunities for students, nearly half have results that are no different than those of the local public school, and 37 percent show charter school students as performing significantly lower than their counterparts in neighboring traditional public schools (CREDO 2009).

Some studies examine the effects of charters on high-achieving students compared to low-achieving students. Based on a sample of thirty-six charter schools in fifteen states, Phillip Gleason, Melissa Clark, and Emily Dwoyer (2010) found that charter schools serving more low-income or low-achieving students had statistically significant positive effects on math test scores, while charter schools serving more advantaged students—those with higher income and prior achievement—had significant negative effects on math test scores. Studies of the Knowledge Is Power Program (KIPP) report similar results (Angrist et al. 2010). LEP students, special-needs students, and students with low-baseline scores benefit more from time spent in KIPP schools than do other students, with reading gains coming almost entirely from the LEP group. This line of research suggest that charters seem to serve low-income students better than they serve well-to-do students (CREDO 2009).

Susan Therriault et al. (2010) suggest that middle and high school students in Boston who attend charter schools significantly outperform their counterparts attending traditional schools. The authors dismiss the criticism that charter schools "skim" the best students from neighboring traditional public schools. Instead, like Joshua Angrist et al. (2010), Therriault and her colleagues find that several factors account for performance differences: selective teacher hiring and retention, strict behavior norms, a focus on traditional reading and math skills, the amount of time students spend in charter schools, and the greater amount of personal attention they receive.

Martin Carnoy et al. (2005) present opposite conclusions. Based on their analysis of nineteen studies, conducted in eleven states and the District of Columbia, these authors conclude there is no evidence on average that charter schools outper-form regular public schools. Zimmer et al. (2009) also find few differences in test scores between nonprimary charter schools and public schools nearby, but charter high schools seem to have a positive association with high school graduation and college enrollment.

In sum, the available evidence on charter school–conventional public school comparisons is mixed. One can find as many studies that suggest charter schools outperform conventional schools as one can find evidence in the opposite direction. So, too, the claims that charter schools exacerbate segregation or foster competition and improvement in conventional public schools find as much support as do the opposite claims. However, the vast majority of these studies are "single point in time" assessments that compare entire student cohorts from one year to the next without considering patterns of student transience and transfer. Because this year's sixth-graders may not be the same children as last year's fifth-graders in the schools being compared, we do not know if students within schools are improving academically. Schoolwide averages, rather than student-student comparisons, also reveal nothing about whether *all* students achieve at about the same level or whether *some* students are achieving a great deal more than others.

These studies tend to treat charter schools in the aggregate. An accurate as-sessment of school effectiveness requires information on student performance from at least two points in time (Center for Educational Reform 2004; Betts and Hill 2006). The most foolproof method to compare the performance of students in charter schools and regular public schools would be an experiment (or "quasi-experiment") in which students are randomly offered admission to charter schools; those not ac-cepted into the school by lottery would return to their public schools, thus enabling a student-student comparison through time. Julian Betts and Paul Hill (2006) call attention to two randomized quasi-experiments. We discussed one of these, by Larry McClure et al. (2005), conducted at The Preuss School, earlier in this chapter. Follow-up studies have shown that Preuss graduates enroll in four-year colleges at a substantially greater rate than students in the randomly selected comparison group (McClure et al. 2005; see also Strick 2009). A more recently published randomized admissions study (Gleason, Clark, and Dwoyer 2010) found that charter middle schools that hold lotteries are neither more nor less successful than traditional public schools in improving student achievement, behavior, and school progress.

The way we treat charter schools in this book departs from the approach of correlational and aggregate studies. We analyze the actual processes involved in creating and sustaining two charter schools—Preuss and Gompers—that seek to institute a college-going culture of learning for low-income students of color. We trust that the dilemmas, institutional constraints, and political tensions—as well as the creative strategies and counter-maneuvers—highlighted in our study will contribute to a deeper understanding of the special possibilities and challenges associated with this provocative approach to educational improvement.

SUMMARY

In this chapter we described the three schools that serve as the sites for our investigation of the constitutive processes involved in constructing a pathway to enhanced life choices for students of color from low-income backgrounds. We contextualized the background and characteristics of The Preuss School on the UCSD campus, and Gompers Preparatory Academy and Lincoln High School in southeastern San Diego, in terms of the challenges facing many public colleges and universities as they attempt to increase diversity on their campuses, a goal further complicated by the imposition in many states of a ban on the use of affirmative action in admissions decisions.

Actions taken by the University of California system and by the UC San Diego campus to increase diversity and improve students' life chances in the face of significant demographic shifts and political actions provide additional context for our study. Reinforced by political and financial support from the state legislature, the University of California responded to the ban on using race and ethnicity in admissions decisions by adopting a new paradigm of outreach to underserved student populations. The new paradigm encouraged campuses to form partnerships with underperforming schools to increase the college eligibility of students underrepresented on campuses. Unfortunately, both the political and the financial support were short lived, resulting in the dismantling of many school-university partnerships. This in turn confirmed suspicions in communities of color that the University of California could be counted on to renege on its promises.

UC San Diego adopted a more radical strategy to increase diversity and the life chances of underserved youth. After a contentious debate about the responsibility of the campus to engage K–12 schools intimately to improve students' life chances,

The Preuss School and the Center for Research in Educational Equity, Access, and Teaching Excellence were approved. Preuss's mission is both to prepare underrepresented students for college and to serve as a model for other urban schools wishing to prepare low-income students of color for college admissions. CREATE is responsible for the broader approach to outreach that emerged from the debate over the university's role in the community, including responding to community requests to form comprehensive partnerships. Community activism, coupled with the support of the outgoing superintendent of San Diego schools, overcame the resistance of the SDUSD school board and segments of the UCSD administration, enabling the formation of partnerships with Gompers and Lincoln High School.

In Chapter 3 we provide examples of how parents and community members advocated for radical changes in their school, thereby illustrating the ways in which street-level activists can push back against often rigid bureaucratic tendencies. In Chapter 4, we compare the organizational development and student performance of Preuss and Gompers, which are charter schools, with Lincoln, which is configured as four theme-based, small schools. This comparison enables us to evaluate the claim that charter school status is required in order for schools to make significant improvements. In Chapter 5, we trace the change in aspirations and accomplishments of Preuss students while they are in high school and college, which enables us to reconsider Bourdieu's theorizing about the permanence of people's dispositions and social standing.

NOTES

1. "Competitively eligible" students have academic records that enable them to enroll in the most selective UC campuses: Berkeley, Los Angeles, and San Diego.

2. Mehan participated in weekly meetings of the UCSD Outreach Task Force held in the summer of 1997 that led to the formation of CREATE and Preuss. He continues to participate in meetings with Preuss administrators and the board of directors and makes informal visits to classrooms.

Chapter 3

Pushing Back against the Power-Preserving Tendencies of Bureaucracies

I don't mind a few crises to heighten a sense of urgency. But a constant flow is crazy.
—Vincent Riveroll, Director, Gompers Preparatory Academy, 2008

In this chapter we describe the complicated, obstacle-laden process through which an energetic and committed group of parents, community leaders, educators, and university collaborators reinvented the conventional middle school component of Gompers Secondary School as a college-prep charter school. Federal, state, university, and school district policies all are explicitly framed as designed to help improve K–12 education. Often, however, perhaps unintentionally, when such policies are translated into practices, they operate more to preserve than to change the status quo in organizations.

The actions surrounding the formation and development of Gompers from 2005 to the present illustrate aptly how people on the ground can resist the power-preserving or oligarchic tendencies of large bureaucracies. After explicating the idea of oligarchy, we examine the influence that public policies and organizations' formal and informal procedures and practices have had on the development of Gompers. We divide the discussion into two parts. In the first part we describe the influence of district policies and the practices that derive from them. In the second, we describe the influence of federal, state, and university policies and procedures. In both parts we show that a coalition of parents, teachers, university representatives, and community leaders pushed back against those policies and practices, thereby demonstrating that the retention of power in large bureaucracies is neither automatic nor permanent. Push-back can open cracks in the seemingly smooth exercise of power.

THE OLIGARCHIC TENDENCIES OF BUREAUCRACIES

The history of innovations in educational and other institutions shows a remarkable and consistent pattern: faced with changing circumstances, organizations seek, often desperately, to retain their power and influence (Michels 1915; M. Weber 1958). Robert Michels's (1915) account of Germany's Social Democratic Party was perhaps the first to identify one rule of oligarchy—the adaptability of formal organizations to changing circumstances in order to retain power. Writing about the Tennessee Valley Authority, Phillip Selznick (1949) described an example of organizational adaptability aimed at preservation. According to Mayer Zald and Patricia Denton (1963), a similar process occurred within the YMCA. As the organization expanded, its rules rigidified, and its mission changed from evangelical Christian outreach to a more general and secular social-service orientation. An ethos of managerial efficiency replaced particularistic leadership at the YMCA, and the organization survived.

Public institutions dedicated to social reform also have modified their goals to remain in business. For example, during the early years of the twentieth century, in a spirited moment of reform, progressives in the United States attempted to rehabilitate prisons and juvenile courts and to reform mental asylums. Within decades, however, the initial innovations, designed to improve the lot of criminals, delinquents, and the mentally ill, had been transformed into routine bureaucratic procedures that sustained administrative rather than humanitarian interests (Rothman 1980).

We see the same process in education. Innovations—especially those proposed from outside educational institutions—are often absorbed into the culture of schooling. The result is a virtually unchanged system. Public Law 94-142, the Education for All Handicapped Students Act, is a case in point. This federal mandate, passed by Congress in 1975, called for a change in the education of special-needs students. Instead of being segregated in self-contained programs, they would be placed in the "mainstream" of regular classrooms or in the "least restrictive" educational environments available. In addition, this law mandated expanded decisionmaking, notably including parents as essential partners in the special-education placement process. In everyday practice, however, educators soon began modifying these mandates, adapting them to existing district and school site routines and standard operating procedures (Mehan et al. 1986; Mehan, Mercer, and Rueda 2002). Today, educators once again routinely place special-needs students in available programs, obtain waivers for parental consent, and establish informal procedures that circumvent the formal procedures mandated by federal law.

Response to the No Child Left Behind (NCLB) legislation presents a similarly consequential scenario. Under the provisions of NCLB, students and schools are required to show "adequate yearly progress" on standardized tests or face negative sanctions, including school closure. Testing experts say that schools, districts, and even entire states work around this federal requirement by using simpler tests (Haney 2000; Kohn 2002; Medina 2010). This strategy compromises the demands of federal law even as it helps keep bureaucratic regimes in power.

Changes to AVID (Advancement Via Individual Determination), an academic program designed to propel students toward college, provide a look at a deliberate—and successful—adaptation undertaken to ensure organizational survival. The program began in California in the 1980s and focused on meeting the needs of high school students with high academic potential who came from low-income families and ethnic backgrounds historically underrepresented in colleges and universities. Challenges posed by affirmative action bans beginning in the mid-1990s, as well as concerns raised by educators and school communities as the program spread across the country, prompted major changes in AVID's mission. The program redefined the population of students it serves to include all groups, with an emphasis on reaching "the least served students in the academic middle," and expanded its coverage to include elementary as well as secondary grades (for further information on AVID, see www.avid.org/abo_whatisavid.html). These changes increase the program's appeal and thus enlarge the number of potential adopters. For instance, in Kentucky and Virginia high schools with AVID programs, educators recruit students without taking race or ethnicity into account. From their perspective, this is preferable because depicting AVID in racialized terms might offend white parents and other community members, who would likely see the program as engaged in reverse discrimination. AVID's redefinition of its target population is a particularly vivid case of an educational design team adapting its organizational forms and reform models in order to maintain their program's powerful position in the reform nexus (Mehan et al. 1996).

The history of the junior high school provides another instructive example of how organizations go about preserving the position they enjoyed before an innovation was introduced. Junior highs were designed to bring about a fundamental change in schooling. Over time, they have become merely a modest addition to the high school. A more recent effort to correct the flaws in junior high schools through the middle school movement seems only to have initiated a new cycle of brief innovation followed by a re-establishing of the status quo. Reforms of the junior high school curriculum and its tracking practices have been adapted to the existing social architecture of the school (Cuban 1992).

Despite the power-preserving tendencies of educational organizations illustrated by these examples, organizational change can and does take place. The Gompers story shows ways in which even a large and powerful bureaucracy can be pushed into actions that it would prefer to avoid.

EFFECTS OF SDUSD ACTIONS
ON THE FORMATION OF GOMPERS

This section examines actions taken by the San Diego Unified School District (SDUSD), Superintendent Alan Bersin, and the SDUSD Board of Education that sometimes enabled and other times constrained the efforts of Gompers Middle School supporters as they worked throughout the 2004–2005 academic year to convert the failing school to charter status. These enabling and constraining actions occurred during the conversion process and, as we explain later in this chapter, continued after Gompers became a charter school.[1]

The Mixed Blessing of Superintendent Bersin's Blessing

From 1998 through 2005 the SDUSD engaged in a dramatic, daring, and possibly unprecedented reform. As prominent displays throughout the district asserted, "The mission of the San Diego Unified School District is to improve student achievement by supporting teaching and learning in the classroom." To reach that commendable goal, the district, under newly appointed Superintendent Alan Bersin, implemented a content-driven, centralized, comprehensive, and fast-paced reform (Mehan, Hubbard, and Stein 2005; Hubbard, Mehan, and Stein 2006). Bersin's commitment to this approach to reform initially led him to oppose charter proposals that did not conform to the district's new "Blueprint for Student Success." By the end of his term in office, however, he had become convinced that variation in school design and curricular implementation was acceptable, even desirable (Mehan, Hubbard, and Stein 2005; Hubbard, Mehan, and Stein 2006). Consistent with this new embrace of variation, Bersin began avidly supporting the conversion of failing schools to charter status.

This enthusiastic support was a mixed blessing, however. In the wake of the November 2004 elections, the composition of the SDUSD school board changed. Previously, a 3–2 majority had supported Superintendent Bersin's reform policies. After the elections, a 3–2 majority opposed his policies. This political shift led to the removal of Bersin as superintendent and also significantly affected the formation of Gompers. Because the newly elected board seemed to reflexively oppose any policy that Bersin supported, his endorsement did not help Gompers win board approval for conversion to charter status.

Despite his own diminished power vis-à-vis the school board, Superintendent Bersin was able to orchestrate district support for schools seeking charter status. He instructed Brian Bennett, director of the district's Office of School Choice, and a practicing lawyer, to help Gompers and the other schools traverse the often-murky district policies and state and federal laws covering governance, finance, and teachers' rights. Bennett boldly confronted the school board and the teachers' union on matters relating to teachers' status with the district, their benefits, and their rights to return to district schools from charter schools without loss of benefits. He met often with the Gompers working group to offer moral support and informal advice on writing the charter proposal and solving new problems that seemed to emerge weekly. Bennett's support and advice facilitated the development and approval of the Gompers charter, but it may also have contributed to the end of his career with the district. He was terminated by Carl Cohn, who became superintendent after Bersin's departure.

Other organizations assisted with the formation of Gompers, frequently encouraged by Superintendent Bersin. The California Charter Schools Association

(CCSA) provides start-up funds to help with school conversions. CCSA staff members supplied advice on preparing charter documents for school board approval and suggested strategies for navigating the political landscape. The Girard Foundation provided funding for the first Gompers "culture camp" (described below) and helped with the costs of providing the school's board members with training in the areas of charter school law and financing. The Girard Foundation also brought Gompers to the attention of other foundations, which led to much-needed financial support in subsequent years.

Board Actions: Changing the Rules of the Game

While the Gompers community was in the process of establishing Gompers Charter Middle School (GCMS), the San Diego school board redefined the charter process; removed Vincent Riveroll, the popular and charismatic Gompers school principal and leader of the conversion process; and delayed approval of the charter. In fall 2004 the school board defined three local schools (King-Chavez, Gompers, and Keiller) as "start-up" charter schools. This designation requires charter petitioners to gather signatures from at least 50 percent of the parents of children who would likely be enrolled if the conventional public school were restructured as a charter. A coalition of black and Latino parents, along with some Gompers teachers, canvassed Gompers' neighborhood on behalf of the charter petition. They secured 700 signatures of the 960 parents of potential students—more than 70 percent.

On January 7, 2005, the school board, with its newly elected members present, overturned the previous board's decision. Reinterpreting the laws governing charters, the new board redefined the petitioning schools as conversion charters, not start-up charters. This imposed a new demand on the petitioners: they had to secure signatures from at least 50 percent of the permanent (unionized) teachers then on staff at the three schools seeking charter status—and they had to do so within two weeks.

This new demand placed teachers at King-Chavez, Gompers, and Keiller in a difficult situation. If they voted in favor of the conversion, their jobs would not be guaranteed. Charter leaders at each school planned to treat all faculty positions as open and interview all applicants—regardless of whether they had taught at the school before. Union representatives from the San Diego Education Association (SDEA) headquarters met with teachers and provided arguments against the conversion to charter status. Some Gompers teachers were told, falsely, that they would lose their health and retirement benefits and the right to return to teaching positions within the district should they choose to leave Gompers.

In a stunning display of professionalism and commitment to the idea of developing a new culture of learning, Sharletta Richardson, an educator who had been associated with Gompers for more than twenty-five years—and a past SDEA representative—was the first to sign the charter petition. She encouraged her colleagues to do the same. Addressing school board members in March, before they made their final decision regarding the charter for Gompers, Richardson explained her actions this way:

For 29 years I have commuted from Mira Mesa to teach at Gompers … when it was one of the leading academic schools in the district. In those past years I have seen neighborhood students graduate from Gompers and go on to become teachers, lawyers, doctors, and engineers. I know our neighborhood students can achieve like that again. But because our demographics are different, and because we have very special needs, we need to do things differently. And Mr. deBeck [board member], that is why my name was the first on the list to support the Gompers Middle School charter. (Richardson 2005)

In the end, charter petitioners successfully met the requirement to obtain the approval of more than 50 percent of the teachers (Gao 2005a).

Board Actions: Decapitating the Movement's Leadership

The district's opposition to the conversion of Gompers Middle School to charter status did not end with the board's demand that petitioners obtain both teachers' and parents' signatures. In what looked like an attempt to destroy the growing momentum of the Gompers working group, school board members decided on February 8, 2005 (in a closed session), to direct Superintendent Bersin to "transfer" Principal Vincent Riveroll from Gompers Middle School to the SDUSD central office, reclassifying him as a "mentor principal" (Gao 2005a; see also Chapter 2). Beginning in the fall of 2004, when then-superintendent Bersin appointed Riveroll as principal of Gompers, he began instituting dramatic changes to the school's structure and culture. Riveroll was a strong supporter of the conversion of Gompers to a charter school. For many, the decision by the school board to remove this charismatic leader of the conversion movement embodied the board members' general opposition to charter schools—an "antipathy shared by a teachers' union that is adamantly opposed to the charter schools' exemption from union rules on teacher assignments and pay" (Sutton 2005: 1).

After hearing about the school board's decision to transfer Riveroll, Gompers supporters first erupted in angry protest. On February 14, 2005, community members met at the Chollas View Methodist Church, located across the street from the school. They deplored the unwarranted removal of Riveroll, but undaunted, they also pledged to continue their efforts on behalf of the charter. Thus, the district's attempt to scuttle the charter by decapitating the leadership failed. In fact, this heavy-handed action seemed to energize rather than sabotage efforts to convert Gompers Middle School to charter status. Supporters organized letter-writing and e-mail campaigns aimed at convincing the school board to approve the charter.

Board Approval

The campaign to convert Gompers to a charter school in partnership with UCSD and community groups such as the Jackie Robinson YMCA, the Parent Institute for Quality Education (PIQE), and the San Diego Urban League, culminated on March

1, 2005, at a meeting of the SDUSD school board. Community leaders, Gompers parents, and UCSD faculty urged the board to "give their children a way out of the trap of poverty, crime and despair; to give them a chance for a decent education" (Sutton 2005: 2). Cecil Steppe, president of the Urban League of San Diego County and parent of three graduates of Gompers, stated that the board should "stay within the law" by granting the charter to Gompers supporters, who had obtained more than 70 percent of parental signatures, collected over 50 percent of the teachers' signatures additionally requested by the board, and had "come back to you at least on two occasions and fulfilled every requirement that you laid on their plate." He further noted, "It seems to me with all of the struggles over the past, that it makes absolutely no sense in my mind for you to say no to an opportunity to bring a whole new way of doing business to a school that has been on the failure list for far too long" (Steppe 2005).

The charter proposal was not approved quietly. In public commentary at the meeting, one Gompers teacher claimed that she had signed the charter petition without "the opportunity to look at it hard enough or deeply enough to give feedback or ask questions about it" because of "all the chaos … that was going on at Gompers." She wanted to withdraw her name from the petition. Before a vote was taken, board member deBeck addressed this teacher's concern:

> We go back to the signature thing…. I've only heard one, one person who came and said that they weren't sure about their signature. So, that's not going to cut it for me…. You have a community support that's strong, and [you met] the charter regulations that we provided. I find it very difficult for me to vote against this charter with this situation. (deBeck 2005)

Shirley Weber, professor and chair of the Department of Africana Studies at San Diego State University, and a member of the San Diego school board from 1988 to 1996, expressed reservations about the four charter proposals before the board. She said she had seen "this board approve and reapprove charters that have failed year after year after year, without the guts to cut them off." "Most of the conversion charters [in low-income areas] have not been successful," she continued, " so that's a tremendous challenge to take one and make it successful." She acknowledged Lytle's commitment as " true and honest" and the charter school as not necessarily a bad concept. Nevertheless, Weber pointed out that the Gompers charter document did not include a provision for parents on the governance team. Further, she wondered about the consequences for students whose parents fail to meet the requirements laid out in the charter: "When you say a parent must have 15 hours of volunteer, volunteerism, what happens if they don't? When you say they must come to open house, what happens if they don't?" (S. Weber 2005). These arguments were reiterated from the podium by board member Sheila Jackson. Ultimately, though, Jackson voted to grant the charter to Gompers.

Hence, after months of debate and several detours, the school board unanimously (5–0) approved the petition to extend the charter of Memorial Academy and to enable Gompers Middle School, King-Chavez Elementary School, and Keiller Middle School to restructure as five-year charters. The GCMS charter called for enrolling students in grades 6, 7, and 8. As soon as the board members finished their voting, the auditorium erupted in raucous approval and applause. Charter status finally obtained, Gompers was free to "move from a culture of survival to a culture of learning" (Riveroll, quoted in Gao 2005d: A1).

Bringing GCMS to Life: A Transformation at Top Speed

The time available for celebrating was short. The leadership team had only six months to take all the actions needed to start a school. Even before taking steps such as sprucing up the campus or recruiting and hiring teachers, however, Gompers leadership needed to create a governing structure. Charter schools are often governed by boards of directors. Discussions about the general configuration and specific membership of the Gompers board began immediately after the school board approved the charter petition. The UCSD members of the Gompers working group were asked to serve as an ad hoc committee to prepare a slate of board members that would include parents, teachers, community members, and UCSD faculty/staff. However, exactly which individuals should fill those slots, especially the ones for "community representatives," proved contentious. Some members of the working group lobbied for community members who represented local groups, while the ad hoc committee advocated for representatives with greater state and national visibility.

During an intense working group meeting, the issue was settled in favor of selecting former State Senator Dede Alpert, the Urban League's Cecil Steppe, and PIQE President David Valladolid—community representatives with state, regional, and national reputations. In addition to the three community representatives, the board includes three parents, three educators, and three UCSD representatives. At its initial meeting on May 28, 2005, held on the UCSD campus, the newly formed GCMS board of directors quickly and unanimously elected Cecil Steppe as chair and appointed Vincent Riveroll director of Gompers Charter Middle School. Because Gompers is an independent 301c3 organization, the school's governing board is more autonomous than is the Preuss board, which is integrated into the UCSD governance structure. The Gompers board sets budgetary and administrative policy, and assigns to the principal authority over personnel matters, professional development, and the enactment of the school's academic plan.

Because time was critically short, and because the lack of high-quality teachers at the "old" Gompers had been a key factor in mobilizing parents to push for changing the school to a charter, even as the governing board was being composed, GCMS leaders began trying to secure an initial high-quality teaching staff. The SDUSD school board's reassignment of Riveroll to the district office removed him from Gompers and limited his ability to recruit and interview prospective teachers. He believed it would be unethical to conduct Gompers business during his regular SDUSD workday. Thus, Riveroll and an ad hoc personnel committee composed of GCMS administrators, parents, and UCSD CREATE personnel conducted recruitment interviews at UCSD from 6:30 a.m. to 8:00 a.m., and from 5:30 p.m. to 8:00 p.m., weekdays—and also often on Saturdays—from March to July 2005. Among the teachers who previously had taught at Gompers and applied for positions at the new charter school, eight were hired. Thirty-nine of forty-seven teachers were new to the school, and of these, thirty-four were new to the teaching profession.

With a governing board in place, and personnel interviewing and hiring begun, more attention could be directed toward other crucial start-up tasks: securing books and educational materials; securing funding; designing a curriculum students would find challenging and exciting; and developing a college-going culture for students who, in most cases, would not have been exposed to such a program previously (details about GCMS curriculum and culture are provided in Chapter 4). To ensure that the new teaching staff shared the same understanding of and commitment to providing all GCMS students with a college-prep curriculum and helping them develop a college-going culture, school leadership conducted a two-week professional development activity before school opened. Its purpose was to develop a common language, common expectations, and common ways in which teachers and support staff would interact with students (Chapter 4 discusses this "culture camp" more fully).

EFFECTS OF SDUSD ACTIONS ON THE DEVELOPMENT OF GOMPERS

In the previous sections we described the frequently negative impact that district and school board policy and practice had on the *formation* of GCMS and the determination with which people associated with Gompers reacted to both setbacks and opportunities. In the next two sections we describe how Gompers supporters responded to district-level decisionmaking with respect to Gompers' *development*. We use two disputes over facilities to illustrate how the actions of social actors on the ground can shape policy formulated in more distant bureaucratic settings.

Resisting District Policies Concerning Educational Facilities

Under the provisions of Proposition 39, passed by California voters in 2000 and implemented in 2003, charter schools that serve at least eighty in-district students are entitled to seek facilities from the district that authorized their charters. From 2006–2007 to the present, twenty-one of the schools chartered by the SDUSD have engaged in a running battle with the district about space allocation and the cost of renting classroom and administrative space.

The dispute started in February 2006, when the district office sent contradictory messages to charter schools. The SDUSD Office of School Choice gave charter schools a week to inform the district about their intended use of facilities for the 2006–2007 school year. Meanwhile, the district's legal counsel had assured the schools that they would retain their existing classroom and administrative space.[2]

The dispute intensified when representatives from the Office of School Choice proposed pairing up charter schools on the same campus and cutting back facilities, based on SDUSD-generated enrollment projections—figures that were in every case lower than what the charter schools projected. The proposal required GCMS to share libraries, cafeteria, office space, and so on with another charter school. Each school would have separate classrooms. GCMS board members Alpert, Steppe, and others spoke eloquently to the school board on February 6, 2006, about the current and potential damage associated with the fast-paced and heavy-handed manner in which the district's preliminary decisions had been presented:

> You need to sit down and talk with people. If you move today, you're going to find that you have so many dissatisfied people, and I think appropriately so, because time has not been spent … to come up with the very best possible solution. This is not yet soup—not only for Gompers but for so many of the charter schools here today. To have just received this information and suggestions about who would be paired with whom … it seems to me you need more time. (D. Alpert 2006)

Despite these comments (and those of others) and vocal opposition from charter school supporters in the audience, board members voted 3–2 to accept the preliminary proposal. One senior board member voted against the motion. The *San Diego Union Tribune* and *Voice of San Diego,* both strong charter school supporters, savaged the board's decision in editorials (*San Diego Union Tribune* 2006; Sutton 2006a, 2006b). Calling the decision "disgraceful," "capricious," "an amoral assault on the public interest," and one that "was certainly illegal," the *Union Tribune* editorial attributed the decision to an "arrogant refusal to work with charters." The editorial tied that refusal to an effort on the part of the board majority to close charters in the wake of the district's diminishing financial resources, a decline linked to falling enrollments in the city's conventional public schools.

The Gompers board responded to the SDUSD action with a counterproposal: they would modify the GCMS charter to make the school available to students in grades 6–9 for one year—that is, until the new Lincoln High campus opened. This temporary change would enlarge the student body sufficiently to enable GCMS to retain its current facilities, and would sidestep the contentious issue of the validity of the SDUSD's projected enrollment figures for the charter schools. GCMS Board Chair Steppe presented this idea to Superintendent Cohn when he visited GCMS on March 6, 2006.[3]

On March 8, 2006, in a brief e-mail to Steppe, Superintendent Cohn endorsed key aspects of the GCMS proposal:

> I'm OK with your two main requests that GCMS serve grades 6–9 and that Gompers Senior serve 9–12. I would like the parties to explore a special contract or MOU [memorandum of understanding] on the operation of the 9th grade program at GCMS so that we can start advancing the notion that high standards in dress, behavior, and achievement can be realized outside of the charter format. (Steppe 2006)

With this memo, three top officials—a senior school board member, the superintendent, and the district counsel—each had indicated support for Gompers. But events that transpired next indicate that top-level support does not always translate into standard operating procedures implemented by mid-level staff. The school board met to review charter plans on March 28, 2006. Between the February 28 and March 28 board meetings, SDUSD officials had met with charter school leaders; 200 charter school supporters had rallied at the San Diego education center before and during the February board meeting (Magee 2006); and GCMS parents had organized plans to enroll their students outside their neighborhood schools.

The political pressure applied by community organizations, parents, and the press seemed to have an effect. District officials modified the initial proposal; schools were allocated more space. But in the case of GCMS, the newly allocated space was not equal to that of the previous year; the formula was based on a 30:1 student-teacher ratio, whereas the charter schools had reduced student-teacher ratios to 25:1 to improve instructional quality. And there was to be an increased charge for any space used over-and-above the original charter agreement. The district did agree, however, to an MOU that enabled ninth-graders to be educated at GCMS until Lincoln High School's new campus opened.

Because under the provisions of Proposition 39 charter facilities must be allocated annually, discussions between charter school leaders and district officials continued into the 2007–2008 and 2008–2009 school years. As was the case in 2006–2007, the district made initial proposals, and some, but not all, charter schools made counterproposals. The district then modified its initial proposals in the face of resistance. Those schools that resisted the most strenuously obtained the best deal; schools that acquiesced fared less well.

For the 2007–2008 school year, this ritualized, kabuki-style dance officially resumed on February 16, 2007, when seventeen charter schools were offered greatly reduced space, and four schools were denied space entirely. GCMS and KIPP were supposed to share a campus. Because the district plan was based on a 30:1 rather than a 25:1 student-teacher ratio, and used a projected enrollment figure of 539 students in grades 6–8 compared to the GCMS-calculated figure of 782 students, the plan slashed the classroom allocation for GCMS from fifty-three to twenty-six.

The goal of enrolling 750 or more students in fall 2007 posed a challenge, exacerbated by other district actions. The district office did not explicitly forbid Gompers representatives from informing students who were attending local elementary schools, and their parents, about the academic program at Gompers. The district did make the recruitment process difficult, however. For example, a letter sent to elementary school parents in the Gompers catchment area listed the schools that children could attend. Names, addresses, and phone numbers of traditional middle schools were included; but information about Gompers was not included. To stimulate enrollment in the face of this kind of passive resistance from the SDUSD, Gompers initiated a vigorous door-to-door campaign to inform parents that they had the option of enrolling their children at GCMS, and to explain the school's academic plan to them.

In spring 2008 the district proposed that GCMS and other charter schools be assessed at $4.25 per square foot for the use of facilities. GCMS Chief of Staff Allison Kenda negotiated aggressively with the SDUSD director of facilities planning. Those actions, accompanied by public appeals to the school board by prominent members of the GCMS board, led to a proposed reduction in charges for the 2008–2009 school year. GCMS was allocated thirty-three classrooms at $1 per square foot, and the remaining twenty classrooms at $2.75 per square foot. While this compromise reduced the cost of facilities considerably from the previous year and from the district's original position, GCMS was not ready to capitulate to what continued to seem unfair treatment. Citing California Education Code paragraph 47614, which reads, "public school facilities should be shared fairly among all public school pupils, including those in charter schools," Kenda pushed to have the district allocate facilities using the same formula it uses for traditional schools and to take into account GCMS's commitment to smaller class size and the specialized educational programs instituted at the school to accelerate students' learning. She succeeded in convincing the SDUSD to charge $1.00 per square foot for all GCMS facilities. This successful bargaining saved GCMS over $200,000 in rent—no small amount in troubled budget times. But this achievement entailed costs of its own: it required a huge investment of hours of administrative time that would otherwise have been spent on the challenges of developing the academic dimensions of this fledgling school.

Resisting District Plans to Place Another School on Gompers Property

Turf battles between charters and the SDUSD were not limited to the cost of renting facilities. In 2007 the district began exploring plans to place Millennial Tech Middle School (MTM), a proposed science-technology-engineering-math (STEM) magnet school on a section of the property known as the East Gompers campus—space that had been abandoned when the high school component of Gompers closed and Lincoln High School opened (fall 2007). On April 22, 2008, the school board approved the placement of MTM on Gompers' east campus. Funding for MTM was to be bolstered by a $2.1 million grant from the federal government for advanced technology, equipment, instructional supplies, curriculum, and staff development. Funds for renovating the site—expected to cost in excess of $2 million—were supposed to come from another source. MTM opened in fall 2008 with 250 students in grades 6–8.

An architectural firm prepared preliminary site plans for Gompers Preparatory Academy (GPA), as GCMS, now configured to become a grades 6–12 charter school, was to be known. The district-proposed site plans for MTM and for a new bus turnaround facility would doom that expansion. The bus facility would co-opt space Gompers hoped to use for high school buildings; and temporary bungalows for MTM that the district intended to place on existing Gompers athletic fields would scuttle Gompers' plan to share the playing fields with MTM.

Gompers staff met with district staff often during the 2008–2009 academic year to try to settle the issue. Unable to achieve an equitable solution, the Gompers board ramped up pressure. Letters to the school board, meetings with district staff, meetings with individual school board members, and articles in the *Voice of San Diego* (Sutton 2009b) did not break the impasse. In an attempt to focus public attention on the conflict, Gompers held a rally and press conference on the site of the proposed athletic field on July 1, 2009.

The softball field backstop on the decomposed granite field east of the school was adorned with a GPA banner and architectural drawings of the future Gompers. By the time members of the press, parents, students, teachers, and community members finished wandering in, seventy-five people were assembled on bleachers facing the podium situated in front of the banner and drawings. Director Riveroll welcomed the audience, reminding those assembled that this event was an exercise in democracy; dialogue and debate can settle contentious issues, he asserted. This event also became a teaching moment, as one after the other, students, teachers, and parents voiced their concerns. Instead of one or two well-established and well-recognized leaders chronicling the perceived injustices, the task was distributed among people not practiced in public speaking. Much as when students are encouraged to write letters to newspapers and post to blogs about perceived injustices, the opportunity for students to address members of the press and the community enabled them to practice public speaking before an authentic audience.

The theme of the rally was "Save Our Field." Coaches and teachers connected athletics and academics. The audience and press were informed that Gompers students who participate in sports must maintain a 2.5 GPA (the district requirement is 2.0) and that athletes have mandatory study hall before practices. The opportunity to participate in sports encourages some students to do well in class—and to avoid gangs. Student Body President Isaac Ramos drew an analogy between people putting a path through a neighbor's backyard garden without permission to the district's decision to place bungalows on the athletic field without consultation. A Gompers teacher who had grown up in the neighborhood and attended Gompers many years earlier pointed out an irony. When the school was struggling, the district paid no attention to the athletic fields, but now that Gompers was succeeding, the SDUSD was paying attention—but only in negative and unproductive ways.

At the July 21, 2009, school board meeting, students, parents, faculty, staff, and Gompers board members presented reasons why the placement of eleven temporary classrooms and a bus turnaround on Gompers property would negatively impact the school's academic and athletic development. Two of the school board's five members expressed surprise and dismay at the lack of long-term planning for the MTM site and deplored not being presented with a range of alternatives to consider. They resented being given a fait accompli by district staff. After a lengthy and often contentious debate over the substance of the proposal and the procedure by which it was presented, the school board voted 5–0 to instruct district staff to meet with MTM and Gompers leadership to develop alternative plans that would be acceptable to both schools by July 28, one week later.

The meeting took place on July 24. District staff presented three scenarios covering the placement of MTM temporary classrooms. Gompers representatives argued forcefully for a fourth possibility—placing all eleven temporary classrooms on the abandoned volleyball courts located north of GPA classrooms. A compromise scenario was agreed upon: four temporary classrooms would be placed on Gompers fields for one year. At the same time, the south end of the school's decomposed granite fields would be prepared for a multipurpose playing field, to accommodate CIF-level soccer, field hockey, and football. Concurrently, the "volleyball courts" area would be prepared to accommodate seven other temporary MTM classrooms in summer 2010. Arrangements would be made to move San Diego County mental health officials from offices they occupied on the MTM campus, in order to provide that school with further growth potential. When the four temporary classrooms are removed from Gompers playing fields, a regulation softball and baseball field will be installed.

District staff members were instructed to prepare drawings, cost estimates, and timelines for these scenarios for presentation at a school board workshop scheduled for July 28. At that special meeting, district staff presented three scenarios to the board. Gompers Board of Directors Chair Steppe presented a fourth option, preferred by Gompers, namely placing all eleven temporary classrooms on the unused volleyball courts, but reluctantly agreed to the alternative plan assembled during the previous week. The school board voted unanimously (5–0) to accept the revised plan, which provided for placing four temporary classrooms on Gompers' playing fields for one year, starting the development of a multipurpose field, placing seven additional temporary classrooms on the volleyball courts, and developing softball and baseball fields as soon as the temporary classrooms were removed. The disposition of the bus turnaround was referred to a planning team to be convened in September 2009.

As this resolution demonstrates, actions from below can influence decisions made at the top of a bureaucracy. There was not just one possible location for the temporary classrooms for MTM. In one week, representatives from MTM and Gompers, working with district staff, produced four viable alternatives for the development of MTM classrooms and playing fields to be shared by the two schools. By contrast, district staff had produced only one scenario during the previous twelve months—one that precluded the development of athletic fields.

Subsequent events led to a more equitable solution. That same September, Bill Kowba, who previously had operational responsibilities within the district, became acting superintendent when Terry Grier (who had replaced Carl Cohn) left the post. Kowba convened a "design task force" to hammer out a long-range master plan for MTM and Gompers facilities. The task force directed the district to use state school facility funds to construct athletic fields for baseball, softball, soccer, and football that would meet CIF standards, and to seek funds for a multistory academic building and gymnasium for Gompers. Equally important, the task force responded positively to Gompers' request to relocate the disputed bus turnaround. Instead of occupying space intended for Gompers' academic and athletic buildings, it is now planned for the eastern edge of the Gompers field, away from classrooms and physical education areas.

The actions taken by the district under the direction of Acting Superintendent Kowba in response to demands formulated by Gompers staff stand in contrast to those of previous administrations (Flanagan 2008). Although this cooperation is a welcome relief, it is not clear as of this writing whether it represents a more permanent change in district policy toward charter schools or is a brief interruption in a constant flow of antagonisms seemingly designed to retain power and influence in the face of challenges from "below."

THE CONSEQUENCES OF GOVERNMENT ACTIONS AND UNIVERSITY POLICIES

Actions taken and decisions made by federal, state, and county governments also impact charter schools. We discuss one federal law, two state actions, and one county grand jury investigation to illustrate how governmental regulations, fiscal policies, and legal remedies sometimes constrain and sometimes assist charter schools. Because Gompers is a charter school in partnership with the University of California San Diego, we also review here the university's role in helping and hindering this charter school. In addition, we examine the actions educators took in response to the constraints and opportunities posed by all of these entities.

The Enabling and Constraining Influence of NCLB

The stated goal of No Child Left Behind is to have 100 percent of the nation's students demonstrating academic proficiency in mathematics and English language arts by 2014. To determine the progress of schools in achieving this goal, NCLB requires states to administer standardized reading and mathematics tests each year to all public school students in grades 3–8, and once to all public high school students. States set "adequate yearly progress" (AYP) targets to benchmark districts' and schools' progress toward the 2014 goal. If schools do not meet AYP goals as measured by their students' performance on standardized tests, then they are subject to discipline and punishment. In the most extreme cases, underperforming schools that receive Title I funds face restructuring—that is, conversion into charter schools, or takeover by the state or a private company.

NCLB supporters (e.g., Tucker and Codding 1998; Education Trust 2003a, 2003b; Hanushek and Raymond 2004) call attention to its outcome-based definition of equality. Instead of measuring equal educational opportunity in terms of inputs (federal or state aid, for instance), NCLB measures equality in terms of outputs (universal achievement goals, measured primarily through standardized tests). Furthermore, supporters of NCLB assert that accountability systems give the public substantial knowledge about the status of their local schools in comparison to state and national standards. In addition to enabling parents to make more informed choices regarding the education of their children, this knowledge also puts public pressure on low-performing schools to improve their quality or suffer negative consequences. Publicity, in fact, has positively benefited low-performing schools. Many have made significant improvements in the wake of public scrutiny (Education Trust 2003a,

2003b). Martin Carnoy et al. (2005) report that the greater the sanctions imposed by a state, the better black students (but not Latinos) perform on high-stakes tests. Although test scores improved, graduation rates did not, leading these authors to question the overall utility of high-stakes regimens.

Critics of the practice of using standardized tests in high-stakes accountability regimens (e.g., McNeil 1998; Haney 2000; Kohn 2002; Amrein and Berliner 2002; White and Rosenbaum 2008; Ravitch 2010a; Hinchey 2010) have lodged a number of complaints. By taking only standardized scores into account, most current accountability systems automatically reward schools in affluent areas because parents' income is highly correlated with students' academic performance (Linn 2000; Haney 2000; Betts, Rueben, and Danenberg 2000; Powers 2004). Although using any single measure of student learning is not good practice, relying on short, timed, multiple-choice tests is especially problematic, critics say, because such tests do not measure creativity, problem solving, or critical thinking—the very skills needed for lifelong learning and active participation in a democratic society; worse, they demoralize test-takers who are not fluent in English.

From most teachers' point of view, high-stakes tests are problematic because they are not always aligned well with the state standards they are presumed to inform. Fearful of recriminations, teachers often dumb down their curriculum in order to "teach to the test," thereby subtracting precious time from much-needed instruction. For example, Joseph Pedulla and George F. Madaus (2004) report that 76 percent of teachers facing the highest stakes and 63 percent of those encountering the lowest sanctions said that mandatory testing led to teaching in ways that contradicted their own ideas of sound educational practice. Worse, some teachers encourage poor-performing students to stay away from school on test days (White and Rosenbaum 2008), or change students' answers to inflate results (Jacob and Levitt 2003; Amrein and Berliner 2002). Teachers also complain that test results are not calculated and reported back to them quickly enough to be a help in diagnosing students' learning needs and modifying curriculum and instruction accordingly.

Low-performing schools react to the accountability component of NCLB by suspending normal instruction and engaging in extensive and frantic test preparation procedures (McNeil 1998; Amrein and Berliner 2002; Berliner 2005). During its first few years, Gompers did not succumb to these tendencies; instead, school leaders hired a nationally recognized expert on literacy coaching (Casey 2006) to instruct the faculty on ways to embed test prep within the context of ordinary lessons. These strategies included formatting quizzes to match those of the standardized tests that students would encounter and posing the types of problems students are likely to find on the California Standards Test (CST) throughout the school year. This incremental approach to test prep minimizes the seemingly inevitable frenzy just before test time. The improvement in students' performance on mandated tests seems to confirm the usefulness of embedded test preparation (see Chapter 2, Table 2.4).

Despite these gains, Gompers faculty is fearful that the upward trajectory cannot be sustained; indeed, it needs to be intensified if the school is to reach the coveted 800-plus mark on the CSTs within its first five years as a charter. For example, special-education students would have to gain sixty points each year for four years to reach that goal. Students with limited English proficiency would have to gain seventy points each year—an incredible feat, given that they made only a forty-point gain in the first year of the school's existence. Cognizant of these challenges, the school has intensified its test-prep efforts. Classroom time is now set aside for test-prep practice; family services staff call upon students who are absent on test day; rallies encouraging excellent test performance are staged in the days running up to test day. Gompers must now be vigilant to ensure that teachers do not start dumbing down their curriculum in order to "teach to the test" and/or begin replacing valuable instructional time with test-prep exercises.

Struggling with the State Budget Crisis, 2008–2011

On September 23, 2008, about three months after its due date, Governor Arnold Schwarzenegger signed the 2008–2009 budget. He reported that the state faced a $14–16 billion gap between income and expenses for the 2008–2009 fiscal year, a projected $24 billion shortfall for 2009–2010, and an additional $10 billion gap for 2010–2011 (Schwarzenegger 2009). State revenue per pupil has declined from a high of $7,000 per pupil in 2007 to a projected low of $6,000 for 2011–2012 (ExEd 2011). Gompers, like other public schools, reacted to the possibility of drastically reduced revenue, and its leadership team redoubled efforts to secure outside funding. Successful in securing "start-up" funding from the California Charter Schools Association, the school still has had to, reluctantly, cut its operating budget, including teachers and support staff. Sadly, this combination of revenue enhancement and program reduction is not proving adequate.

Indeed, the state's continuing fiscal crisis threatens to eliminate key ingredients in Gompers' detracking model. The school has been able to continue operating its family services center, extending the school day, embedding teacher professional development in the fabric of the school day, and offering an "academic and culture camp" at the beginning of the school year (because of a generous donation from the Girard Foundation). Many of the extra scaffolds installed to assist struggling students have had to be reduced or eliminated entirely, however. Notably, the class-size ratio has been increased from 24:1 to 32:1, and important tutoring programs, such as Encore, Math Lab, and Saturday Academy, have been curtailed. The master calendar, originally modified to provide more instructional time to core courses in mathematics and English language arts through elaborate team-teaching arrangements, now distributes instructional time equally across subjects. The leadership team has shrunk from its original configuration of six educators each responsible for monitoring and improving instruction in subject-matter disciplines to four educators who split their time between classroom teaching and providing schoolwide leadership.

In short, so many of the vital and defining components of the school's theory of action have been reduced or eliminated that Gompers Preparatory Academy is in danger of losing its distinctive character and becoming indistinguishable from conventional public schools. If this downward spiral of financial investment by the state continues, the consequences are predictable. Struggling but motivated under-represented minority students will witness the removal of yet another opportunity structure designed to improve their life chances.

Complying with the Williams Remedies

Several California state laws impact charter schools. Notable among them are those written since the landmark *Brown* decision that assert states are legally responsible for ensuring that all children in their jurisdiction have access to the "bare essentials required of a free and common school education"—trained teachers, current text-books, and adequate and safe facilities (Rosenbaum et al. 2000a: 6, quoted in Powers 2004: 764; Oakes 2003). Disparities in these educational resources are fundamentally unfair. *Williams v. State of California,* settled in 2004, "order[s] the State to develop a system that prevents, detects, and cures unequal access to basic educational neces-sities," including the distribution of credentialed teachers, the condition of facilities, and the quality and supply of textbooks (Rosenbaum et al. 2000b: 324, quoted in Powers 2004: 766). By focusing on "how dollars are actually used within classrooms and schools to produce desirable educational outcomes" (Grubb and Goe 2002: 5), the *Williams* case and other legal challenges both affirm the promise of equal edu-cational opportunity that is at the heart of the *Brown* decision and transform it by demanding material redress of the deep inequities in the distribution of educational resources in public education (Powers 2004).

Often when legal precedents are translated into the practicalities of enforce-ment, lofty statements are reduced to mundane checklists. This has certainly been the case with the enforcement of the *Williams* remedies. Officials representing the state descend on schools without prior notice and inspect classrooms for the presence of textbooks and heat, and the absence of broken windows; they check bathrooms for the absence of leaks and presence of toilet paper. Much less attention has been paid to the quality of the teaching staff, and even less to the subtleties of teacher-student interaction and the depth of student learning.

The first surprise visit of the *Williams* team to GCMS in October 2005 reported shortages of critical material resources. Chagrined, the GCMS staff prepared for the next surprise visit by ensuring that each student's desk displayed the appropriate course books, restrooms were spotless, and windows were clean. This preparation paid off on the second *Williams* surprise visit September 2006, when GCMS received high praise. The report singled out manicured landscaping, clean facilities, a quiet campus, and student engagement in learning. In this case, preparing to comply with a state regulation reaped benefits.

The intent of the *Williams* settlement is to equalize educational resources, the most important of which is instruction. But because measuring the quality of instruction is a difficult, time-consuming undertaking, the *Williams* test has been reduced to tangible and superficial measures, such as checking for the presence of textbooks and absence of broken windows. Though the actions of educators can ensure compliance with a checklist, inspections that measure superficial school features do little, in and of themselves, to improve instruction or revitalize schools.

Surviving a Grand Jury Investigation: "Phoenix Rising"

San Diego County laws as well as state laws impacted Gompers' early development. To everyone's surprise, the San Diego County Grand Jury investigated GCMS during the 2005–2006 academic year. To be sure, Gompers has had a less than distinguished history, but no grand jury had ever paid attention to the dismal situation at Gompers before the school converted to a charter. Furthermore, the "new Gompers" had been open only a month when the investigation commenced. The investigation consisted of jury members' unannounced visits to campus and classrooms and perusal of documents and records. These activities would have been burdensome under any circumstances, but given that they occurred just after the school opened, they were especially distracting. GCMS educators did not openly resist this imposition; they interrupted their daily duties and responsibilities to comply with the visitors' requests for documents and interviews.

In its final report, released in May 2006, the Grand Jury reported favorably on the GCMS educational program. It applauded the efforts of the staff, parents, and students for their dedication to student achievement and commended the GCMS board of directors, the GCMS leadership team, and the staff for creating a college-going culture and learning environment. The report was not without criticisms, however. The Grand Jury recommended that the school increase its security and its counseling personnel, and that it correct spelling and grammatical errors in the charter document. The Grand Jury's report concluded that becoming a charter was indeed in the best interest of the students because "GCMS is a rising phoenix in public education."

Allying with the University: Drawbacks and Benefits

UCSD's presence was, in many ways, at the heart of the initial Gompers charter school debate. Many Gompers neighborhood parents supported UCSD's involvement and welcomed the resources UCSD promised. Other actors, however, including members of the UCSD administration, some community members, and an ambivalent school board, were concerned about the extent of the university's involvement and the depth of its commitment. Some UCSD administrators, in a manner reminiscent of the debate over the creation of The Preuss School, expressed concern about the extent of UCSD's financial commitment to the charter school effort at Gompers and questioned whether that effort was consistent with the university's mission.

School board members also worried that not enough faculty and staff members at the university endorsed UCSD's involvement with the same level of enthusiasm as Cecil Lytle and Hugh Mehan. Through CREATE, UCSD promised to bring to Gompers material and intellectual resources, many of which have been derived from successful developments at Preuss. Intellectual resources include advice on how to restructure and reculture the school to enable rigorous college-prep instruction for all students (Alvarez and Mehan 2006). Material resources include UCSD students, who serve as tutors before school, during classes, and after school; professional development experts; researchers who compile and analyze information on students' performance and the development of the school; teaching interns in math, science, and English/LEP; events and materials designed to provide opportunities for parents to learn about higher educational options for their children when they finish high school, as well as concrete advice on how to achieve higher educational goals and obtain funding for college; and faculty who serve on the Gompers board of directors.

CONCLUSIONS: "A CONSTANT FLOW OF CRISES" INHIBITS REFORM

Opening a new school for 800-plus students with only six months' lead time is a staggeringly difficult task. In the case of Gompers Charter Middle School, the job required recruiting, interviewing, and hiring an entire teaching and support staff, refurbishing facilities, designing a college-going culture for a neighborhood without such a program previously, coaching teachers in that academic plan, and then making learning challenging and exciting for students. But that already-daunting scenario was further exacerbated by external constraints that generated "a constant flow of crises" (Riveroll 2008).

To understand the struggles over power and control that took place among Gompers, the district, various government agencies, and the university, it is instructive to place the struggles in the context of the dispute over the value of charter schools in the school reform movement. Recall from Chapter 2 that advocates of charter schools claim they provide the possibility of innovative alternatives to stodgy and inflexible public schools, whereas opponents fear that charter schools are a step down the slippery slope to privatization. Charter schools are touted as laboratories or models—places where new educational ideas can be tried out. If such experiments are successful, then the lessons learned can be adapted in other contexts. Following that logic, if Gompers Charter Middle School became successful—boosting the educational achievement of the most socioeconomically disadvantaged groups—then the district could take full credit for this innovation and bask in the reflected glory of the school. Moreover, the district could then apply the lessons learned to new educational contexts.

"Charter schools as models" was not the narrative guiding the relations between charters and the SDUSD from 2005 to 2008, however. After years of acrimonious exchanges between the school and a revolving door of superintendents, tendentious interventions by legal experts, and inflamed editorial commentaries, the district and Gompers came to tenuous compromises. Sanctioned by the current superintendent, Bill Kowba, Gompers retains its classroom, cafeteria, auditorium, and office space without the need to share with another charter school. The neighboring magnet middle school will occupy buildings on the other side of the fence that divides the two school campuses. Athletic fields will be shared with MTM. Teachers have the right to return to schools in the San Diego Unified District if they leave Gompers.

The formation of Gompers provides a counterexample to the privatization narrative that dominates the debate over charter schools. Critics of charter schools fear that they will undercut public education because private schools outside state control will proliferate. Private school advocates were nowhere to be seen when activist parents in southeastern San Diego clamored for a new school. Instead, these parents, tired of what they perceived as persistent neglect from the SDUSD and the school board, set about forming a charter school independent of the district. They energized the local community, reached out to the departing school superintendent, and persuaded UCSD to pledge material and intellectual assistance.

Examined from the point of view of supporters of the conversion of Gompers Middle School to a charter school, the actions of the San Diego Unified School District school board are inexplicable, even inexcusable. Examining these actions from the point of view of the school district or the teachers' union, however, reveals understandable motivations. Charter schools can be perceived as undercutting the centralized power and authority that bureaucracies such as school districts seek to preserve. In that sense, charter schools are a potential threat to conventional public schools and their teachers' unions. They also pose a more immediate and concrete challenge: funds that would normally go to the SDUSD central office flow directly to charter schools. The district receives about $5,100 per pupil from the state. With just over 12,000 students enrolled in charter schools—about 10 percent of the district's total school population—SDUSD loses about $61 million annually to its charter schools (Sutton 2006a). This is an especially serious issue for the district because of a general decline in enrollment—from 140,000 to 130,000 in the past few years (McEntree 2007).

Concomitant with fiscal considerations is the matter of control. As schools become charters, they are less dependent on the central administration for services and are less subject to central office authority. So, the district's lack of support for charters can be seen as an expression of the fear of losing control of schools in their inventory. This is an issue of special importance in the part of the district where Gompers is located. The area has many conventional public elementary schools but few conventional public middle and high schools. Some comprehensive high schools are converting to small schools; others are magnets. Schools that send students to Lincoln High School are charters; no conventional public middle school is a feeder for Lincoln.

Charter schools are not required to unionize, which diminishes union membership and the hard-earned power to bargain on behalf of teachers. Soon after they were advised by the SDUSD district that they needed to restructure, the four schools considering charter status in 2005 sought a waiver from the SDEA's contract with the district. The schools wanted to be able to offer teachers contracts directly, without activating the seniority-based personnel policy centered at the district office. The SDEA did not grant a waiver of the "post and bid" process, citing procedural violations (Williams and Toch 2006). By the time the four schools petitioned the school board for charter status, there were thirty-five charter schools already established in the district; the 13,000 students they enrolled accounted for a loss to the district of $70 million in state funding. Most of the charters were established in low-income neighborhoods; thirty of thirty-five were located south of Interstate 8—the symbolic and material boundary between the well-to-do neighborhoods and the less-well-off neighborhoods in San Diego (*Voice of San Diego* 2008).

Some district leaders, perhaps fearful that charter schools are a step toward the privatization of public schools, subtract needed funds from district coffers, and challenge the central authority of the district, attempted to contain the expansion of charter schools in general, and Gompers in particular. The strategy began with a move to charge charters exceedingly high rents for facilities use; next came a decision to place Millennial Tech Middle School, a STEM magnet, on adjacent property, followed by plans to expand MTM onto Gompers' property. The dramas these actions engendered exposed the clumsy manner in which the SDUSD as an organization attempted to preserve its power. The district's actions constitute a crude example of the more general power-preserving tendencies inherent in many large bureaucracies.

In the case of the turf war between MTM and Gompers, several, but not all, school board members clung to a single course of action and attempted to keep that decision from public scrutiny. District staff acquiesced to that limited vision instead of doing due diligence and presenting a range of alternatives for all school board members' consideration. A well-orchestrated political action campaign composed of vocal and articulate parents, students, teachers, university representatives, and community members caught the attention of a board member who was willing to challenge the board president's agenda-setting authority. This opened discourse space for the consideration of alternatives to what appeared to be a final decision. Once that debate was opened, the flaws in the original conception were revealed. The full board's rejection of the president's preferred version undercut her authority and revealed her limited vision.

Board members often expressed their concern about the increasing number of charter schools in the district—especially those located "south of 8." Thus, in 2004, when the idea of re-creating Gompers as a charter school was first posed to the board, members appealed to Gompers parents to restructure their school under the guidance of the district. However, parents and teachers dismissed the idea of simply tinkering with educational programs or grade configurations. Repelled by a history of teacher vacancies and chaotic conditions, which they blamed in part on district-union bargaining agreements, the Gompers working group was convinced that reopening the school as a charter was the only viable option.

The district's actions toward charter schools under the direction of Superintendent Kowba's two immediate predecessors appear to have been predicated on a divide-and-conquer or attrition strategy. The district would lay down a challenge and wait to see if and how the schools responded; then the district would lay down another challenge and wait to see if and how the schools responded, and so on. The schools' responses differed; in some cases, the district's strategy paid off, and in some cases it did not. Some of the well-endowed charter schools, like Keillor Leadership Academy, KIPP, and Gompers, had the financial resources and human capital needed in order to fight back. Their resistance proved productive. The political pressure applied by community organizations, parents, and newspapers seemed to have an effect, in that the district modified its initial proposals. In the end, schools paid less rent and were allocated more facilities.

Other, less well-endowed charter schools were unable to retaliate. Weary of the battle, they withdrew their requests to use district facilities or begrudgingly accepted the district's financial demands. As a result, some of these schools may close entirely—not necessarily due to any failure of their academic plans or ability to attract students, but because they have been worn down. One consequence of this attrition strategy is that it divides and diminishes the charter school community. Even though all of the charter schools have certain interests in common, in order to protect themselves, the stronger schools separate themselves from the weaker ones. When the weaker ones close, they often leave unpaid bills in their wake (E. Alpert 2007)—which produces a loss for all concerned.

These locally generated constraints have been compounded by state and federal policies and practices. The Gompers detracking model, with its rigorous curriculum supported by extensive academic and social scaffolds, requires an extended school year and a lower student-teacher ratio. The shifting state policy on charters and the statewide budget crisis that required Gompers—and all public schools—to plan for significant reductions in state funds starting in 2008–2009 cut into the Gompers theory of action even before it was solidified.

The accountability provisions of NCLB lurk in the background, affecting all urban schools, including Gompers. Important innovations such as installing a rigorous college-prep curriculum reinforced by academic and social supports require time to instantiate. The NCLB's demands for annual yearly progress on cognitively limited standardized tests with ever-increasing standards inhibits plans to restructure and reculture what was previously a failing school. In very practical terms, Gompers' extensive academic plan collides with the accountability imperative when teachers feel compelled to direct attention away from instruction and toward test prep.

UCSD's partnership with Gompers, while helpful, also has produced its own troubles. On the one hand, faculty and staff associated with CREATE were able to assist Gompers in navigating through the uncertainties of the political process and to direct considerable resources (tutors, research, professional development, and governance expertise) to the school. On the other hand, the university's uneven record in communities of color and the less-than-enthusiastic commitment of UCSD's central administration toward community engagement required CREATE to negotiate trust cautiously and repeatedly.

One can never be sure of the motives of actors in the political arena (Brzezinski 2007). Publicly stated motives do not always align with the actions that flow from them, but publicly stated motives also may be at odds with those stated behind closed doors (Mills 1940). Although the motivations guiding the actions of individuals in positions of power in the cases described in this chapter may not be clear, it seems their ideological positions served to preserve the district's position concerning its relation to charter schools.

To be sure, large bureaucracies such as school districts attempt to consolidate and thereby retain their power and authority by issuing directives from the top. But educators, parents, and community members are not compliant actors, passively responding to directives mandated from higher levels of bureaucracies. Instead, they are active agents. As we have seen, educators, parents, and community members may act in a variety of ways in response to actions directed from the top. They comply with some directives and resist or even actively subvert others. Too, as they did in the turf war described here, they may initiate alternatives, such as plans for reduced rental fees or different bungalow placement. In short, grassroots political action can thwart, or at least slow down, the power-preserving tendencies of entrenched bureaucracies.

NOTES

1. Our participation in the formation of Gompers led us to attend approximately twenty weekly (and sometimes twice-weekly) working group meetings composed of school personnel, parents, and community members; four school board meetings; seven one-on-one meetings with charter association members, school board members, district staff, and the district superintendent; and thirteen small group meetings with UCSD faculty members, students, and faculty.

2. SDUSD Assistant General Counsel Jose González had notified Gompers Director Riveroll in 2005 that GCMS did not have to "apply for facilities under Proposition 39 because that process is not applicable to your charter school." The letter also said, "Your charter school will be housed in ... the same facilities that Gompers Middle School was housed in" (González 2005).

3. On that day, Cohn was treated to a full-dress demonstration of the Gompers "culture": a slide show displaying the development of GCMS—led by a student; a song sung by the Associated Student Body (ASB)—dressed in their new uniforms of skirts/trousers, sweaters, ties, and white shirts; and classroom visits. Everyone was on good behavior. The schoolyard was spotless. The hallways were empty; only students and teachers walking purposefully were visible. Cohn saw a parent meeting led by Michelle Evans and facilitated by Rafael Hernandez, and he attended a final meeting with the ASB. There, students asked him questions about what he liked about Gompers. He responded that he had been impressed by the commitment to a "culture of learning," the respectful behavior on the part of students, and the orderliness of the school. He commented on classrooms—all visits occurred during "prelude," an opening period in which students gather on a rug, sitting in a whole-group configuration, and receive instructions for the day. Teachers were on task, he said, with instructions on display, and lots of questions asked and answered by students. Before leaving, Cohn summarized his reactions to his day at the school by saying that the goals of high standards and academic achievement were commendable—and were reinforced by commitment to standards governing behavior and dress.

Chapter 4

Trying to Bend the Bars of the Iron Cage

The Possibilities and Limitations of Charter Schools as Models for Successful School Reform

Hugh Mehan and Makeba Jones

US public schools are charged with the responsibility for achieving two paired goals: academic excellence and educational equity. The former entails educating students to their highest potential. The latter entails ensuring that all students have an equal educational opportunity to reach their highest potential. Achieving both goals has challenged public schools since their inception. In the long history of educational reform "tinkering toward utopia" (Tyack and Cuban 1995), some reforms, such as gifted-and-talented programs and No Child Left Behind legislation, have emphasized academic excellence more than equity, while others, such as desegregation, special education, the GI Bill, and bilingual education provisions, have put educational equity in the foreground and pushed academic excellence more to the background.

Scrambling to improve their standing in comparison to European and Asian nations and to "close the achievement gap" here at home, public schools have experimented with a variety of reforms. Charter schools have emerged as an innovation with the potential to educate students better and to provide models traditional public schools can emulate. Their proponents' critique of public schools as being overly bureaucratic and thus stifling creativity tacitly invokes a major observation the German sociologist Max Weber made about industrial society generally. Weber noted that as societies became more urbanized and industrialized, social life grew increasingly bureaucratized. He argued that social control rationalized on the grounds of rules and regulations, efficiency, and accountability was preferable to social control based on tradition or on a cult of personality. But he also cautioned that a rule-governed social order was susceptible to ossification, impersonalization, and hyper-routinized behavior. In such an over-bureaucratized social order, Weber predicted, people are likely to become trapped in an "iron cage," a "polar night of icy darkness" (M. Weber 1994: xvi).

Rigid bureaucratic rules and countless regulations—the bars in the iron cage—have often been cited as the reason for public schools' failure to fulfill the twin goals of educating all students to their highest level of expertise, and doing so equitably. Charter school advocates claim that administrators, whether they are in local school district offices, state capitols, and/or Washington, DC, are so distant from the everyday reality of local schools that they do not—or cannot—respond to even the most basic requests from principals and teachers. Freed from the dictates of remote bureaucracies, educators can experiment with new teaching methods and curriculum that, charter proponents assert, may help all students achieve greater academic success.

The educational situation in San Diego affords a unique opportunity to examine the claims and counterclaims concerning the potential of charter schools to stimulate innovation. The Preuss School on the UCSD campus takes full advantage of the bureaucratic flexibility its charter status affords. From the beginning, it was designed to significantly modify the culture and structure of traditional public high schools. Consciously bending the bars of the iron cage, Preuss planners designed—and the school has put into practice—unique academic, governance, financial, and personnel policies. In addition, The Preuss School is intended to serve as a model for the revitalization of local and national public schools.

In the next section, we begin by recounting key aspects of the debate over the value of charter schools as a means of stimulating public school reform efforts. We then describe the organization of The Preuss School and follow that with a discussion of adaptations of the Preuss model at Gompers Charter Middle School and the newly restructured (but noncharter) Lincoln High School. Finally, we speculate about the reasons the two schools have differed in their adaptation of the Preuss model and consider whether it is necessary for schools to "go charter" in order to make significant improvements.

CLAIMS AND COUNTERCLAIMS CONCERNING CHARTER SCHOOLS AS MODELS FOR REFORM

Charter schools are celebrated for their bureaucratic flexibility. They can and do make significant changes—in personnel, governance, curriculum, and instruction—that are often difficult to implement in traditional public schools (Payne and Knowles 2009). Charter schools have the power to choose and promote their faculty and staff; they are able to assemble a team that is dedicated to the mission of the school and hold each member accountable for the students' academic and social development. Charter school authorities also can dismiss teachers who are not performing well. This practice—although startling in education—is the norm in many firms in business or industry. Local control over personnel decisions is superior to prevailing practice, charter school proponents argue, where poorly performing teachers are shuttled from classroom to classroom, school to school, eventually settling into a position of least resistance—which all too often is in a school in a low-income neighborhood. To be sure, local control of personnel decisions can be subject to abuse. Teachers' unions raise legitimate concerns that charter school administrators can dismiss teachers who challenge their authority, disagree with local policy, or, because of years of service, become "too expensive" to retain.

Control over the use of time is an equally important component of flexibility that is available in charter schools:

> The scarcest resource teachers and principals possess is time. This resource is systematically eroded by district mandates, the churn of new programs and policies, and incessant demands for compliance. While each demand may have a logical rationale, taken together they create a tsunami of activity in schooling. The demands detract from the core enterprises of teaching, learning, and leadership and systematically drive good people out the door. (Payne and Knowles 2009: 230)

Charter schools can modify the time devoted to instruction by lengthening the school day and school year, or by modifying the length of time devoted to certain subjects. Educational disparities (commonly referred to as the "achievement gap") between well-to-do and less-well-to-do students, and between US students and students in all other industrialized countries, prompts many educators to push for lengthening instructional time. Whereas the average American school year is 180 days, in European and Asian nations the average is closer to 220 days. Schools—charters or traditional—that serve students who are far below grade level can benefit from increased instructional opportunities afforded by the ability to manipulate instructional time within the school day, the school week, or the school year. Of course, any increased time must be improved qualitatively, not simply added quantitatively.

In California, charter schools have budgetary autonomy; instead of managing highly proscribed budgets, they receive lump sums. This arrangement creates room for fiscal rearrangements, mid-course corrections, and innovations to meet the needs of the students and families they serve. Charters also typically have a governance structure that differs significantly from that of conventional public schools. Many have a locally constituted board of directors that includes parents and community members. These innovations enable voices that have been stifled by distant and ossified bureaucratic structures to be heard. Local control is not a panacea, of course, as the painful history of local governance of schools in Brooklyn's Bedford-Stuyvesant neighborhood and in Chicago's southside communities attest. A significant peril facing local boards is their members' lack of familiarity with the relevant educational codes and laws that govern charter schools. Local boards may lack expertise in accounting practices and fundraising, limitations that can doom start-up charter schools (California Charter Schools Association 2011).

Proponents say charter schools provide new educational opportunities for children and families in low-income neighborhoods who have had limited choices in the past. State and local educational policies generally impose restrictions on access to public schools other than those located in students' own neighborhood. Charter school laws enable parents to more easily enroll their children in schools outside district-established attendance boundaries.

Finally, charter school advocates see these alternative institutions as models for nearby public schools. Their innovations in governance, flexibility in forming academic plans, and control over personnel decisions could spread to conventional schools. If parents choose to enroll their children in charter schools rather than in regular public schools they judge to be less effective, the latter will have to improve in order to retain students. Failing public schools either will improve or close, according to this argument.

Critics of charter schools counter these claims (see Chapter 2 and the comprehensive review in Hubbard and Kulkarni 2009). They point to studies that suggest public schools and charter schools do not learn from each other (Wells 1998; Carnoy et al. 2005; Zimmer et al. 2009) and that charter schools do not appear to foster competition among local regular public schools (Carnoy et al. 2005; Zimmer et al. 2009). The lack of job security for school personnel and the high turnover of charter school staff also are cited by critics as drawbacks to charters (Stuit and Smith 2009).

In the next section, we describe The Preuss School and examine its influence on Gompers Charter Middle School and Lincoln High School. These two schools' experiences adapting the Preuss model allow us to test the "charter school as innovator" hypothesis. Developments at Gompers and Lincoln help answer the still-open question of whether traditional public schools can engage successfully in systematic change and improvement, or whether charter status is necessary in order to revitalize failing public schools.

COMPARING THEORIES OF ACTION

Many commentators (Oakes 1992; Oakes et al. 1999; Jones et al. 2002; Yonezawa, Jones, and Mehan 2001; Mehan, Hubbard, and Stein 2005; Hubbard, Mehan, and Stein 2006) suggest that educational change and school improvement efforts have technical, cultural, and political components. The "technical" category includes efforts such as making schools safe and attractive; adding new science labs, equipment, or curriculum materials; and/or enhancing professional development activities. The purpose of these technical efforts is to improve teachers' classroom instruction. Such structural changes as rearranging the manner in which students are organized for instruction, reducing class size, or shifting to small schools from large comprehensive ones also fall into this category. The "cultural" category incorporates efforts to change teachers' beliefs, practices, and norms, often concerning controversial topics, such as teachers' expectations about the performance of students from different racial or ethnic groups, school tracking, and testing practices. In the "political" category are actions taken by stakeholders to forge political alliances to obtain, increase, or consolidate power. For example, educators may work to build productive relationships with community groups or attempt to galvanize key elected officials as a way of increasing their school's quality.

Jeannie Oakes (2003) suggests that an excellent and equitable education is enhanced by safe school facilities, rigorous academic curriculum, qualified teachers, intensive academic and social supports, a college-going school culture, opportunities for students to develop a multicultural college-going identity, and strong family-neighborhood-school connections. Each of these schooling attributes has technical, cultural, and political dimensions, and in practice, these dimensions seldom act independently of one another (Hubbard et al. 2006). For instance, although reducing school size appears to be a straightforward technical reform, taking this step may require political and cultural changes. Gilbert Conchas and Louie Rodriguez (2006) point out, for example, that in smaller schools, teachers (a political constituency) may need to revise their standard operating procedures and their beliefs about students' abilities (cultural changes). Likewise, trying to install a college-going school culture and providing students with opportunities to develop a multicultural college-going identity are clearly cultural moves, but to fully transform a school, technical changes (e.g., smaller class size) and political changes (e.g., convincing teacher and parent constituencies that a rigorous academic curriculum for *all* students is appropriate and beneficial) also must take place.

When educators plan to open a new school, or reform an existing one, they explicitly or implicitly activate some or all of these dimensions of change as part of a "theory of action" for achieving equitable education. According to Chris Argyris and Donald Schön (1978), the norms, strategies, and assumptions rooted in an organization's practice comprise its theory of action. What the organization publically *says is done* is the "espoused" theory; what *actually is done* is the "theory-in-use" or the "enacted theory."

To help evaluate whether conversion to charter school status is necessary in order to effect significant improvement, we describe here the strategies that educators at Preuss, Gompers, and Lincoln deployed to achieve reform goals. The leaders of these three CREATE partnership schools approached the opening of their respective schools with explicit plans. But, as we explain below, each school's theory of action emphasized different dimensions of change.

THE PREUSS SCHOOL THEORY OF ACTION: DEVELOPING A "COLLEGE-GOING CULTURE OF LEARNING"

The Preuss School developed as a response to the UC Regents' decision to eliminate affirmative action in undergraduate admissions decisions. Its two main missions are to help remedy the lack of diversity on UC campuses by preparing students from backgrounds underrepresented in the UC system for admission to college and, assisted by CREATE, to develop a successful model for educating underrepresented minority students, and then to make that model available to other public schools for adaptation to their site-specific conditions.

From the start, Preuss educators, led by Doris Alvarez—the school's founding principal and winner of a national principal of the year award—were committed to establishing a college-going culture of learning (Oakes 2003) for students of color from low-income families. The planning group began by developing rigorous college-prep courses, making provisions for academic and social scaffolds to support students, and hiring highly qualified teachers. (Unlike educators in many inner-city schools, Preuss leaders were able to make safety issues a lower priority because students would be bussed from their neighborhoods to the UCSD campus–based school.) In order to ensure that the norms, expectations, and practices of a college-going culture of learning were internalized by educators, parents, and students, the school enrolled fifty students in each of the sixth, seventh, and eighth grades in the first year (1999) and added a new sixth grade each year thereafter until it reached its goal of approximately 750 students. The first senior class graduated in 2004.

Establishing Rigorous Academic Curricula

Research shows that students who take higher-level courses perform better than those who take lower-level courses (e.g., Oakes 2003). Accordingly, Preuss offers students only courses that fulfill or exceed the University of California and California State University (UC/CSU A-G) entry requirements. Courses include four years of English, four years of math, four years of science (including three lab sciences), four years of a foreign language, and one year of a visual and/or performing art. The college-prep curriculum embodies the school's high expectations for each student. These expectations in turn emphasize the college-going culture of learning being instantiated at the school.

The evaluation practices of the school are more extensive than the norm. In addition to taking the required regimen of state-mandated standardized tests and UC/CSU mandated college entrance exams, Preuss students are expected to present an exhibition of their work annually by participating in the local citywide science fair. In the students' senior year, the exhibition is more extensive; students make a written and an oral presentation to a panel of judges (usually a Preuss faculty member, a UCSD faculty member, and a parent or community member) about their senior-year research project, internship, and public service work. This portfolio of measures—test scores, students' course work, grades, exhibitions—affords a more comprehensive view of students' academic progress than can be established with high-stakes tests alone. It also exposes students to the types of evaluations they are likely to encounter in college.

Providing Intensive Academic and Social Supports

Preuss students are not typical of the private or affluent public school students who routinely take college-prep courses and then apply to college. Some speak English as a second language; some were not academically successful in elementary or middle school; none has parents or guardians who have graduated from college (or even from high school, in some cases). Given the differences in their students' backgrounds, Preuss educators have instituted a variety of academic and social scaffolds to provide students with assistance as they contend with the curriculum required for entering four-year colleges and universities. Most notably, the school extends its year by eighteen days to give students more time and opportunities to excel. UCSD students who serve as tutors in class and after school assist Preuss students with their academic work and serve as role models. Additional academic help is provided to those who need it during "Saturday Academies."

Preuss students are assigned an advisory teacher, with whom they meet regularly during an advisory class. Advisory teachers serve as advocate and counselor for the same group of students from the time they enter the school (grade 6) until they graduate (grade 12). Modeled after the successful AVID program (Mehan et al. 1996), the advisory class is a regular feature in the students' schedule, thereby emphasizing its importance. This class aims to develop trusting relationships among teachers and students (Noddings 1984) and to provide a means of closely monitoring student progress (Meier 1995; Sizer 1992).

Research on the college preparation practices of well-to-do students and of elite schools (Cookson and Persell 1985; McDonough 1997; Lareau 2011) shows that parents and counselors invest considerable energy in developing students' portfolios and making connections with college admissions officers. Because the parents of Preuss School students have not graduated from college, they often lack the cultural and social capital needed to undertake this kind of work. Advisory teachers, and the school's college-preparation counselor, assume these responsibilities on behalf of Preuss students. They try to ensure that their advisees take the requisite admissions tests, secure fee waivers, obtain letters of recommendation, and apply to multiple colleges (at least one CSU, one UC, and one private college or university). The college-preparation counselor and teachers often encourage students to explore different types of colleges and to learn about requirements, costs, and potential sources of support. To this end, the students tour college campuses and interact with their undergraduate tutors during and after school.

Hiring Quality Teachers

Strapped by high start-up costs and limited funds, many new charter schools are forced to hire only newly credentialed teachers. The Preuss School, as the recipient of a special infusion of funds from the UC Regents, was able to hire an initial group of teachers with extensive teaching experience, led by Jan Gabay, a national teacher-of-the-year award winner. Over time, as the school has expanded its enrollment, faculty with a range of experience (and therefore of pay levels, as well) have been employed. This arrangement has the advantage of enabling more-experienced teachers to mentor less-experienced ones.

To increase the faculty's teaching expertise, Preuss School teachers engage in professional development activities at the school site during the school day. Once a

week, school starts later than usual; the delayed start creates time for teacher professional development. Teachers meet in grade level or department teams to plan and
examine students' work collaboratively (Lewis 2002; Alvarez and Mehan 2006).

Creating Safe and Inviting School Facilities

The Preuss School is located on the UCSD campus, which sits on a mesa above La
Jolla, one of the most affluent communities in Southern California. The school has
up-to-date science, computer, music, and art facilities for 800-plus middle school
and high school students. Classrooms, built to accommodate twenty-five students
each, have specially designed spaces for one-to-one and group tutoring.

The school's physical and cultural distance from the low-income neighborhoods in which its students live cuts two ways. On the one hand, its location provides
a safe environment for learning, and the surrounding campus offers a symbolic
connection to the students' intended future as college-goers. On the other hand,
its far-from-home location is the source of both physical and cultural stress. The
students must commute—often by bus and trolley—forty-five to sixty minutes to
and from school. This causes fatigue and increases separation from neighborhood
friends—and sometimes even from family members (see Chapter 5).

Summary

In planning the school, Preuss leaders took full advantage of the bureaucratic flexibility provided by its charter status as decisions were reached about location, composition of the student body, budget, governance, and guiding principles for developing
a college-going culture of learning. Although the aforementioned description may
make it seem as if the school took shape smoothly, in fact, conflict accompanied the
process at each step (Rosen and Mehan 2003; Lytle 2007).

Because it is a charter school, Preuss is able to define its student population.
The school enrolls *only* low-income students with high potential but underdeveloped
skills. "Low income" is defined as a family income that is no more than twice the
federal level for free- or reduced-lunch eligibility. Neither parents nor guardians can
be graduates of a four-year college or university. In addition, unlike a conventional
public school, Preuss is able to cap enrollment at approximately one hundred students
per grade level. Because more students apply to the school than can be enrolled,
Preuss operates a lottery annually to select students randomly. By prior agreement,
students not accepted through the lottery become members of a "comparison group,"
which enables CREATE to conduct research that compares the academic progress
of students accepted and not accepted into the school.

Because it is a charter school, Preuss is able to modify the conventional public
school academic plan. The school's designers successfully lobbied for the incor-
poration of detracking principles (Alvarez and Mehan 2006). Students take only
college-prep classes. Recognizing that not all entering students are prepared to meet
the demands of a college-prep curriculum, the school provides academic and social

support. Many of these scaffolds involve the modification of time. These and others, such as using university students as tutors and providing extensive counseling, are innovations any school could adopt. The trappings of a college-going school culture (Oakes 2003) also are prominent features of the school.

As a charter, Preuss enjoys a unique governance structure. Because it is a unit of UCSD, Preuss is related to the administration in the same way as academic departments, organized research units, the library, and so on. As a result, the chancellor has ultimate authority over the school. A board of directors, composed of UCSD faculty, administrators, parents, and community members, provides advice to the chancellor on budgetary matters, the school's academic plan, students' progress, and personnel matters. In addition, CREATE provides annual and periodic reports on the academic performance of Preuss students compared to those students who were not accepted through the lottery (e.g., McClure et al. 2005; Bohren and McClure 2009).

Structural modifications such as the longer school day, longer school week, and longer school year necessitate a nimble personnel and budget plan. Taking advantage of the flexibility afforded by freedom from collective bargaining agreements, Preuss adjusts faculty and staff pay to take into account the longer time teachers and staff devote to the students' education.

THE GOMPERS THEORY OF ACTION: CREATING A SAFE ENVIRONMENT, CONNECTING WITH THE NEIGHBORHOOD, AND BUILDING COMMON EXPECTATIONS FOR STUDENT LEARNING AND BEHAVIOR

Like their counterparts at The Preuss School, Gompers Charter Middle School leaders aimed to incorporate the factors Oakes (2003) enumerated as contributing to an education that is both academically excellent and equitable. Also like Preuss planners, the Gompers team had to make choices and establish priorities. The working group grappled with the overlapping technical, cultural, and political dimensions of change as they developed a new vision for the school and set about trying to put that vision into practice. The Gompers theory of action emphasized three key goals during the school's first several years: ensuring school safety; establishing among faculty, staff, and students a common culture of expectations for behavior and learning; and connecting the school more closely to its neighborhood. Achieving these milestones would, over time, propel the school toward attaining its overarching goal of developing a college-going culture of learning among all its students.

Making School Facilities Safe and Inviting

Gompers is located in a neighborhood characterized by high unemployment, gang violence, and very limited socioeconomic possibilities. School leaders immediately took actions aimed at countering these threatening conditions. To make Gompers safer and more inviting, they hired security guards who patrol the campus. Local gangs and drug dealers lay claim to many of the routes students take to and from school. Project Safe Way (a community-initiated neighborhood safety program) volunteers monitor students as they travel to and from school. The San Diego police department helped by intensifying patrols before and after school and warning known gang members to avoid the campus and the paths students traverse (Williamson 2008).

Recruiting and Retaining Quality Teachers

With charter status, Gompers leaders control personnel decisions. They are able to hire, promote, retain, and dismiss teachers as needed; the school is exempt from district personnel policies that award teaching positions on the basis of seniority. This level of control was especially important because the lack of quality teachers at the "old" Gompers was an important reason why parents mobilized to change the school. The "new" Gompers recruits teachers who want to be there, are committed to the education of Gompers students, and are willing to contribute the extra time and energy it takes to improve the learning of underperforming students.

The school board accepted the Gompers charter proposal on March 1, 2005. With opening day scheduled for September 5, 2005, the school's leaders engaged in a period of intense and rapid-fire hiring (described in Chapter 3). By the time school started, a teaching staff of forty-seven was in place, along with a senior leadership team composed of a director, a deputy director, a chief of staff, and a group of resource teachers in math, English language arts, and science.

Instilling Common Expectations among Teachers and Students

Faced with an almost completely new faculty and staff, Gompers leadership instituted a new practice, which it called "culture camp." The camp was designed to instill a common culture among all school personnel. It was held in the weeks immediately preceding the opening of the school in fall 2005; modified versions of the camp have continued ever since. The goal is to develop a common language, common expectations, and common ways for teachers and support staff (including custodians and safety officers) to interact with students. Gompers educators believe that a stable and predictable learning environment contributes to students' academic development and teachers' professional development. The pre-school culture camp, along with refresher sessions held during the school year, helps achieve that environment.

In addition to holding the same high expectations for students, and knowing and consistently enforcing the same rules, Gompers teachers are expected to have similar ways of organizing the physical layout of classrooms, conducting lessons during the school day, assigning and receiving homework, and monitoring absences, tardiness, and students' between-class movements. For example, all classrooms are expected to set aside a special place, usually a rug, where students gather informally for discussions; and all teachers are encouraged to hang posters on their classroom walls depicting learning strategies and material learned so that students can consult these visual aids in the context of subsequent classroom lessons.

Conventional teacher union contracts with school districts often limit the number of days teachers can attend professional development workshops. Gompers' charter status makes it possible to offer extensive professional development activities annually, before school opens (and to require that all teachers participate) and also during the school year. Educators at Gompers, like those at Preuss, recognize that the most effective professional development occurs at the school site and is embedded in actual classroom practice (Darling-Hammond 1997, 2010). Gompers delays the start of school one day per week to provide time for professional development and also sets aside a specific time during the school day to enable teachers to meet in grade level or department teams to evaluate student work and progress, plan and assess lessons, and develop curriculum in common.

Building Visible Signs of a College-Going School Culture

Motivational signs and other visible symbols displayed inside and outside Gompers are intended to reinforce the school's commitment to establishing a college-going culture of learning. College pennants adorn classroom and hallway walls. Students enter the school through "the Gates of Wisdom," an entry adorned with a large, inviting sign inscribed, THROUGH THIS GATE WALK THE FINEST PEOPLE IN THE WORLD. A banner underneath the sign reads, A UCSD PARTNERSHIP SCHOOL. The school motto, REACH, which stands for "Respect, Enthusiasm, Achievement, Citizenship, and Hard work," is posted ubiquitously. All students' parents or guardians are asked to sign and return a copy of the school's code of conduct. The code includes an explanation of the policies concerning parents' volunteering, uniforms, student behavior, and attendance, and outlines the consequences for noncompliance. Students are expected to be able to recite and explain the school mission when asked to do so by school personnel or visitors.

Campus attire is another visible symbol of the nascent college-going culture at GCMS. The teaching and administrative staff wear "professional dress." Students wear school uniforms. Both forms of dress are intended to signal to the students—and the community—that serious business occurs at Gompers. Not surprisingly, school uniforms have elicited some resistance from students (and some parents). Students are sometimes reluctant to wear their uniforms in the neighborhood, mainly for fear of reprisal from local gang members. As a result, students can be observed changing from "street clothes" to school uniforms on their way to and from school. For example, as boys approach the school, they can be seen pulling up their sagging, khaki-colored trousers and tucking in their white shirts. They reverse the process on the way home.

Students and staff often negotiate appropriate standards of dress on campus. A student who arrives at school dressed in something other than the uniform, or wearing an incomplete uniform, is not sent home. To ensure no loss of class time for a violation of a behavioral expectation, the student is loaned a uniform (or parts of a uniform) for the day. During the school's first two years, one staff member, positioned at the school entrance, was assigned the responsibility of enforcing the dress code. As students passed through the Gates of Wisdom, they were admonished to tuck in their shirts, straighten their ties. Although the need for an official "uniform policeman" has diminished over time, and students have increasingly conformed to the school's expectation for appropriate dress, faculty and staff can still be heard imploring students to "straighten up." Jocular exchanges now accompany attempts by staff to rebuff students' inevitable resistance to the dress code.

Establishing a Rigorous Curriculum Supported by Academic and Social Scaffolds

Gompers, like Preuss, offers a college-prep curriculum to its students and, also like Preuss, has instituted practices designed to support student learning in rigorous courses. When the school first opened as a charter serving grades 6–8, many of the incoming students were below grade level according to state and federal standards. To better support these students, class time allotments varied across academic subjects. Math and English language arts were offered for ninety minutes each, five days a week. Afternoon classes were organized in a modified block plan, where science, social science, language, and PE courses were given on alternating days, with instruction in ninety-minute blocks. To decrease the teacher-student ratio, subject matter teachers assisted the math and English teachers in the morning; roles were reversed in afternoon classes. This master schedule was maintained until 2008, when Gompers expanded to a high school and the California budget crisis necessitated program cuts at the school.

Gompers leaders also added minutes to the length of the school day to provide more time without needing either to start the school year earlier than the traditional day after Labor Day, or to end it later than the traditional mid-June (adjustments that would put the school out of synch with other local schools, potentially causing problems for students' families). The last thirty-minute period of each day was designated as "encore." Students who were performing well in their classes participated in an extracurricular activity; students who are not performing well are assigned to additional tutoring sessions. Extracurricular activities and tutoring both continue into the after-school hours. This increases the possibility of better engaging students than if they went home after last period and were expected to return for additional work.

When interim assessments during the academic year identify specific students as not making sufficient gains, these students are expected to participate in extra tutoring before school, during classes, after school, and during Saturday Academy. UCSD students serve as tutors at these times. These extra scaffolds for struggling students are facilitated by the local control over time and resources provided by charter status.

The academic arrangements at Gompers are not conventional. The school day is longer. Teachers have differentiated assignments—some have more contact time with students than do others—and all teachers serve as both teachers and assistants. Some tutor students during the encore period; others offer extracurricular activities. Teachers' pay varies according to their assignments, a practice seldom possible under collective bargaining agreements between traditional public schools and teachers' unions.

Connecting with the Neighborhood

Gompers established a Family Support Center whose staff interacts with parents (using English or Spanish, as needed), helping them understand the unique features of the school, including the courses students take, the extended-day plan, and the school uniform policy. In addition, the staff counsels parents on many extracurricular issues, such as how to secure transportation, health care, and child care.

LINCOLN HIGH SCHOOL'S THEORY OF ACTION: A SMALL-SCHOOLS APPROACH TO BETTER EDUCATION

Lincoln High School is located a few blocks from Gompers and, like Gompers, serves an economically depressed, largely residential area with some commercial enterprise. To help stimulate economic revitalization in the many neighborhoods served by Gompers and Lincoln, the Jacobs Family Foundation, a San Diego–based philanthropy, has invested in a community resource center and a shopping plaza. Neighborhood residents can buy shares in the enterprise, and local entrepreneurs are encouraged to open businesses in the plaza.

A middle school when it opened in 1948, Lincoln added a grade each year until it became a grades 7–12 school. When a population explosion in the 1950s led to the opening of Gompers as a junior high school, Lincoln became a grades 10–12 senior high school. A magnet program, a medical/health center, and a structured basic skills program in math and reading were installed one after the other at Lincoln in the 1960s and 1970s, but none of these enhancements resulted in academic excellence. The number of students who lived in the neighborhoods in the 1990s ranged between 2,031 and 2,790; yet enrollments varied from 770 to 986, in large part because many parents sent their children to schools outside their community under the provisions of the district's voluntary ethnic enrollment program. Students who stayed in the neighborhood and attended Lincoln were often tardy, absent, or struggling academically.

By 1998, when Alan Bersin became superintendent, Lincoln was hopelessly underperforming. Bersin proposed a fresh start: the district would rebuild the school from the ground up, with new facilities, new leaders, new teachers, and a new educational focus. An extensive district-community planning process ensued. With substantial funding from the Bill & Melinda Gates Foundation and the support of Superintendent Bersin, community members and educators associated with the redevelopment of Lincoln High School adopted a structural approach to school improvement. The large, comprehensive high school would be converted to a collection of small schools. Demolition of the old facilities began in 2003. The school reopened in fall 2007, configured as four small schools, each with a distinctive theme: the Center for Social Justice, the Center for Public Safety, the Center for Science and Engineering, and the Center for the Arts. Each is led by an administrator (two schools have principals; two have vice principals); all four administrators are supervised by an executive principal. The Center for Social Justice is open to freshmen (ninth-graders) only; the other three centers serve students in grades 10–12.

When construction delays postponed Lincoln's reopening by a year, parents and community members were aggravated, but for the district's new superintendent, Carl Cohn, and Lincoln's Executive Principal Mel Collins and his staff, the delay meant more time to prepare for the opening. A school advisory steering committee had been established in 2007 by the executive principal. Committee members included representatives of neighborhood community organizations, CREATE, parents, and educators. The American Institutes of Research, the organization designated by the Bill & Melinda Gates Foundation to monitor small schools funding and development in the district, hosted the planning meetings and helped facilitate the process. When the four small-school administrators were hired, they joined the advisory steering committee. Like planners at Gompers, Lincoln stakeholders had to prioritize some aspects of school improvement over others. Establishing safe and inviting facilities, recruiting qualified teachers, developing a college-going culture and a rigorous curriculum, and strengthening family-school connections were important aspects of Lincoln's theory of action. Unfortunately, as we explain below, in the end, actions taken and decisions made outside the planning team's control constrained the full enactment of their vision.[1]

Building Safe and Inviting Facilities

Lincoln stakeholders are justifiably proud of their new top-notch facilities. The restructured school boasts a modern library/media center, state-of-the-art theater, modern athletic fields, technologically "smart" classrooms, computer labs, and laptop carts with wireless capability for many classrooms on the school's twenty-three-acre campus. These beautiful amenities certainly make Lincoln an inviting educational environment.

In response to the ubiquitous concern for student safety prompted by the continued presence of gang activity in the neighborhood, the school is surrounded by a sturdy metal fence. Entrance to the campus is controlled by the on-campus security staff and is available only at strategic points. The presence of Project Safe Way volunteers near the school has significantly deterred gangs and drug dealers. Parents, especially those who cannot drive their children to and from Lincoln, greatly appreciate this added protection. The combination of excellent facilities and strong safety measures makes the extensive Lincoln campus an oasis for many students.

Recruiting and Retaining Qualified Teachers

Lincoln planners considered "phasing in" the school, such that there would be a ninth grade the first year, tenth the second, and so forth. This plan, successfully adopted at

Preuss on pedagogical grounds, and ongoing at Gompers, was not possible at Lincoln, however, for political reasons. Community members, eager for the school to reopen after being closed for several years, and disappointed at the year-long delay, wanted the school to open immediately and completely. Prospective students' parents, many of whom were Lincoln alumni, simply would not stand for a phased-in plan. Thus, a full faculty and staff needed to be in place when the school opened.

Student demographics and budgetary constraints also influenced the hiring (and retention) of teachers. The new facilities were built to house up to 2,400 students (600 maximum per center). The district's enrollment projection for the school's opening was 1,800–1,900. This estimate was grossly low: Lincoln opened with an enrollment of 2,289. A steady stream of new arrivals pushed enrollment to a staggering 2,300 students. Students returning to Lincoln had attended seventy-seven different schools the previous year, which made the accumulation and analysis of student records and the placement and counseling of students an overwhelming task. Moreover, class sizes throughout the four centers were much larger than anticipated because the district's teacher allocation, based on projected enrollment, was not sufficient to meet the student demand. Administrators desperately sought substitute teachers to try to ease the worst of the overcrowding. Books, furniture, and instructional equipment also were in short supply, particularly in science, until November.

More than 90 percent of the students enrolling in the reconstituted Lincoln High School qualified for federally funded free or reduced-cost meals. Overall, 24.5 percent were classified as English-language learners (ELL). Of the 295 students classified as in need of special-education services, 147 students were designated as needing mild/moderate special-education services; 17 students qualified for moderate/severe special-education services; 83 students required special day class services; 25 students needed special day services for the emotionally disturbed; 15 students received integrated life skill services; and 8 students received services for the medically and physically challenged. The unexpectedly large number of ELL and special-education students placed a heavy burden on a teaching staff that was already seriously taxed by the overcrowding of classrooms and the shortage of books and other materials.

Like their colleagues at Preuss and Gompers—and throughout the profession—planners at Lincoln recognized the value of qualified teachers for enhancing students' learning. But educators in traditional public schools operate under different constraints than their colleagues in charter schools. The collective bargaining agreement between the SDUSD and the teachers' union (SDEA) stipulates that "post and bid" procedures govern the hiring of new teachers. That is, when an open teaching position is advertised ("posted"), teachers with the most seniority have first rights to interview ("bid") for that position. Furthermore, when a school is closed, teachers from the closed school have first priority for positions in newly opened schools.

The Lincoln advisory steering committee carefully crafted a description of the kind of teachers the school wanted. Characteristics included experience working with at-risk students, engaging and varied instructional strategies, high expectations, and

commitment to student success. The team proposed an alternative teacher recruitment plan—one that would enable the leaders of Lincoln's centers to make hiring
decisions independent of seniority rules. They sought a waiver of the union contract,
arguing that Lincoln would be a "hard to staff" school. SDEA representatives attending advisory steering committee meetings tried to place the Lincoln situation
in a broader context. The union's broader mission is to achieve consistent personnel
policies across all district schools. However noble the goal of achieving an equitable
education for low-income students of color, making an exception for Lincoln, they
argued, might set a dangerous precedent.

After a contentious debate, a compromise was reached. Lincoln could hire
20 percent of the teachers outside the post-and-bid process. This compromise
applied only to the first year, however; no concessions were reached concerning
teacher hiring, retention, or removal in subsequent years. Although their teaching
responsibilities would not begin until summer 2007, teachers were hired on a rolling
basis throughout the planning year. Three special hiring cycles filled a majority of
the teaching positions in the four centers. The screening process used during the
first two cycles, held in spring and summer, was elaborate, and the new hires from
those cycles were asked to participate in a Lincoln orientation program that laid
out the vision and mission of the school, and the role of teachers in the school's "no
excuses" approach to supporting academic engagement and success. Teachers hired
in the third cycle, which occurred well into the new school year, were not subject to
as much screening and did not have the benefit of participating in the orientation
program. As we explain further below, these differences contributed to divisions
among the faculty over time.

Lincoln's three tenth- through twelfth-grade centers had few problems hiring
faculty. The Center for Social Justice ninth-grade teaching positions were harder to
fill. When the conventional post-and-bid process was exhausted, that center was able
to hire teachers from outside the district. This produced teachers with considerable
experience teaching social justice courses, and teaching freshmen in particular, but
the process had a down side. Teachers hired from outside the district, even those
with many years of experience, are classified as "provisional." This made faculty
at the ninth-grade center vulnerable when the state budget took a fiscal downturn
starting in spring 2007 and continuing to the present. The Center for Social Justice's
predominantly provisional positions were cut in the spring of each year, and then
reinstated by the school board in the summer. Uncertainty over the composition of
the teaching staff dampened the enthusiasm of both teachers and administrators
and undercut attempts to ensure continuity.

Creating a College-Going School Culture

Early in the planning for Lincoln's opening, advisory steering committee members
agreed that the presence of a strong college-going school culture should be the
foundation for the redevelopment. Planners held passionate discussions about the
kinds of positive and proactive student beliefs and high expectations they wanted

the school culture to promote. These discussions overlapped with ones about high-quality teaching and rigorous academic curricula. Mission and vision statements were drafted to focus the planning around these structural elements. All agreed on the paramount importance of academic excellence and high student engagement at the new Lincoln. Planners were well aware of the potential challenges in enacting these high expectations as many students would likely, and, in fact, did, enter Lincoln performing significantly below grade level. To help make students' initial transition into a high school with this kind of emphasis on academic excellence less daunting, the executive principal and district area superintendent designated the Center for Social Justice as open to freshmen only. (Additional schoolwide academic supports also were put in place; these are discussed below.)

Successfully developing and sustaining a college-going culture of learning requires a strong commitment among the teaching staff. It is especially important that teachers, counselors, and administrative staff share a common culture of expectations and practices. Frequent and regular professional development activities—ideally, ones built into the school day, as at Preuss and Gompers—help ensure that teachers teach at the same high level of expertise, hold the same high expectations for student achievement, and present common academic values to students.

Structural constraints hampered the development of a college-going culture at Lincoln. Although the four small schools are on the same site, they are some distance apart. The very practical matter of the physical separation of counseling offices, for example, made it difficult for counselors to coordinate schedules, provide backup, and ensure that students and their families received similar guidance and advice. In addition to the contractual limits on hiring mentioned earlier, collective bargaining agreements between the district and the local teachers' union limited the extent to which existing approaches to professional development could be changed. SDEA teachers' contracts specify not only the amount of time (number of days and times of day) devoted to teacher professional development but also the length of the school day and the distribution of instructional time. Contracts further state that teachers are expected to teach the same length of time. Thus, a longer school day with time for professional development and more instructional time devoted to some subjects over others challenged existing union contract provisions.

Complicating Lincoln's fledgling school culture even further was the fact that some faculty used the teacher union contract to block administrators' proposals for professional development conducted outside the school day. Although teachers were offered additional compensation for this work, many refused to participate, citing contractual provisions. This response narrowed the possibilities for ongoing improvement of classroom instruction and student engagement. Lincoln's leaders did not abandon their commitment to establishing a campus culture of high expectations for student success, however. They crafted a plan to offer teacher professional development during teachers' contracted work time, and CREATE helped with this effort by placing UCSD students in classrooms to offer teacher support through tutoring. CREATE also organized teacher professional development activities that took place within the calendared professional development days.

During Lincoln's second year (2008–2009), there was a campuswide effort to improve students' writing and critical thinking with respect both to classroom coursework and to state standardized tests. To improve these skills across the curriculum, the San Diego Area Writing Project (SDAWP) was asked to work with all content-area teachers during Lincoln's monthly two-hour professional development time. Improving writing instruction requires content expertise as well as consistent and frequent time for teachers to digest what they are learning and experiment with new techniques. Short monthly meetings did not afford nearly enough time to accomplish these tasks. Whereas Preuss and Gompers teachers enjoyed weekly half-day professional development, contract stipulations prevented Lincoln from establishing a similar schedule.

The SDAWP organized the sessions to focus on rigorous writing instruction and curriculum to support Lincoln's mission of academic excellence. However, there was backlash from teachers who, perhaps because they doubted the ability of Lincoln students to meet high academic standards, resented the mandatory professional development time. Many were disengaged during the sessions, visibly counting the minutes until their contracted time was finished and they could leave for the day. CREATE and the SDAWP succeeded in convincing Lincoln leaders that a "one size fits all" approach to improving student writing might not make sense across all content areas, particularly in math and science. Teachers in those areas, therefore, took part in a study-group form of development in which they read professional texts about the role of writing in learning math and science. The shift in format for this group reduced their resistance to the professional development work. Other teachers clearly found the regular SDAWP-led sessions helpful; in their end-of-session reflections, they noted that they had learned a great deal about improving their writing instruction.

Providing Rigorous Curriculum and Academic Supports

Union policies and contractual agreements with the SDUSD influenced other aspects of the Lincoln High School plan of action, as well. Committed to offering college-prep classes while realizing the need to provide struggling students with additional academic supports, Lincoln planners considered modifying the academic calendar along the lines implemented at Gompers and Preuss. They proposed to devote morning instructional time primarily to English language arts and math, and use afternoon class time for art, music, humanities, history, and natural science courses. Instead, Lincoln opted for a "4x4" course schedule. In this approach, courses are offered on alternating days during the week and course time is lengthened from the conventional fifty-five minutes to almost ninety minutes. Lincoln's academic year calendar also was modified, dividing it into three rather than two semesters. Given the extended class time in subject courses each trimester, students could complete more courses during the school year than was possible within the conventional two-semester plan.

By the end of Lincoln's second year, however, many teachers were unhappy with the 4x4 trimester setup. They seemed overwhelmed by the enormity of the challenges they faced trying to enact Lincoln's ambitious theory of action. Invoking a provision in the SDEA-SDUSD contract, teachers called for a vote on the course schedule; a two-thirds majority of Lincoln's faculty approved a change. As a result, Lincoln opened its third year with a traditional six-period, two-semester schedule, an arrangement most teachers felt better enabled them to meet students' needs.

Lincoln planners wanted rigorous curricula that prepared students to meet college entrance requirements. Accordingly, the school offers a full range of UC/CSU A-G courses, including Advanced Placement (AP) courses, and has an open-enrollment policy to encourage all Lincoln students to take AP classes. Lincoln educators worked with the College Board in developing the college-prep curricula in all courses. Elements from the College Board Springboard materials are incorporated into course work in order to prepare students for AP classes as upperclassmen. Based on research on mathematics teaching and learning, the Center for Social Justice eliminated all remedial math classes and enrolls the members of its all-freshmen student body in geometry. Teachers must remediate basic math skills in the context of teaching that course. Those who do not necessarily have high expectations of Lincoln students have had a difficult time with the concept of integrating basic skills at the same time as they teach new mathematical concepts.

To assist students with the academic demands of courses and support classroom teachers, UCSD students have served as tutors at Lincoln since its reopening. They offer help before school, in classes, and after school. In 2007–2008 an average of twenty-two students per quarter worked at Lincoln; in 2008–2009 the average was forty-four students per quarter. Budget constraints forced CREATE to withdraw its shuttle service from campus to Gompers and Lincoln for the 2009–2010 academic year, causing a drop in the number of tutors to twenty-seven per quarter.

Forging Family-School-Neighborhood Connections

Lincoln's theory of action recognized the importance of connecting the school to its surrounding community. When the school reopened, Lincoln's family and community liaison team did double duty, taking care of campus operations and creating plans to engage the parent community. During the school's first year, the team hosted numerous parent informational meetings and social events, such as yoga and cooking classes.

In response to a request for assistance with parent engagement, UCSD dispatched talented staff members from the campus's Early Academic Outreach Program (EAOP) to work with Lincoln students and their families. EAOP staff offer advice about appropriate courses for college preparation, sources of funds to finance college, and college-entrance testing requirements. The program also arranges trips for students and parents who want to visit such colleges as UCLA, USC, Stanford, and UC Berkeley. Parents especially value these excursions because they come away more informed about entrance requirements, funding opportunities, and details about campus life.

EAOP Director Rafael Hernandez formed a parent book club in 2008–2009 to involve parents directly in the educational process of their students. Reading (or listening to audio recordings) of the books assigned to their children in class (e.g., *To Kill a Mockingbird*) and then discussing the readings at meetings empowers parents to actively participate in conversations about assigned class reading with their children at home. Parents have enjoyed this program and have expanded their readings to include nonclassroom material of interest to them, such as *Como Agua Para Chocolate* (Like Water for Chocolate) and *Cien Anos de Soledad* (One Hundred Years of Solitude).

In 2010, when the family and community outreach coordinator and school nurse grew increasingly concerned about the overall health of Lincoln students and their families, CREATE responded to their appeal for help by contacting the UCSD School of Medicine. With assistance from UCSD physicians, the San Ysidro Comprehensive Health Center, a not-for-profit community health organization, established an on-site health clinic within the school's spacious health facility. Physicians from the San Ysidro center offer Lincoln students various primary-care services, referrals to nearby clinics for other treatment, and certain specialty services, such as therapeutic counseling. UCSD medical students who are part of the Program in Medical Education (PRIME) offer health education activities in Lincoln classrooms to inform youth about at-risk behaviors such as substance abuse, unprotected sex, and poor nutrition. In 2010 the school nurse started a leadership group called the Youth Health Council. The approximately twenty-five students in that group receive leadership training about adolescent health. The goal is for the council members to become campus leaders who will educate their peers about making healthy choices in their lives.

As in many places across the country, the economy's downward spiral has hit southeastern San Diego families hard. Both unemployment and homelessness have increased; families now struggle more than ever to provide such basic needs as sufficient food and clothing. The toll on Lincoln families was apparent in an increase in the sale and use of drugs on campus, and in a rise in mental and emotional stress. UCSD responded to the visible crisis among local families by partnering with Project Safe Way to host a "community market" in 2010. The event offered approximately 250 families free food (e.g., canned goods, fresh produce) and free clothing. The one-day market provided a way to extend help to all neighborhood families, whether or not they had children attending partnership schools.

Summary

Lincoln planners tried to address the technical, cultural, and political dynamics of school reform. Their efforts often were hobbled, both by the inevitable overlapping of the three dimensions of change and by specific external constraints beyond the planners' control. Delays in facilities construction, district leadership changes, union policies, and collective bargaining stipulations all created obstacles that limited the extent to which the new vision for Lincoln could be enacted. Technical problems such as dramatic and unexpected overcrowding when the school opened and shortages of books and other materials taxed staff and led to rushed hiring and reliance on substitute teachers. This in turn undercut efforts to create a common culture of high expectations and shared commitments to providing students with an excellent, equitable educational experience. Political issues, especially impasses with the teachers' union over altering instruction time and incorporating more professional development activities, forced planners to abandon some innovations that had helped sustain a college-going culture at Preuss and Gompers, and to significantly revise others. Lincoln's leaders have refused to give up, however, and a campus culture of academic excellence and expected success is understood to be a work in progress.

CONCLUSIONS

We return here to evaluate claims about the value of charter schools, using CRE-ATE's experiences with local educational reform in San Diego as our gauge. Advocates claim that charters have unique properties that enable them to innovate in order to improve the quality of education and increase the possibility of equitable opportunity for their students. Most notable among these features is bureaucratic flexibility. Charter schools have full control over hiring, retaining, and removing their teaching and administrative staff—and holding them accountable for the academic and social progress of the students attending the school. The schools are also free to design their academic plans—especially the time devoted to various activities, control budgets, and design governance structures. Equally important, they provide new educational opportunities for children and families in low-income neighborhoods who have had limited choices in the past. Finally, proponents of charter schools say they serve as models for nearby public schools. Their innovations in governance, flexibility in forming academic plans, and control over personnel decisions can spread to conventional schools.

Our work with Gompers and Lincoln cannot contribute much evidence either for or against the claim that charters can serve as a model, stimulating competition among nearby schools. Our two partnership schools are in the same neighborhood, draw from a similar student population, and were reconstituted at nearly the same time (within two years of each other). However, our experiences with Gompers and Lincoln clearly sustain the claim that charters offer new opportunities for the residents of low-income neighborhoods. The conversion of Gompers into a college-prep charter school, coupled with the reopening of Lincoln as a cluster of four theme-based small schools, gives parents in southeastern San Diego many more choices for the education of their children than they have ever enjoyed before.

The flexibility afforded by charter school status facilitated the development of innovative structural and cultural arrangements at Gompers. A variety of factors, some generated by the challenging conditions on the ground (e.g., opening a school with more than 2,000 students, coordinating the academic plans and governance of four small schools), and others beyond the control of the Lincoln planners, swamped the possibility of significant organizational change at Lincoln. Gompers modified the length of the school day, school week, and school year and incorporated teacher professional development activities into the core of the school day, rather than relegating them to after-school time. Gompers also engaged the teaching staff in extensive professional development activities before school opened each fall to assist teachers in implementing a common set of practices and expectations for students' learning and behavior.

The Lincoln planning committee, although composed of community members, union representatives, school district employees, and UCSD faculty and staff, had no real authority to make important decisions. The SDUSD administration's decision to retain a conventional academic plan (including a 180-day school year and a school day of six periods of equal length) in the four small schools limited the possibility of carrying out many of the detracking measures implemented at Preuss and Gompers. The district teachers' union collective bargaining agreement constrained the school administrators' ability to recruit and hire teachers who would meet their criteria and advance their agenda.

The lessons we have learned from our work with Preuss, Gompers, and Lincoln suggest that certain critical conditions must be in place to accelerate the academic progress of students from low-income neighborhoods. These include a rigorous curriculum for all students, supported by a wide range of academic and social scaffolds; high-quality teachers; safe and inviting school facilities; and strong family-neighborhood-school connections (Oakes 2003). And we should not overlook the importance of outside funding. Each of these schools benefited from significant start-up funds provided by outside agencies: Preuss drew on a special allotment from the California legislature, Gompers from a grant from the California Charter Schools Association, and Lincoln from a grant from the Bill & Melinda Gates Foundation.

Schools attempting to instantiate these important conditions may begin with any of the dimensions of change—technical, cultural, or political—but in the final analysis, all three must be put into play. Though many schools may espouse a similar theory of action, each school engaging in reform does so in a different setting, with different features. A comparison of the Lincoln and Gompers cases points out the importance of the relation between setting and theory. The technical, cultural, and political dimensions of educational change and school improvement efforts do not operate independently; rather, they interact with one another. As we have seen, converting a failing school to a charter and reconstituting a large comprehensive high school into smaller ones simultaneously affects the culture and politics of the school. For example, teachers have to change their standard operating procedures and beliefs about students' abilities in smaller or charter schools. Certain political constituencies (such as teachers' unions and parents) have to be convinced that such change is beneficial to them. Counselors in each of the small schools must coordinate their policies and practices so that students and their families receive similar advice and guidance. In short, site-specific features constrain the theory of action, and the choice of a theory of action influences the possibilities for modifying the features of individual settings.

The bureaucratic flexibility afforded to a school by its charter status certainly speeds the installation of these critical conditions for change. It is not clear, however, that conventional public schools must be converted to charters in order to establish these conditions. Detracking a conventional school is a much longer and a much more arduous process than starting one from scratch, as Carol Burris, Kevin G. Welner, and Jennifer Bezoza (2009) show. This more lengthy and complex process requires an unwavering commitment on the part of public school educators and visionary community and union leaders to center their priorities on the twin goals of educational equity and excellence, without losing sight of the need to secure fair treatment of teachers in the profession. For example, the collective bargaining agreement between the SDUSD and the SDEA stipulates seniority-based hiring. But such contract provisions do not constitute the only model for teacher personnel decisions. The Los Angeles Unified School District and other districts in San Diego County delegate much more responsibility for teacher hiring and retention to school sites. A school-based collective bargaining agreement does not require charter status; it does require recognizing that even entrenched features of school structure are not necessarily permanent. They can be revised, or even removed, by concerted social action.

The relevant constituencies—schools, districts, families, unions—must be willing to try to bend the bars of the bureaucratic cage that holds public education hostage. If educators are reluctant to rattle this iron cage, then another generation of students will remain trapped in the vicious cycles of economic disadvantage, low and depleted expectations, and underachievement. "Going charter" is one way to rejuvenate schools, and that reform strategy can be implemented relatively quickly. But charters are not the only means to try to achieve the twin goals of educational excellence and educational equity. If traditional public schools—in collaboration with teachers' unions—can manifest the flexibility necessary for nurturing innovative ideas and establishing promising instructional programs, then they will be well positioned to finally fulfill the equity and excellence promises of American public education.

NOTE

1. Jones, Mehan, and other CREATE colleagues observed classrooms with members of the school's leadership team and have participated in research and governance activities since Lincoln was designed for reopening. We participated in weekly steering committee meetings and offered advice on curriculum, especially in the Center for Social Justice. Jones facilitated the introduction of teacher professional development activities and a student health service.

Chapter 5

Changes in Students' Aspirations and Conduct

THE ROLE OF INSTITUTIONAL ARRANGEMENTS

Hugh Mehan and Season S. Mussey

Regardless of the measure employed—school dropout rates, school completion rates, national or state comparisons of test scores, college enrollment rates, and others— students of color from low-income backgrounds perform poorly when compared to their more well-to-do peers. And, this social fact is reproduced from one generation to the next. As explained in Chapter 1, in our view, the cultural reproduction theory associated with Pierre Bourdieu and his interpreters provides the most robust account of educational inequality in the United States. It is more subtle and comprehensive than competing accounts—such as biological reproduction theories (these overemphasize the racial basis of educational disparities) and economic reproduction theories (these overemphasize the degree to which schooling recapitulates the relations of authority between capitalist and worker).

Of course, the cultural reproduction theory, too, has its drawbacks. Bourdieu has been rightly criticized for underestimating the possibility of social mobility (Apple 1982; Giroux 1988; MacLeod 1995; McLaren 1997), for not identifying the processes or mechanisms by which inequality is reproduced from one generation to the next (Mehan 1992, 2009), and for minimizing the possibility that individuals can modify their habitus (Horvat and Davis 2010). Even with these limitations, however, we find Bourdieu's insights, particularly his concepts of habitus and cultural capital, to be useful tools in understanding how the practices of schooling can shape

91

the aspirations and actual social trajectories of individual students. In this chapter, we use these concepts to examine features of The Preuss School that present opportunities for breaking the cycle of reproduction.

SCHOOLS AS SITES OF REPRODUCTION AND POSSIBILITY

Many scholars have documented the ways in which schools are socially organized to contribute to educational disparities that break out by social class and ethnicity (Bowles and Gintis 1976; Willis 1977; Cicourel and Mehan 1985; Wilcox 1982; MacLeod 1995; Fine 1991; Foley 2010; Oakes 2005; Mehan et al. 1996). Not all schools are inexorable reproducers of social inequality, however. Studies show that some schools and some programs are sites of liberation and possibility. Notable examples are the schools associated with the Harlem Children's Zone Project (Tough 2008) and the Knowledge Is Power Program (Mathews 2009).

The Harlem Children's Zone Project (HCZ) works to improve the life chances of low-income youth living in a one-hundred-block area of central Harlem, New York, by "going beyond the walls of the classroom." HCZ unites health, education, and economic resources, rallying community health care professionals, law enforcement officials, and parents to support the education of children in specially designed charter schools (Tough 2008). The students who attend the Promise Neighborhood elementary and secondary schools associated with HCZ show significant academic achievement gains on state-mandated tests (www.hcz.org/programs/promise-academy-charter-schools).

The Knowledge Is Power Program (KIPP) is a national network consisting mainly of middle-school-level public schools. The schools, located in twenty states and the District of Columbia, enroll more than 26,000 students. Over 90 percent of KIPP students are African American or Latino, and more than 80 percent are eligible for the federal free or reduced-price meals program. The schools offer a rigorous college-prep curriculum and try to build a strong culture of support. As at The Preuss School, KIPP schools extend both the academic day and year. Most are in session from early morning to late afternoon, Monday through Friday and on some Saturdays. Summer school is also offered. Teachers are expected to be available to students after as well as during school hours (Mathews 2009). Christina Tuttle et al. (2010) used a matched comparison group design to evaluate KIPP students' achievement. They report that the standardized test scores of students in the vast majority of KIPP schools were positive, statistically significant, and educationally substantial. Other observers (Carnoy et al. 2005) say that KIPP's admission policies and practices over-select motivated and compliant students who come from families that are motivated and compliant—which minimizes the generalizability of findings about these students' positive achievement.

Within-school programs also show promise as a means of disrupting the cycle of educational inequality. Hugh Mehan et al. (1996) describe how AVID (see also Appendix 1) supports the college-going aspirations of low-income youth by building in extra academic time, providing explicit instruction on the hidden curriculum, and encouraging teachers to serve as advocates for students within the school and between the school and colleges. Carol Lee (2001) documents the utility of appropriating street language and culture into classroom lessons by high school teachers who then guide students through a sequence of learning steps to an appreciation and understanding of literary classics. In a similar vein, Norma González, Luis C. Moll, and Cathy Amanti (2004) show how elementary school teachers successfully appropriate a wide range of the "funds of knowledge" from Latino communities to invigorate classroom lessons. Erin Horvat and James Davis (2010) describe YouthBuild, an educational program that assists high school dropouts in learning new skills and finding employment in the construction industry. As a result of intense intervention efforts, YouthBuild participants modify their expectations and aspirations, join the workforce, earn wages (albeit low ones) and pay taxes, and avoid both prison and welfare.

These innovations are not fleeting. They have disrupted the cross-generational reproduction of inequality for significant periods of time. Juxtaposing the literature that shows that schools contribute to the reproduction of inequality with the admittedly smaller literature that shows that schools contribute to social change reveals that schools are complex systems. They can be sites where existing hierarchies are reproduced, and they can be places where these same hierarchies are disrupted and possibilities for social mobility are created (Horvat and Davis 2010)—often at the same time. Unfortunately, we know very little about *the processes* within schools that construct the possibility of social mobility.

The remainder of this chapter is directed toward filling in some of this gap in our understanding by looking closely at specific aspects of The Preuss School. These institutional arrangements seem to be helping students develop skills and aspirations that lead them toward a wider range of life choices and positive outcomes. Our analysis draws on Bourdieu's concepts of habitus and cultural capital (see also Chapter 1). The habitus, a "system of lasting transposable dispositions" (Bourdieu 1977: 82), guides our actions in social space. A disposition includes a person's outlook on life, values, and aspirations for the future. It is acquired early in life by experiencing the attitudes and beliefs of the people in one's social space. The emphasis in Bourdieu's formulation is on *lasting* dispositions, that is, on permanent values and aspirations. He does allow for the possibility that a person's habitus can change as a result of practices implemented in total institutions (Goffman 1961)—such as prisons, nunneries, and military boot camp. But apart from the effects of total institutions, Bourdieu seems insistent that once formed, dispositions learned at an early age within families and neighborhoods remain relatively stable and persistent (Horvat and Davis 2010). William Sewell (1992: 15) puts it this way: "In Bourdieu's habitus, schemas and resources so powerfully reproduce one another that even the most cunning or improvisational actions taken by agents necessarily reproduce the structure."

Furthermore, as we noted in Chapter 1, Bourdieu claims that distinctive cultural knowledge, skills, manners, norms, dress, style of interaction, and linguistic facility are transmitted by the families of each social class. Children of the elite classes thus inherit substantially different "cultural capital" than do the sons and daughters of the lower classes. Schools contribute to the reproduction of inequality by organizing instruction so it rewards the cultural capital of the elite classes and systematically devalues that of the lower classes.

CHANGES IN PREUSS STUDENTS' ASPIRATIONS AND CONDUCT

As previous chapters have explained, Preuss students are encouraged to believe that they can achieve academically, walk in the front door of a college, and obtain a degree. However, they struggle with the need to reconcile the expectations and values acquired at home with the new values and expectations they experience in their college-prep school. Here, we examine how students' lives are impacted by their daily navigation between the different and sometimes conflicting demands of home and school. This section contributes to the dialogue about the academic performance of low-income black and Latino students by revealing some of the institutional arrangements that contribute to changes in students' values and aspirations as well as to their academic performance.[1]

Students' Changing Academic Outlook: "We Want to Be Somebody"

"Aspirations reflect an individual's view of his or her own chances for getting ahead and are an internalization of objective possibilities" (MacLeod 1995: 13). During interviews, Preuss students repeatedly informed us that they had high aspirations for later in life: "We want to be somebody" (see also Suárez-Orozco and Suárez-Orozco 1997). More specifically, they want to go to college and "get ahead":

> **NK:** Is there a typical Preuss student?
> **Mariana:** Yes and no. Because I think we're really different, everybody here is so different, and that makes it fun that we're all different. But in a way we're all the same because we're all here for the same reason, and we all share the same mentality. *Everybody here, they all want to go to a university, a good university or a good college or something like that.* And everybody here wants to get ahead in their grades; everybody here worries about school. So I think we are the same, kind of, because the typical Preuss student worries about school, worries about grades, worries about their future, and how they're going to get there.[2]

Angelica also concluded that college leads you to "be something":

> **Angelica:** Yeah, like my friend, she's my next door neighbor, she goes to Desert Sands High and she's like, "why are you working so hard?" and I tell her it's school … *there's a purpose, for me to get somewhere.* But she doesn't understand that. It's something that's not in her future, I guess. She doesn't really want to study and do work and have a future, I guess. I don't know, I guess she sees things different.

A future orientation has been associated with the "achievement ideology." That belief system, deeply engrained in American society, asserts that hard work leads inexorably to success later in life (Turner 1960). During interviews, Preuss students articulated a willingness to postpone immediate gratification for gratification later in life. They said they studied hard now in order to prepare for the future. Furthermore, they distinguished their own future orientation from the orientation of their friends. They perceive the latter as living in the present and not making plans for the future:

> LUCY: I guess here, my friends here, they talk more about their futures and stuff but *my friends outside of school they talk, live in the present.*
>
> MARIANA: If I wasn't at Preuss, I'd have more time for my friends, but I'd have less time for me and for my future. And that's a tradeoff. And I think it's really changed me in that way.

Gabriela thinks that because most students at Preuss are focused on the future, there is less peer pressure to pursue immediate pleasures:

> GABRIELA: *At every school there's peer pressure* but the thing is that at this school, if you say "no," they'll just leave you alone, like say "whatever" and "fine." People are not into stuff like drugs. And I'm not saying people don't have boyfriends and girlfriends, it's not like they don't, but it's like we don't have the pressure of it.
>
> NK: How come?
>
> GABRIELA: I know their parents, like Nam here, his parents are just like, "it's school, school, Nam; school, school" ... so *everybody's, like, thinking about the future.* It's just, ok, why am I going to do something stupid that's gonna give me pleasure for what, one day, two days, a week, month maybe? But if you look at it in the long run, it's not going to help me out. And I guess it's just the different kids that you're around kinda has that influence on you.

Their newly formed future orientation influences Preuss students' relations with their neighborhood peers. The longer they attend Preuss, the more students associate with their school peers and the less they do so with their neighborhood peers. On our questionnaire, 65 percent of Preuss students reported that they associated primarily with school peers when they were away from school. Information obtained from interviews gave us insight into students' reasons for this choice. Preuss students said they associated more with their school peers because they were more academic and future oriented than their neighborhood peers:

> NK: Do you keep in contact with friends you don't go to school with?
>
> ANGELICA: Not anymore, no. Well, I lost touch with them, because, yeah, they changed a lot.
>
> NK: And what kind of things are you talking about?
>
> LATOYA: *They want to party,* and you want to party too, *but you have to work hard* so you really just hang out with more kids here at school.

> DORA: The kids in my community are going to schools that aren't as good, and *they just want to hang out all the time and go to parties and stuff.*

Latoya and Maria suggest that the intense academic schedule at Preuss influenced their outlook. The lack of leisure time keeps Preuss students from doing "stupid" things:

> NK: Are Preuss students different than neighborhood students?
> LATOYA: When I talk to my friends from other schools, a lot of kids are sexually active, or in gangs, or staying out all night—those kind of things. When it comes to us, we have to work, *we don't have time to be in a gang or be doing other things that could ruin your future.* So in that way, I think we're a lot different than kids from other schools, because we don't have that leisure time to just, when you don't have anything to do, what are you going to do, get into trouble.... Like, why we get out so late, so we don't go home and go, "hey what am I going to do, go hang out with my friends and get into trouble?" We don't have time to do that.
> MARIA: And I just feel that this school helps out by, *since the hours are so long, we can't get into gangs or go make trouble.* You're mainly in the house, you do homework. And I think other schools are like, you have so much time between school and the nighttime or whatever, allowing them to go do bad things. I think the school [Preuss] kind of prevents it.

In sum, most—but not all—Preuss students "want to be somebody" and see college as the vehicle for success later in life. They believe that working hard leads to good grades, which in turn can be parlayed into access to college and good jobs. The experiences and attitudes these Preuss students describe are very much like those related by people who shift their political, cultural, or educational orientation (Hurtado 1994). They change peer and reference groups, and start associating with people who share their orientations.

The retreat from neighborhood friendships and the development of new values did not occur immediately. These shifts developed over time, as the students became more captivated by academic pursuits, while their neighborhood friends remained more focused on parties. This slow transformation suggests that Preuss students' habitus was not fully formed when they entered the school in the sixth grade. Instead, it was modified during their school years, in large part by the institutional arrangements of the school, including the formation of densely populated, academically oriented peer groups.

Conflicts between Home and School: "They Just Don't Understand What I'm Going Through"

The gradual formation of new peer and reference group associations reinforced the college-going culture emphasized by Preuss teachers. This development was not without costs, however. Franz Schultheis (2010) reports that Bourdieu himself felt a sense of alienation as he ascended in French intellectual circles. The more prominent he became in the academic and public policy worlds, the more alienated Bourdieu felt from his previous, more private world of family and culture in Denguin, the village in the Pyrénees district of southwestern France where he was born. Similarly, Preuss students lamented the loss of previous associations even as they valued their new ones. And they struggled with the often-painful emotional labor needed to navigate the cultural and geographic space between home and school. During interviews, students shared their feelings about coping with parents who did not seem to understand either the fatigue induced by the forty-five to sixty minutes it took to travel to and from school each day, or the stress they experienced from contending with the difficult academic material (AP classes, testing, daily homework) associated with the college-going culture being cultivated at Preuss. They expended considerable emotional energy balancing their academic responsibilities with the desires of the family to spend more time together, and reconciling their newly found academic ambitions with their parents' wishes that they stay close to home after high school graduation.

Among the 182 students who completed our questionnaires, 87 percent of twelfth-grade students, 88 percent of eighth-grade students, and 77.6 percent of eleventh-grade students agreed with the statement "My parents understand what it takes to succeed at The Preuss School." But students who participated in one-on-one follow-up interviews and focus groups relayed a more complex story. They detailed the difficulties experienced as they tried to meet both school and home expectations. When asked to elaborate, students said their parents often did not understand the specifics of the demands placed on them at Preuss. This led to misalignments between what was expected from students at school and at home.

Our interviewees often used the phrase "they don't understand what I am going through" in describing parents' reactions to the tension that resulted from trying to meet the expectations of home and school. Shantell's comments are typical:

> SHANTELL: They have an idea that, yeah, you have to have a little something different if you want to survive in that school, but *I don't think they understand the magnitude, in what it takes out of you to be at this school.* I go home, I get on the bus, I come here, I'm here all day, and then I get home around 5 o'clock. And then if someone were to clean up, do chores, do this, do that, help my brothers with homework, and cook dinner and stuff like that, but, I still have homework too. And then try to maintain a social life, it's kinda hard.

Preuss students recognized that subscribing to the new values associated with the school's college-going culture required them to make their academic responsibilities a top priority. That choice, however, sometimes conflicted with their parents' expectations about how much time family members should spend together:

> CLARISA: The whole point about coming here, with having to stay after school, you really don't have time for other stuff. It just has to be Preuss. Your whole life is Preuss. That is how it was for me.

Others echoed this "Preuss is your life" theme, describing a school experience that demanded they fill their Monday through Friday (and sometimes Saturday) schedule with academic activities, often to the exclusion of family, friends, and time for themselves. Whether it was commuting to and from school, taking college-prep courses, participating in academically oriented student clubs, devoting one to two hours a day to homework projects, or engaging in community service, many Preuss students worked on their emerging "college-bound" identity on a daily basis, all year long.

Isaac detailed for us how academic responsibilities often led him to isolate himself from his family. Sometimes this involved locking himself up in his room for several hours each night, in an attempt to focus on schoolwork; other times, he missed out on specific family events because of his academic workload. Isaac found that his relationships with his parents and brother fragmented because of his absence. He felt pulled in opposite directions by his conflicting desires:

> ISAAC: I like spending time with my family a lot. It's fun and we mess around, and then it is kind of hard 'cuz I want to be with my family, but I know I can't 'cuz I have to do homework. The only way for me to do homework is to lock myself in and isolate myself and don't pay attention to them. Yeah, *I want to go kick it with my mom and go watch a movie, or kick it with my dad and go watch the game. Go see the Charger game or something, but I just can't no more.* I just tell them I have to stay and do homework. An example, like for this Christmas, they want me to go to Mexico. I would go but I can't ... I need my rest, I need to do my applications, I have to worry about school. I would be more than happy to go to Mexico, I just can't. I am trying to explain that to them, but *they can't understand 'cuz they are not in my shoes.*

Students reported that their parents often scolded them for failing to fulfill their responsibilities at home. Chores such as babysitting younger siblings and cleaning the house and yard went undone when they competed with academic responsibilities. Students felt they were caught in the middle. If they fulfilled their assigned responsibilities at home, their academic responsibilities would go unmet or not met in full. If they opted to meet their academic responsibilities, they would disappoint or possibly anger their parents.

Isabel described a different aspect of parents' lack of familiarity with the college-bound culture their children were acquiring at The Preuss School. She explained how frustrating and painful she found it that her mom seemed to have no interest in hearing about "school stuff":

> ISABEL: With my mom, I would be like, "Oh, this happened today at school, it was so cool," and she would be there cooking or doing something and wouldn't talk to me or anything. And I would just look at her and be like, "Never mind, never mind, I am talking to myself." She would be like, "Yeah, I am hearing you, I am listening to you." So I would [prompt her,] "Say something. Like 'How was it?'" Like my mom wasn't really involved, so I never took the time to tell her this happened today, *cause she wouldn't understand.* She would say,

"OK, *que bueno.*" [Alright, how wonderful.] And she'd keep driving or doing whatever she was doing.

JCM: What did that feel like?

ISABEL: It felt bad because it seemed like she really doesn't care, but it was because she never went to college or anything. She never had an education, so she doesn't know anything, and the times I did try to talk to her, she wouldn't know what to tell me. She'd be like, "*No sé que decirte,* good job?" [I don't know what to tell you, good job?] And so then, I found someone else telling me, "Oh, good job."

Isabel's painful experience of not obtaining coveted praise at home and feeling that her mother lacked any interest in her school life resonated with that of many other students we interviewed. It was common to hear that students approached their parents and neighborhood peers enthusiastically regarding school matters, eager to share stories about their experiences and to gain understanding, assistance, or praise, only to find those desires unfulfilled.

Gerardo recalled his mother's reaction when he told her that he had submitted an application to attend UC Riverside. To his surprise, instead of praising him for his efforts, his mother questioned how realistic it would be for him to attend that university. In her view, Gerardo's attending a school away from home only meant more expenses, something that the family could not afford:

GERARDO: "Oh mom, I sent the application," and she was like, "OK" [imitating a timid, uninterested voice]. I thought she was going to make like a bigger deal 'cuz I am the first one [to go to college]. I was like, "I might go to UC Merced," but I didn't end up applying 'cuz I didn't get the fee waiver, so I just put down UC Riverside and UC San Diego. "I put UC Riverside," and then she is like, "Are you actually going to go to Riverside and live over there? I mean, the only way you are going to be over there is if you get accepted with a scholarship or some money that ends up paying for school." I am like OK, instead of helping out and telling me, "Oh, you're going to make it," you are here telling, "Are you actually going to go over there and study, or are you just wasting money by the application and stuff." I was like OK, I am not telling them anything anymore. Like whatever, I am sticking to my own stuff, telling my friends.

Teresa and Claudia appeared to have had an especially difficult time reconciling their newly found academic ambitions with their parents' expectations. For Teresa, the "battle" consisted of convincing her mother that gaining independence was a reasonable aspiration for a young woman, even if it meant going against her mother's deep-rooted cultural beliefs that a young girl should stay close to the immediate family:

TERESA: I want to move out of San Diego because I want to have my own independence. That's the reason why me and my mom have a battle about this, because of that [independence]. I see that as the American dream.

JCM: What's that?

TERESA: Finding independence and having the independence. And my mom, she's like, "No. You and your American style." She wants me to stay at home, not leave the house until I'm married. But I'm atheist, so I'm eventually not going to marry through the church. Also, if possible, she'd like me to bring my family in with hers. And that's not happening at all! *She's used to the Mexican tradition of having the grandma, the* nietos *[grandsons] and* nietas *[granddaughters], and everything. But I see myself in college, playing soccer for sure.*

Claudia encountered a resistant mother when she announced that she wanted to pursue university studies on the East Coast. Claudia's mother focused on two ways her daughter was likely to fail. First, Claudia's high objectives were beyond her reach and thus her hopes eventually would be crushed. Second, being away from the safety net of her home would lead Claudia into trouble:

CLAUDIA: Yeah, my mom thinks—I don't know. It's so weird. It's kind of sad to me, in a way, because she thinks I'm setting myself [up] for failure. *She thinks I'm not going to make it, especially on the East Coast. She wants me to stay here.*
JCM: What do you think your mom means by failure and not making it?
CLAUDIA: Getting pregnant and then giving up everything because she sees that, oh, she sees everything I want to do because my goals are super high. And she just listens to me, and sometimes I don't even, like, tell her anymore. Because I know she doesn't believe it, because she still is stuck on this idea that if I leave San Diego, if I leave home, I'm going to get pregnant. And I'm going to give up everything and get left by my partner and be a single parent and have to struggle. She's going to have to come pick up for me. That's what she thinks. I've always told her that she doesn't understand, and as much as I try to explain it to her, it ends up in fights and stuff. So I'm tired of that. Maybe that's why I want to get out. It's motivation. It's a bigger push for me to leave San Diego. I just need to isolate myself from that for a little while and learn about myself. Honestly, I see young girls, you know, who do get pregnant and do give everything up. I totally understand. I understand why my mom says that, but I don't understand why she expects that from me. And then I always tell her, "Mom, you think I'm going to give everything up? You think after all I've done and gone to Preuss, you think I'm going to give everything up?" I tell her, "Why did I go to Preuss, if you think that? If you think I'm going to go and get pregnant? Why would I have gone to Preuss and sacrificed everything?"
JCM: Did she support you in seventh, eighth grade, ninth grade, tenth grade, your being here?
CLAUDIA: Yeah, up until I had a boyfriend. I got a boyfriend here and then she wanted me to get out of this school. She really seriously did want me to get out, but I said, "No, Mom. You're the one who's going to ruin it, if anything—you're the one who's going to mess me up."

Students developed strategies for resolving conflicts that developed when parents felt their importance in their children's lives waning. Becoming a lower priority than their children's academic pursuits was an especially difficult transition for parents. Amanda poignantly explained that often it was easier to simply go to her room and take care of her schoolwork than it was to try to overcome her mother's resentment over losing the close connection the family had shared:

> AMANDA: My mom *me regañaba* [she would yell at me], "You are not spending enough time with us. Sometimes you spend more time with people outside of school versus spending time with the family." She would get mad at me. I would just say I am sorry, or sometimes I would just get home and sleep. And she is like, "Oh, you don't want to talk to me." At first, even up until last year, it did affect a little bit my family relationships, especially with my sister. She would ask for help, but I would have to do this [referring to Preuss] first [and she would complain,] "Oh, you never help me." It was hard for me to balance that time out. This year I've done a better job of balancing time out. I am trying to spend more time with my family. I do give myself some off-time [from schoolwork] during the weekends.

Other students resolved this dilemma by privileging activities with highest value. They ensured that test preparation, school projects, and the activities most valued on college applications were completed consistently, while routine homework was completed haphazardly or not completed at all. At home, students selected family events, chores, and activities that communicated to the family that they were making a genuine effort to participate actively. This approach, though, left students trying to please those around them while leaving little time for themselves.

These quotes exemplify the painful conflicts associated with students' efforts to negotiate the differences between expectations expressed at home and the burgeoning aspirations they were acquiring at school. On the one hand, students' recently crystallized academic aspirations encouraged them to venture off the traditional cultural pathways traveled by their neighborhood peers and some family members. On the other hand, students struggled with negative reactions from family members who expected them to conform to cultural norms when considering their future opportunities. These conflicts often left students pivoting between whom they had been and whom they had become. Making the situation even more difficult was the fact that the students' parents, because they lacked the requisite knowledge about the arcane college-going process, did not seem to grasp how much time and effort it had cost their daughters and sons to succeed at Preuss.

Preuss Peers Understand What "We're Going Through"

Friends and family members may not have been able to understand Preuss students' school lives, but their classmates usually did. Among those Preuss students who responded to our questionnaire, 67 percent felt that their school peers understood their school lives, and 66 percent said their neighborhood peers did not. This view was reinforced in one-on-one interviews with thirty eleventh-graders. They believed that a deep level of understanding existed among students at Preuss because they all "go through" similar experiences at home and at school. The phrase "going through" appears often in reference to their peers:

> **NK**: Is Preuss different socially from other high schools?
>
> **PERLA**: I guess we interact better because we have a lot of the same classes together, we've known each other sometimes since sixth grade, so I think we mesh well together. So, as opposed to other high schools, I don't think it's too much different, but I think it's just that we work better together because we are all in the same situation as far as financially, in our cultural backgrounds, *what we've been through, a lot of this is the same,* so I think that common ground allows us to come together more.
>
> **NICOLE**: We've known each other for so long, and we know everything there is to know about each other, kind of. We're like a family, we're not just classmates, we know each other on a deeper level, I guess. And *we go through the same stuff, so we relate.*
>
> **ANGELICA**: We all know each other, *we all know what we're going through,* we're all going through the same thing. Unlike other schools, where you don't know what the other person is doing or going through.

Border-Crossing and Code-Switching Strategies

In addition to experiencing conflicts between home and school demands, academically oriented low-income students often come from friendship groups in neighborhoods where an academic orientation is not commonplace. In such circumstances, many students engage in academic pursuits with their friends at school and engage in recreational pursuits with their neighborhood friends after school and on weekends. Other research indicates that "border crossing" or "cultural straddling" strategies like these seem to be effective for Latino and African American students and for recent immigrants to the United States (Gibson 1988; Mehan et al. 1996; Carter 2006a, 2006b). Border-crossing strategies enable students to develop enough confidence to engage in academic pursuits in school and to recognize the elements of compatibility between those aspirations and their neighborhood-based selves (Carter 2006a, 2006b; Rumbaut and Ima 1988).

When Preuss students talk about how they negotiate home, neighborhood, and school demands, they are describing border-crossing strategies. Over time, they have learned to express the appropriate language and behavior in each setting: a way of talking and acting that is appropriate for the school setting and a way of talking and acting that is appropriate for home and neighborhood settings. While on campus, students understand that to interact properly, a certain way of talking is required, but they report that when they return home to their families and community, they do not hesitate to switch to the speech patterns and behavior expected there. Teresa articulated clearly what sociolinguists call "code-switching" (Gumperz 1982), a technique many Preuss students have mastered:

JCM: Do you feel you need to act differently on campus?

TERESA: *I probably interact differently,* but I still act the same, just probably here because the education levels, they're different here than they are at home. So I probably have to talk more like, not ghetto, but like more at their level.

JCM: At their level, as teachers or staff?

TERESA: Yeah, well, here probably I know more educational stuff than other seniors at other high schools do. Like some words that aren't even that complicated, they don't even know the definition of it.

JCM: Have you ever been caught in that situation where you ...

TERESA: I have. *So I have to, like, watch out how I'm using the language,* that kind of thing. Well, my mom and my dad, they at least finished high school, so that they know their Spanish words very well. But like my uncles and stuff, they don't, so I need to be careful how I talk and stuff, so I won't offend them.

JCM: The academic Spanish?

TERESA: Yeah, the academic Spanish. Like *los acentos* [the accents] and all of that.

For the most part, Teresa said, she has learned to maneuver through the new linguistic demands of the academic setting; but from time to time, she still catches herself policing her "ghetto" self. On the other hand, she tries to taper off her academic Spanish with family and not use what her friends call "school girl" speech in her neighborhood.

Preuss students did not view the adoption of an academic register as a form of culture stripping. They did not feel that they were being asked to sacrifice their home-based cultural language and practices. Instead, the students we interviewed experienced achieving in the academic setting as a normal process. They had come to realize and adapt to the fact that they participate in two distinct worlds—one at home and the other at school. Latino students in particular reinforced each others' beliefs that pursuing academic success and "being Latino" is normal. Students reported that maintaining their home language and culture was facilitated by occupying common space with classmates who shared many similar cultural beliefs, customs, and interests.

Students also asserted a desire to overcome the widely accepted stereotype that depicts minority students as failures. When Efrain was asked if expressing his Mexican-American identity ever poses any challenges, he responded, "It only comes up when it is stereotyping, that can be a challenge. Like [when people say] Mexican people, Hispanic people, they don't go to college. It is like a little challenge, 'Oh, I am going to prove you wrong.'"

The Latino students we interviewed also said that returning to neighborhoods and communities where people primarily speak Spanish enables them to more easily maintain a deep-rooted connection with their cultural traditions. Though they often described the process as painful and the costs as high, students believed they benefited from participating in two worlds. At Preuss, they gained the academic preparation and social support necessary to go to college; at home they remained intimately connected to their family culture, language, and identity. Clarisa spoke for many students when she affirmed the importance of laying claim to one's roots:

> CLARISA: Even though we come to La Jolla, we come to Preuss, we should never forget how we got here or where we are from. That is like my main focus. Don't be ashamed of who you are and where you came from! I think that it is better if you came from the bottom and come to the top than if you came from the top and always being there.

CHANGES IN STUDENTS' CONDUCT: ACADEMIC PERFORMANCE AND COLLEGE ENROLLMENT

Not only are the outlooks of Preuss School students different, but so too is their conduct. As we noted in Chapter 2, they consistently score at the highest levels on California state-mandated tests that measure academic performance. In 2009, for example, Preuss students obtained the highest score among San Diego County high schools on the Academic Performance Index (894); they "fell" to second in 2010 and 2011. Since 2004 they have outpaced students who attend high schools that have a much smaller population of low-income students. They also outscore peers who attend the high schools in Preuss students' home neighborhoods. Moreover, Preuss students enroll in college at rates that are about twice the national average for low-income students of color (Pew 2009). An average of 84 percent of the 685 students from the school's first eight graduating classes signaled their intent in their senior year to enroll in four-year colleges (Bohren and McClure 2009). (See Chapter 2 for additional enrollment data.)

Students' Outlook Tempered by the Realities of College

We have established that Preuss students develop high aspirations for their post–high school lives. But how do they fare once they actually leave Preuss? Do they sustain these high aspirations over time? Does their excellent high school academic record smooth their transition into the demands and complexities of college life? Or, are there circumstances in college that derail their upward trajectory?

Data constraints limit the answers we can provide to these questions. Once students graduate from high school, we no longer have direct access to information about them. We have found information on college enrollment provided by the National Clearinghouse to be helpful in providing aggregate data. But the Clearinghouse is missing records on as many as 10 percent of students in the Preuss and comparison groups. When we try to obtain information from graduates about their college life or careers in the world of work by e-mail or surface mail, we find comparison group students are especially reticent in supplying information once they have left high school. Betsy Strick (2009) estimates that 69 percent of Preuss students who graduated in 2005 and 2006 persisted into the second year of college;

among the comparison group for those years, an estimated 38 percent of students persisted into their sophomore year of college.[3]

Coauthor and former Preuss teacher Season Mussey (2008) reports results from interviews about college life that she conducted with twenty-eight students who graduated from Preuss in 2008.[4] Three topics emerged repeatedly during the interviews. Like freshmen in college everywhere in the United States, many Preuss students expressed surprise about the volume and intensity of college course work. The amount of writing required in literature, humanities, and social sciences courses was a particular shock. Some found that their GPAs dropped. For the most part, though, Preuss students reported that they felt well prepared academically for college, especially when they deployed some of the coping strategies emphasized in high school. However, they were surprised to find they needed to adapt to a new condition: in colleges dominated by well-to-do white students, they suddenly became minority students. Below, we elaborate on each of these points.

Preuss graduates felt comfortable with the material presented in their courses, especially in the natural sciences. Luke's situation is representative of responses recorded by Mussey. He is majoring in microbiology at a top research university in Southern California; his GPA is 3.3. Luke reports that much of what he learned in the introductory courses in college reviewed his advanced classes in high school. He views himself as a "math person." Because he acquired the necessary skills in high school to excel in math, he feels that it is natural to find college classes challenging but manageable:

> SSM: How would you describe a typical science class?
>
> LUKE: It's pretty hard. It is pretty hard, but interesting, because I guess you don't usually talk about science in that kind of depth. So it is pretty interesting.

Others comment on the approach to teaching and learning that they encountered in their college courses. Deborah equates some of the "good teaching" at her university with the teaching she experienced in high school:

> SSM: How were you most prepared for college?
>
> DEBORAH: Preuss is similar to college in its rigor. The material we learn *and how we learn it* at Preuss is similar to the *good* teaching here. I've recognized some of the techniques I learned and practiced at Preuss being taught here—such as the types of hooks for an essay, how to draw Lewis dot structures, partial fractions. There's a lot of thinking to do, and the critical thinking skills from Preuss really help—such as working backwards from the answer, looking at similar problems.

She also notices differences in college teaching methods compared to high school and particularly points out the lack of scaffolds:

> DEBORAH: At Preuss, I feel the teachers really aim to have the students succeed, going over things step-by-step and emphasizing the important parts. Here, I

think the teachers just review and add onto what's in the book, or rely on other means of teaching to teach the student [e.g., smaller sections, independent reading]. *The need for self-motivation and initiative is bigger at college*; just being in class won't be enough to understand the material. In a way, the teacher seems less invested in the student here.

Some students saw their GPAs fall—as much as one grade point (e.g., from a 4.0 in high school to a 3.0 their first year of college). Despite these setbacks, the Preuss students in Mussey's sample were not deterred from their overall aspiration "to be somebody." Deborah's story is representative. She attends a large, highly se-lective, out-of-state private school. She currently maintains between a 3.0–3.5 GPA while majoring in biomedical engineering. Despite this very respectable grade-point average, she is dissatisfied with her current academic achievements. Deborah made straight As in high school and was formally recognized for her academic achieve-ments when she graduated. She was always at the top of her class; now, for the first time in her academic career, she is not. She is certainly achieving success by most standards, but she doesn't always perceive it that way. In part, this is because she feels anonymous at her large institution:

> **SSM:** Do you feel like you have been a successful student? Why or why not?
> **DEBORAH:** Not really, since my grades aren't what they were (and might be getting worse), and I haven't done anything impressive or great. *Most of my teachers don't know me.* I feel like I'm just another number, another nameless face, sometimes.

This feeling of anonymity is lowering Deborah's confidence in her academic abili-ties, an ironic outcome since she attends one of the top colleges in the nation and is learning computer programming, linear algebra, genetics, chemistry, Spanish, and expository writing from what she calls "accomplished professors and teaching fel-lows." As a result of her perceived drop in performance, she worries about her grades when compared to her peers:

> **DEBORAH:** I worry about the students in my classes only when it comes to grading. Scary smart people means there might not be a curve, or I'll be at the lower end of it. Other than that, they're just students.

Preuss students deployed some of the coping strategies explicitly taught to them in high school classes to deal with the heightened expectations they would face with college classes. The value of forming study groups was mentioned by a majority of students in Mussey's study. Naomi and Luke give us insight into the value of studying in groups:

> **SSM:** What are some things you do when you are studying in a group?
> **NAOMI:** When you are with yourself, you tend to study more the things you do. I go over most of the things that I know. You can't get help for what you don't

know. I guess *when you are in a group, it is a better way to learn because they can ask you questions and if you can't answer, then there is your check....* You can say, oh, I don't know that ... if there is more people, everyone knows their little area; you tend to study more of everything than you do by yourself.... Here at my college there are study groups that you can sign up for. Last year, I did a summer group, we became a family, and a lot of them turned out to be in my classes.... SHPE [Society of Hispanic Professional Engineers] offers mentoring and tutoring. And we can assign you with a mentor or a place to study.

SSM: What kinds of things do you do in study groups?

Luke: Problem solving—like, I ask questions about concepts that I don't understand.

SSM: How is that different from what you do when you are studying alone?

Luke: *When I am studying alone, I usually just want to do all of the homework* problems that I got wrong. I also review what other students got wrong, and I guess read the book over.

The average number of students in Preuss classes is twenty-five. Students attending large universities experience a shock when attending lecture classes with hundreds of students. Luke found the anonymity of large lectures so unsettling that he thought about quitting college.

Luke: The first day in Summer Bridge [a program that helps incoming students make the transition to college] I wanted to quit college because of the lecture. I was like, it is so hard.

In addition to noting the challenge presented by large lectures, Luke mentions another significant difference between learning in high school and learning in college: the need to take personal responsibility in college because instructors don't keep close track of students:

SSM: How do you find college different from high school?

Luke: *No one is watching, so you can pretty much do anything you want.* Time management. You have to manage your time, not like high school where they give you the planner, they tell you what is going to be on the board and there is homework assignments every day in high school. They [college professors] just want you to read it, and expect you to read it, so you can talk about it next class. And they may not give you as much time. They expect a lot more from you, and they don't say it. They are just going to say, go ahead. There is no homework, but I want you read this ... and you have to read it on your own. They are going to assign the reading; you have to self-motivate yourself. There is no one to push you. No advisory teacher.... *You gotta' do it by yourself.*

Preuss students distinguished their preparation for the academic demands of college from their preparation for the social life of college. They felt especially ill-prepared to deal with their new status of being a minority in predominantly white colleges and universities. Elizabeth and Naomi describe this "culture shock." Elizabeth attends a community college in Southern California, where she has been admitted to a transfer program, guaranteeing admission to a four-year college upon successful completion of a series of courses at the community college. With a 4.0 GPA, she is currently on track to transfer to a large, top-tier research university in the same city. She will major in biochemistry, in preparation for pursuing a career as an OB/GYN. Elizabeth's comments are typical of the Preuss graduates who say that the social transition is the biggest adjustment they have had to make:

> **SSM**: Some students find the transition from The Preuss School to college difficult. Talk about some of the ways that The Preuss School is different from college. In what ways is Preuss similar to college?
>
> **ELIZABETH**: *The biggest one would be social.* Because you are so used to high school, you know everybody. But then you go to college and everybody is on their own, so basically you sit alone. That is why I study alone. I mean, you do make friends, but it is more of a social transition. Academically, it is not that bad, it's not that different from high school, from what we had here.

Naomi, who is a mechanical engineering major and is currently on academic probation with a below 2.0 GPA at a large, comprehensive public university, echoes Elizabeth's sentiments:

> **SSM**: Part of your high school's mission is to prepare minority students for college because historically black and Latino students have had less access to college. Do you find yourself to be in the minority at your institution?
>
> **NAOMI**: Definitely. There are mostly Caucasians. There are Latinos here. And, I mean, Preuss prepared me to understand like how much, like, I can do, as far as I am [a] bright student and it doesn't matter if I am Mexican or not. I can do these things. *In Preuss there are a lot of Latinos, the majority. And when I come here, it is kind of a culture shock—the majority is Caucasian.* I got involved with SHPE for that reason, because they were Latino and they were engineers. And it's like you build a family.

Naomi also calls out the gender dimension of her newfound minority status:

> **SSM**: Historically, women have been underrepresented in certain fields in college. Do you find yourself, as a woman, to be in the minority at your institution?
>
> **NAOMI**: *At [my university], for one woman, there are ten guys. And so that is a BIG change.* I guess for some people it could be intimidating. I guess in my engineering class, it was intimidating at first.... I am here to learn. And I am going to make these kind of mistakes, but we are all here to learn, and I will ask someone, "Hey, I don't get this. Can you explain it to me?" You know, it makes it easier if you forget about you being a minority and keep participating in class. It makes it easier to think about, that we are all just students.

Many Preuss students reported that they joined affinity groups to cope with their newly experienced minority status. Naomi is typical. In addition to SHPE, she joined two other on-campus organizations, Movimiento Estudiantil Chicano de Aztlán (MEChA), and a Latina sorority. All three organizations are related to Naomi's identification with her ethnicity and her strong commitment to academics. Students developed a social and academic network of peers through participation in these and similar groups. These kinds of networks, even among students who were experiencing academic difficulties, were described as helpful for reinforcing their aspirations to succeed in college.

The Preuss graduates' newly ascribed minority status was especially salient in private colleges populated by well-to-do students, including those from African American and Latino backgrounds. Martha attends a large, highly selective private college. In high school, she was confident, independent, and at the top of her class. She consistently earned above a 3.75 GPA. Now it is below a 2.5. She attributes this steep drop to the fast pace, anonymous nature, and competitive environment of her introductory science classes. Martha's frustration with her academic performance seems to be amplified by her feeling of isolation at this large institution, far from her home. As a low-income student, she perceives herself as in the minority, and she doesn't understand what she calls the "work-hard/play-hard" mentality of her more privileged peers. The result is that she is left feeling like she is struggling in isolation. She believes that most of her peers are performing better academically than she is. Martha terms her efforts to develop her academic identity in this new context an "identity crisis."

> **SSM**: Part of The Preuss School mission is to prepare URM [underrepresented minority] students for college because historically, black and Latino students have had less access to college. Do you find yourself to be in the minority at your institution?
>
> **MARTHA**: It's hard because *I have had a huge identity crisis.* I feel like I can't claim the Latino heritage because of how I look. I may fit in more because I am light skinned. The student population is really diverse, and I didn't see it my freshman year. Now, I am really aware of the race issue, and there are tons of people that I have met because I have looked for them. In one sense, I am in the majority because of how I look. And the way that white people are stereotyped is as sorority girls and frat guys that have so much money I can't wrap my mind around it. How ... I don't even know. I have seven dollars in my bank account. I can't imagine. *The majority isn't white people, it is rich white people. It is not just black people, it is rich black people. It is not just Latino, it is rich Latino. The minorities that are here are wealthy. The financial aid kid is the minority here. I have been trying to identify as the Latino, but even that group is wealthy. I haven't been around "poor minority" kids.*

After she attended a summer language program at a different college, Martha changed her major, and her attitude:

MARTHA: It [the program] was for seven weeks. We couldn't speak English. I wasn't talking to my family or listening to music. There was a huge range of people. I really learned how to study well and to work well. It really opened up my eyes because it wasn't just about taking French classes. It was about how French has an impact on the world. And French-speaking countries in Africa. It gave me more of a global sense than anything in college so far. *It is going to shape what I do in the future.*

SSM: You said you want to go into education....

MARTHA: After I went to Middlebury [for the language program], I am thinking about teaching English to second-language learners, and I found a joint program at Columbia that teaches in inner-city schools in New York City. I think it is important to continue my own studies. *I feel like that is one of the reasons that I want to go to grad school,* especially if I want to teach English or adults. I also know I want to work on myself.

These quotes suggest that Preuss graduates make the academic transition to college more readily than the social transition. They report finding the college experience confusing and even sometimes shocking as they negotiate ways to meld their academic and multicultural identities in a world where they find themselves in the minority, surrounded by students who come from more affluent backgrounds. Another more common coping strategy involves joining affinity groups to try to find a community whose members share a similar background of values and experiences.

When asked how high school could better prepare them to make the social transition to college, Mussey's interviewees called for more school-based opportunities to explicitly "deal with" the gender, social class, and ethnic identity issues that they were contending with in college. Some Preuss graduates were being exposed to this social justice discourse in their college ethnic studies or sociology courses, but they wanted to be exposed to it earlier, in high school. Their appeals invoke discussions of "multicultural education" and "multicultural college-going identity" that reverberate in the research literature and in teachers' training. "Multicultural education" focuses primarily on the formal, explicit school curriculum. One version calls for injecting the cultural, artistic, scientific, and political contributions of underrepresented minorities and women into the existing historical narrative taught in US history courses. A second calls for transforming US history from a "narrative of progress" to a narrative that accentuates the ongoing and never-ending struggle for social justice (for comprehensive reviews, see Banks and Banks 2002; Ayers, Quinn, and Stovall 2009).

Developing a multicultural college-going identity focuses on the student's acquisition of a sense of self as a member of the academic community *and* a member of an ethnic/racial group in the context of a predominantly white society. Enabling students to develop this dual identity entails providing them with the opportunity to master robust academic skills, and a chance to learn to understand and combat the "discourse of power" (Delpit 2006). While not denying the importance of transforming the content of curriculum materials, this perspective encourages teachers to confront the social fact of discrimination based on race, class, and gender in society with their students during classroom instruction and in political actions outside of school (Duncan-Andrade 2009; Yang 2009).

Social justice instruction is especially meaningful when teachers elicit students' lived experiences and use these to ground the topics discussed in class. This approach makes explicit the often implicit ways in which people in positions of power make distinctions between the privileged and the marginalized (Delpit 2006). The details of the language demanded in "gatekeeping encounters," such as job interviews and college applications, are displayed and analyzed (Erickson 2004). The importance of adding formal or academic ways of talking without subtracting local dialects is stressed (Valenzuela 1999), as is the need to switch between formal and informal variants as situations demand (Gumperz 1982; C. Lee 2001).

To some extent, Preuss teachers already help students develop their multi-cultural identities in tandem with their academic skills. In grades 6–11, especially in A-G and AP courses in history, world languages, and English, where the state's content standards accentuate the conventional canon, Preuss teachers organize their instruction to investigate topics that have relevance for their students. This makes it possible to meet state standards while also strengthening students' critical thinking, writing, and oral presentation skills. Some, but not all, of the topics chosen by students emerge from their ethnic cultural background. Teachers attempt to appropriate topics that spring from some aspect of students' experience and move the discussion to social justice issues such as prejudice, discrimination, and structured inequality because they conclude students feel a greater connection to schooling when the work has recognizable relevance for their lives (Gabay 2011; Kovacic 2011).

In senior year, the emphasis shifts. All Preuss seniors conduct small-scale research projects, serve as interns in a campus- or community-based organization, and provide public service in their home communities during that year. This three-part sequence culminates in a year-end presentation to a committee (ideally) composed of a Preuss teacher, a university faculty member, and a community member. These off-campus activities are intended to enable students to explore aspects of their identities and also to engage them in real-world learning experiences in which they are able to indirectly confront the consequences of socioeconomic disparities, environmental degradation, and discrimination.

In their call for a vocabulary to represent and help interpret their lived experiences—especially in the entirely new context of college life—Preuss graduates do *not* seem to be recommending a revision of the school's formal curriculum—one in which Bill Ayers is substituted for William Shakespeare. Nor do they want to jettison the single-track, rigorous curriculum aligned with the College Board AP curricula and the A-G course requirements for college admission. These former students seem to appreciate having been exposed to a college-prep curricula; they recognize that it has put them on par with their college peers, regardless of differences in socioeconomic status or cultural background. But, even as they acknowledge the value of these educational experiences, Preuss graduates also suggest that they are not sufficient preparation for the indignities they are contending with in college.

They seek more robust opportunities to explore issues of equity, diversity, and social justice throughout the grades 6–12 course of study.

There are several take-away lessons in the shock Preuss and other underrepresented minority students experience when confronting challenges to their identity in high school and college. The students' unpreparedness reinforces appeals for educators to examine the cultural and political content of their curriculum materials and modify them as needed to present realistic representations of race relations, structured inequality, discrimination, and the struggles for civil rights. More specifically, educators would do well to intensify the teaching of the discourse of power, and strategies for confronting it during teacher-student interaction and in settings outside of the classroom. Incorporating students' lived experience in such lessons may better assist youth as they confront racism, sexism, and other forms of discrimination when they leave the relatively protective cocoon provided by their high school experience.

CONCLUSIONS

Preuss School students see the geographical and cultural distance they travel to and from school both as an obstacle that sometimes separates them from neighborhood friends and family and as a catalyst that affords them an opportunity to change their aspirations and succeed academically. Accompanying the opportunities and resources available at Preuss are the troubles and challenges of juggling home and academic lives. On the one hand, Preuss students are encouraged to believe that they can achieve academically and obtain a college degree. On the other hand, they struggle with the need to reconcile the norms and expectations routinely found in their homes with those demanded by the school. In this chapter we have shown how students' aspirations and academic performance emerge within their daily navigation between the different and sometimes conflicting worlds of home and school.

While confronting the pain associated with balancing the often-competing demands of home and an academically oriented school, the students attending Preuss incorporate new aspirations and outlooks for the future ("I want to go to college," "I want be somebody") and new forms of conduct (academic achievement in high school, enrollment in college upon graduation) into their habitus. These changes contrast starkly with the low aspirations, depressed outlook, and poor academic record typically associated with students of color from low-income backgrounds. The positive changes in aspirations and educational career path suggest that the social-class trajectory of low-income youth is more malleable than Bourdieu's theory predicts.

Preuss School students enroll in four-year colleges in numbers and percentages that exceed national averages, extending their record of high school accomplishments. Once they enroll in college, they express confidence about their academic preparation but indicate frustration with large, anonymous classes and surprise at suddenly being in the minority, both in terms of gender and ethnicity. The students deploy some of the strategies emphasized at Preuss to cope with these new challenges.

When their grade-point averages drop after they begin college, their aspirations are tempered but not abandoned.

In Bourdieu's formulation, the school serves as a medium of exchange where socially valued cultural capital acquired in the family and neighborhood is parlayed into academic skills. Academic skills are then converted into economic capital in the form of better, more prestigious jobs. Among Preuss students, habitus is being modified and cultural capital is being acquired *in school,* not in the family, which is the traditional source of values and aspirations. That is, changes in students' aspirations and their improved academic record are occurring within a specially designed institutional space. While certainly not a total institution in Goffman's (1961) or Bourdieu's (1977) sense, Preuss has installed significant features that extend the college-going culture of the school further into the lives of students than occurs with more traditional schools.

As we have described in previous chapters, these institutional arrangements include an exclusive college-prep course of study, structural changes in the quantity and quality of instructional time, and a shift in the organizational culture of the school, including carefully selected instructional staff who personalize their interactions with students. All of these arrangements are intended to support a high density of highly motivated students of color from low-income backgrounds. The changes we have observed in students' aspirations and conduct suggest that with the appropriate allocation and arrangement of institutional resources, educational programs and schools can become sites of transformation rather than reproducers of social inequality (see also Horvat and Davis 2010).

Unfortunately, at this point, we simply do not know if these changes indicate that the social-class trajectory of people from humble circumstances can be modified more permanently. Mussey's (2008) research shows that Preuss students parlay the academic and social skills they acquire in high school into the next step on a career ladder—namely, college enrollment. However, we don't know if Preuss graduates will be able to convert their newly acquired cultural capital into more coveted economic benefits, such as well-respected jobs. It is possible that their changes in outlook and performance will be swallowed up by the more intense social pressures of the outside world as time erodes the strength of the extensive academic and social supports they drew on as students in an innovative, thoughtfully designed high school.

NOTES

1. The findings we report in this chapter are drawn from research conducted at The Preuss School during the 2004–2005 and 2008–2009 school years. Two studies based on this research have been published previously. Mehan, Khalil, and Morales (2010) reported on the attitudes of 182 Preuss School students whom Nadia Khalil and J. César Morales interviewed about the challenges these students face as they adapt to the college-going culture of their new school. Khalil's access to students was facilitated by her role as tutor at the school; Morales's access was facilitated by a previous evaluation he had conducted on students' progress (McClure and Morales 2004). Mussey (2008), who was a science and

advisory teacher at Preuss, reported results of a survey she gave a cohort of Preuss students and also described the outlook of twenty-eight of these students when they first encountered college after graduating from Preuss. For this chapter, we employed Bourdieu's key concepts to mine the materials from both studies. By juxtaposing information obtained from surveys with the more intimate responses that emerged during interviews, we are able to provide a richer depiction of students' views regarding their life possibilities than would be possible with a presentation of survey results alone. We use selected student quotes to illustrate points in this chapter; the complete set of quotes appears in Mussey (2008) and Mehan, Khalil, and Morales (2010).

2. Interview data reported in this section were obtained by Preuss insiders Khalil, Morales, and Mussey. In the interview excerpts quoted in this chapter, NK refers to Khalil, JCM to Morales, and SSM to Season S. Mussey. All student names are pseudonyms. Note that in some of the excerpts quoted in the chapter, we use italics on sentences or phrases that highlight the central theme of the quote.

3. Strick obtained this figure by adding the confirmed four-year college enrollment and persistence data with an estimate of the percentage of the students on which the Clearinghouse had no records.

4. Mussey's advisory role connected her with a cohort of students from sixth through twelfth grades. She took advantage of this role to ask her advisees, using questionnaires (N = 78) and follow-up interviews (N = 28), to reflect on their experience in college after they had graduated from Preuss.

Chapter 6

Conclusions

Contributions to a Theory of Educational Inequality, Social Policy, and the Possibility of Educational Equality

The demonstrated success of The Preuss School, the early results for Gompers Preparatory Academy, and the initial promise of Lincoln High School suggest the life chances for students of color from low-income backgrounds can be improved when a college-going culture of learning is made an integral part of the schools they attend. The Preuss School's exceptional college enrollment rate of 84 percent (approximately twice the national average for low-income youth) and high API scores (the school ranks above schools in well-to-do neighborhoods in San Diego) suggest that low-income youth can succeed in academically rigorous college-prep and AP courses when certain critical conditions are met. These include safe and inviting school facilities, rigorous academic curriculum, qualified teachers, intensive academic and social supports, opportunities for students to develop a multicultural college-going identity, and strong family-neighborhood-school connections (Oakes 2003).

Detracking programs reverse the conventional time-curriculum relationship. In the traditional arrangement, students are educated for the same length of time, but the curriculum to which they are exposed varies. This practice leads to tracking (Oakes 2005). By contrast, a "detracked" arrangement establishes high instructional standards and presents rigorous curriculum to all students while at the same time varying academic and social supports as needed in order to enable all students to meet high academic standards. The better the students' academic performance, the fewer scaffolds offered; likewise, the greater the students' academic needs, the more academic and social supports provided.

Some important modifications of the traditional approach to schooling include the flexibility to modify the school day, school week, and school year, to vary the frequency and length of courses, to make crucial personnel decisions locally, and to engage teachers in extended professional development activities at the school site, during the school day, and all year long. These practices contribute to a highly effective pathway to college for underserved students.

These structural and cultural changes to standard operating procedures are most effective when parents are actively engaged and committed to supporting the success of their children. The importance of family involvement is vividly illustrated at The Preuss School. Preuss parents navigate a complicated admissions procedure, make significant sacrifices in time and energy to get their children across town to school, do their best to support their children's efforts to succeed in a demanding academic program, and interact with teachers and administrators. It is parent commitment combined with a school's academic program, then, and not the academic program alone, that must be seen as responsible for the success of a detracking approach.

CULTURE, STRUCTURE, AND AGENCY REDUX: INSTITUTIONAL ARRANGEMENTS AS AGENTS CONSTITUTING CHANGE IN STUDENTS' ASPIRATIONS AND CONDUCT

Our findings suggest that schools can be rearranged to help change students' aspirations and conduct. Bourdieu argues that habitus (dispositions that guide people's outlook, values, and aspirations) is formed early in life, within families and neighborhoods, and that once formed, is relatively stable and permanent. Preuss students develop aspirations that are distinctively different from those generally attributed to low-income students of color. They are encouraged to believe that they can be high academic achievers, walk in the front door of a college, and obtain a degree. Most—but not all—Preuss students "want to be somebody," and they see college as the vehicle for success later in life.

Students reported finding it difficult, and sometimes painful, to juggle the often-competing expectations of their neighborhood friends (who do not necessarily share their college aspirations) and parents (who want them to participate in family events) with the newly encountered demands of their academically oriented school. Nevertheless, they persevered, incorporating new aspirations and outlooks for the future ("I want to go to college," "I want be somebody") and new forms of conduct (stellar academic achievement in high school, enrollment in college upon graduation) into their habitus. With these changes, Preuss students sharply distinguish themselves from the typical profile associated with students of color from low-income backgrounds: depressed aspirations, negative outlook, and poor academic record. The positive change in students' aspirations and educational career path is constituted in large part by the elaborate institutional arrangements installed at the school to achieve a college-going culture of learning.

Our analysis, along with recent work such as that by Erin Horvat and James Davis (2010), shows the usefulness of Bourdieu's concept of habitus for exposing some of the processes of social reproduction and the possibility of social change. People's aspirations and outlook do seem to be established early, but they do not necessarily remain permanent. Intensive and multifaceted programs such as the one Horvat and Davis describe and innovative schools such as Preuss offer preliminary evidence that properly organized institutional arrangements can stimulate long-lasting change. The changes we observe in students' aspirations and conduct suggest that with the appropriate allocation and arrangement of institutional resources, the social-class trajectory of low-income youth is more malleable than Bourdieu's theory predicts. Taken together, these observations suggest that Bourdieu's reproduction theory can be formulated to be less deterministic than some critics have proposed. Among the research questions remaining unanswered, one concerns the relation between changes in habitus and conduct. Do changes in dispositions precede changes in conduct? Or is the relationship reversed, with conduct changing dispositions? Or do the two types of change develop simultaneously, indicating a reflexive relationship?

PUBLIC POLICY AND PRIVATE PREJUDICE

George Lipsitz (1998) argues that public policy and private prejudice combine to create a "possessive investment in whiteness" that contributes substantially to the racialized hierarchies in our society. He uses the term *possessive investment* to account for the advantages that accrue to individuals in positions of power and privilege through such practices as making profits from housing, land, and stock investments secured through discriminatory practices, and allocating unequal education to students of different races.

In the educational realm, such overt discriminatory practices as separate and unequal schools, tracks, and ability groups have been identified and are being dismantled. However, more subtle but no less pernicious social and cultural processes that sustain privileged positions continue to exist. In California, state and UC system decisions to abolish affirmative action policies, and then to disarm bit by bit, piece by piece, the new UC outreach paradigm aimed at better preparing students by improving the cultural and structural conditions of schooling, are actions that protect privilege just as much as do redlining neighborhoods for housing loans and denying minorities access to labor unions, public transport, high-quality schools, and health care.

Particularly galling in this more subtle cultural manifestation of privilege protection is the inverted use of expressions such as "equal opportunity" and "equal rights" to justify and legitimate racist actions. The proponents of Proposition 209 (which eliminated affirmative action) called it the "California Civil Rights Initiative" and borrowed language directly from the 1960s civil rights era to say that they were trying to ensure that all citizens of California had equal opportunities:

> The state shall not discriminate against, or grant preferential treatment to, any individual or group on the basis of race, sex, color, ethnicity, or national origin in the operation of public employment, public education, or public contracting.[1]

Survey research conducted at the time suggested that California voters interpreted this language as protecting the civil rights of the oppressed, when in fact its hidden intent was to eliminate affirmative action as a tool for oppressed groups to achieve mobility and greater access to equal opportunities.

A similar inversion of language and intent occurs in debates over gender equality. Commentators who claim that a "boy crisis" exists, in which the social organization of schooling conspires against boys' "naturally" aggressive tendencies, invoke the discourse of equal opportunity to justify special considerations for boys (Jacob-Almeida 2012). So, too, in the present context, those who argue against race-based scholarships, or early access to course enrollments, or invitations to participate in early academic opportunity programs, do so in the name of equal opportunity. But in invoking the discourse of equal opportunity, they (perhaps unintentionally) in fact protect the rights of the privileged from challenge by the unprivileged, rather than level the playing field for the historically disadvantaged.

Consequences of Shifting the Discourse from Affirmative Action to Academic Preparation

The way University of California policies (and administrators) frame the topics of diversity, our relations with local schools, and students' access to higher education also illustrates the power of language to shape our thoughts and actions. When the UC Regents took affirmative action off the table in July 1995, they challenged the UC system to establish a diverse student body by other means. UCSD responded to this challenge by reformulating the discourse. In our opinion, affirmative action was a political and educational strategy that recognized the lack of diversity on university campuses to be a function of systemic inequality, such as the effects of past group oppression, and those of current discrimination. Thus, in the language of the political campaign to end it, affirmative action was erroneously portrayed as "set asides" and "quotas." This reverse-discrimination representation of affirmative action was convincing to voters.

To avoid politically charged albeit politically effective constructions, we deploy a different discourse, one that emphasizes academic preparation and school change to enable underrepresented youth to walk in the front door of colleges. This emphasis on academic preparation as a strategy to achieve educational equity is not a new idea. More than thirty years ago, the California Round Table on Educational Opportunity called upon educators to focus on providing students with better academic preparation in order to decrease the educational disparities between the less fortunate and more privileged:

> We are convinced that the single most effective step that can be taken toward better representation of low income and ethnic minority students in baccalaureate study, their retention once they are enrolled, and their subsequent entry into post graduate study lies in stronger academic preparation at the junior and senior high school level for all students. Thus, action to improve educational quality will also serve educational justice. (California Round Table on Educational Opportunity, 1981: 2–3; see also Duster et al. 1990)

The shift in discourse from quotas and set-asides to academic preparation appeals to a wide range of the political spectrum. To those on the right, the move toward deeper academic preparation and away from quotas is appealing for three reasons. First, this logic privileges the agency of poor students: hard work, positive attitudes, and individual effort are celebrated as the keys to success. Second, it suppresses objectionable features of affirmative action—set-asides and quotas. Third, it shifts the paradigm from achieving diversity for its own sake to improving academic preparation, with diversity as an anticipated by-product (see also Rosen and Mehan 2003). To some on the left, the discourse shift to academic preparation and school change is reassuring. Many others voice concern that charter schools—the most visible instantiation of the movement toward better preparing students and more creatively organizing schools—will undermine public education (because most charters are not union shops and because their growing popular appeal is interpreted as threatening the already precarious position of public schools). Still, these critics do often begrudgingly support the charter effort because at least a core constituent group—educationally disadvantaged students—continue to be served. Because observers on the political left know that race and class are inexorably linked in the United States, and especially so in urban areas, some view building charter schools to attract and educate low-income students as a clever way to work around the ban on affirmative action.

The academic preparation construction is also productive when talking to K–12 educators about achieving equity and diversity. Whereas affirmative action in university admissions *called attention* to the deleterious effects of social and cultural conditions on individuals' chances for admission, it did little to *actually address* those conditions in classrooms. For instance, the policy neither prepared teachers to teach diverse populations of students nor prepared students to succeed in college once they arrived.

The University of California has considered a variety of strategies to deal with the problem of underrepresentation. Most of these involve changes in the admissions system, including a shift from basing admission almost exclusively on students' GPAs and SAT scores to a comprehensive review of students' application files; "eligibility in the local context" plans; accepting the top 12 percent of students from high schools even if they have not taken the complete set of college-prep courses; and modifying the SAT regimen and A-G curriculum. (For a more thorough discussion of these and other alternatives, see Brown, Rashid, and Stern 2010.)

Although we applaud these attempts to expand admissions criteria to be more inclusive, K–12 educators join us in concluding that in and of themselves, the new criteria will not change the composition of the student bodies on college campuses—especially at our more selective campuses. No matter how we tinker with the admissions system, there are simply not enough underrepresented students in California presently on the pathway to college eligibility to fulfill the UC's mandate to "seek out and enroll, on each of its campuses, a student body that demonstrates high academic achievement or exceptional personal talent, and that encompasses the broad diversity of backgrounds characteristic of California" (UC Regents 2001: 1). We need to help the state's K–12 educational system prepare more students to enroll and succeed in college as one important means of improving the life chances of underrepresented students.

UC'S CONTRADICTORY MESSAGES TO THE COMMUNITY CONCERNING ACCESS

In addition to helping the K–12 system prepare more students for college, the UC system must recognize that it may need to change its policies and practices in order to increase the life chances of low-income students of color. As an institution, the university has a history of sending contradictory messages to the community concerning access to college. The people charged with admissions and the people charged with outreach speak with two different voices—inclusion and exclusion. "The right hand is out recruiting while the left hand is raising the bar," is the way the university's first vice president in charge of educational outreach phrased it (Pister 2000). Outreach, speaking with the voice of inclusion, says, "Come in, join us; you can make it." The admissions office, speaking with the voice of exclusion, proclaims the enforcement of high standards and celebrates arduous work, saying, "This is a difficult place to get admitted. Only the top 12.5% will be invited to enter one of our campuses; only the top 4.5% will be invited to our most selective campuses."

Whereas the outreach voice of inclusion that signals the possibility of access is problematic, the voice of exclusion is backed up by harsh realities. The competition for UC admissions is a zero-sum game. There are only a limited number of seats in any given year for the freshman class on the nine (undergraduate) campuses in the UC system. The fact of limited spaces for students has significant, indeed ironic, consequences if outreach efforts are actually successful, that is, if more and more URM students become eligible for the university. We have to ensure that there will be room for URM students on our campuses as we better prepare them to meet UC admissions standards.

On the one hand, then, the net results of our efforts to diversify our campuses will be positive. Students who have not been well served by the university in the past will have more chances to walk in the front door than they did before we took steps to improve the quality of their education. On the other hand, our access efforts may not produce the full measure of results intended by enabling legislation and university mandates, that is, to increase the absolute number and relative percentages of students from underrepresented backgrounds who are eligible to enroll across all UC campuses. Systemwide, the less competitive campuses are more likely to become more diverse, but the distribution of underrepresented students may remain the same on competitively eligible campuses. The unintended result will be to maintain inequality if socioeconomically advantaged groups seek out qualitatively different educational advantages in order to maintain their privilege, even at quantitatively similar levels of the educational system (Lucas 2001). For example, privileged parents may increasingly seek to enroll their children in elite private colleges rather than state-supported colleges (such as California State University) even though both private and public colleges exist at the same level of the higher education system.

The Contest over Conceptions of Meritocracy

The University of California prides itself on its use of meritocratic grounds for admissions decisions. Based on the conclusions of psychometricians (e.g., Spearman 1927), many educators and policy makers subscribe to the theory that standardized tests uncover or "tap" students' talents (e.g., Tucker and Codding 1998; Education Trust 2003a, 2003b; Hanushek and Raymond 2004). This conventional wisdom is especially reassuring to educators seeking to locate talent that may be hidden or masked in students raised in poverty or those who have suffered from gender or racial discrimination. Accordingly, in the name of meritocracy, UC relies heavily on standardized test scores (SAT, ACT) and grade-point averages when making admissions decisions. These indices presumably give a more objective measure of students' ability than teachers' subjective judgments. The impulse to suppress subjective judgments and overcome any limitations imposed by students' backgrounds or discrimination is clearly commendable. Certainly, it is preferable to the quota system imposed on racial and religious groups that dominated earlier admissions decisions in higher education (Karabel 2005).

It must be acknowledged, however, that UC's present admissions criteria privilege a particular form of merit. Despite the fact that the university now engages in a "comprehensive review" of students' applications, in which students' statements of purpose, letters of recommendation, and evidence of overcoming difficult social circumstances are taken into account, SAT or ACT scores and GPA still matter, and matter a lot. The SAT and ACT, however, like most standardized tests, measure a certain narrow kind of skill. Because these are timed tests, speed of mental processing and the ability to recall tidbits of information, often out of context, is favored over long and more thoughtful analysis and reflection. These of course are "culturally arbitrary" standards (Bourdieu 1977). And standards, in turn, "are nothing more than structured preferences" (Williams 2005: 103):

The mind funnels of Harvard and Yale are called standards. Standards are concrete monuments to socially accepted preference. Standards are like paths picked through fields of equanimity, worn into hard, wide roads over time, used always because of collective habit, expectation, and convenience. The pleasures and perils of picking one's own path through the field are soon forgotten; the logic or illogic of the course of the road is soon rationalized by the mere fact of the road. (Ibid., 99)

The use of standardized tests in high-stakes settings has been roundly criticized (e.g., McNeil 1998; Haney 2000; Kohn 2002; Amrein and Berliner 2002; Ravitch 2010a). Because students' academic performance is highly correlated with parents' income, accountability schemes that take only standardized scores into account inevitably reward schools in affluent areas (Linn 2000; Haney 2000; Betts, Rueben, and Danenberg 2000; Powers 2004). Moreover, short, timed, multiple-choice tests are especially problematic because such tests do not measure creativity, problem solving, or critical thinking—essential skills for lifelong learning and active participation in a democratic society; worse, standardized tests demoralize test-takers who are not fluent in English.

High-stakes tests are problematic from K–12 teachers' perspective because they do not necessarily align with the state standards. Some teachers elect to simply "teach to the test," thereby subtracting time from much-needed everyday instruction (McNeil 1998). Joseph Pedulla and George Madaus (2004) found that the great majority of teachers who faced the highest stakes taught in ways that contradicted their own ideas of good practice. Other studies report that teachers encourage poor-performing students to stay away from school on test days (White and Rosenbaum 2008) or change students' answers to inflate results (Jacob and Levitt 2003; Amrein and Berliner 2002).

By setting admissions standards as measured by standardized tests and by students' completion of a specific sequence of courses, UC tacitly directs high schools to prepare their students for a certain kind of entrance examination and to arrange their curriculum such that their students take the required A-G course work. Educational resources are not evenly distributed across schools and districts. Thus, in preparing for admission to UC, students who attend schools in well-to-do neighborhoods have a built-in advantage over students who attend schools in low-income neighborhoods. Schools in high-income neighborhoods often routinely offer SAT-prep courses as well as far more college-prep (A-G) courses. White and Asian students are overrepresented in college-prep classes while African American and Latino students are significantly underrepresented, regardless of the socioeconomic status of the neighborhood or school (Oakes 2005; Haycock and Navarro 1997). By contrast, African American and Latino students are overrepresented in special-education programs (Mehan et al. 1986) and continuation schools (de Velasco et al. 2008).[2]

This situation is exacerbated by current UC policies concerning Advanced Placement (AP) courses. UC awards extra grade points to students completing AP courses; an "A" grade in an AP course is worth 5.0 on a 4.0 scale, a B is worth 4.0, and so on. This policy enables students in AP-rich schools to accumulate GPAs in excess of 4.5 on a 4.0 scale. In a report prepared for the American Civil Liberties Union to support its lawsuit against the Inglewood, California school district, Jeannie Oakes et al. (2000) show that access to AP course offerings is unevenly distributed across California's high schools. Students attending comprehensive high schools with predominantly African American and Latino/Latina populations have diminished access to AP courses. This differential is most stark in mathematics and science. Students who attend public schools rather than private schools, and/or urban or rural rather than suburban schools, have less access to AP courses in general, and AP courses in math and science in particular (Sadler et al. 2010).

This kind of differential access is recapitulated in AP test-taking patterns. Only 639 students, across twelve very large high schools in low-income neighborhoods in the Inglewood district, sat for the AP exams in math and science in 1999, an average of 53 students per school. Of these, only 117 achieved a passing score. By contrast, at five of the schools in the district's wealthiest neighborhoods, students took 890 math and science exams, an average of 178 exams per school. Of these, 629 achieved a passing score (Oakes et al. 2000). These differences in course offerings and in test-taking limit the educational opportunities of low-income students of color—a stratification in educational resources fueled in part by UC policies.

Protecting Privilege by Other Means

Debates about the meaning and practices of meritocracy in university admissions across the country and attempts by public universities to achieve the diversity goal on their campuses may be exacerbated by the actions of people outside the university. John Dewey (1900: 3) famously commented on the tension between selfish concerns and the public good: "What the best and wisest parent wants for his own child, that must be what the community wants for all of its children. Any other ideal for our schools is narrow and unlovely. Acted upon, it destroys our democracy."

Well-to-do families and the schools their children attend can be expected to respond to the challenges posed by equity-producing practices by making sure that their already advantaged children are positioned even more competitively. Well-to-do parents currently invest in private test-prep courses and hire private counselors to assist them in making connections with prestigious colleges and universities (McDonough 1997). Companies such as Kaplan charge considerable fees to students seeking to improve their test scores on SAT, ACT, MCAT, and LSAT exams required for entrance to four-year colleges and graduate schools. Private counselors help students prepare application essays, ensure that teachers write carefully documented letters of recommendation, and contact colleges directly on behalf of their clients. Well-to-do parents successfully petition the College Board for longer test-taking time for their children. Local educators report that few parents in urban schools seek such waivers, even though a substantial number of students are eligible for them. By contrast, parents in suburban schools apply for and receive these waivers in numbers that exceed the total registered special-education population in the schools their students attend (Ong-Dean 2009).

We must be vigilant, for parents in positions of privilege will deploy other means to protect their position if URM students become better prepared and therefore pose a threat to their children's place in the status and economic hierarchy. They may well invest in even more private courses and test-prep efforts in order to raise their children's chances to enroll in four-year colleges. They may well fight to preserve a tracking system that keeps low-income students of color out of advanced classes (Kohn 1998). In an extreme case in point, parents in New York City are investing hundreds of dollars for test-prep kits to boost their children's chances to enter gifted kindergarten classes—a tactic that low-income parents either don't know about or can't afford (Winerip 2010). The cumulative result of privilege-protecting efforts such as these will be an inflation of the credentials needed to enter higher levels of education, occupations, and professions (Collins 1979; Lucas 2001).

Preuss and other college-prep schools for low-income students of color are attempting to spread an elite practice to underserved members of society. A logical extension of Bourdieu's theory is that these attempts will be challenged. As low-status youth gain access to higher education, the rules of the game may change. A striking example occurred at UCSD recently. The Admissions Committee changed the GPA requirement from a 3.0 GPA to a 3.5 GPA for students transferring to the university from community colleges, effective fall 2011 (UCSD Admissions Committee 2011). The rationale offered for this change in policy was increased workload; the number of applicants has doubled while admissions staff has been cut in response to the budget crisis. This not unreasonable rationale has unintended gatekeeping consequences for URM students. If this criterion had been in effect from 2007 to 2010, the percentage of underrepresented applicants would have been reduced by more than 67 percent; 38 African American students would have been eligible to apply instead of 184; 228 Mexican American students would have been eligible instead of 734.

The fear that elites will change the rules of the game to protect privilege is warranted. Slots at the top of the status hierarchy are limited. Therefore, any attempt to spread an elite practice to all members of society may result in the practice being devalued and replaced by a different sorting mechanism. Because the power structure in society is so strong, simply giving more access to privileged knowledge may result in a new definition of privileged knowledge (Lareau 2003: 277). Students of color from low-income backgrounds may enroll in greater numbers in two-year colleges and less prestigious four-year colleges, while at the same time, students from well-to-do backgrounds will continue to be overrepresented in more prestigious four-year colleges and universities. That is, the credentials of all students may rise, but the relative ranking of ethnic and socioeconomic groups is likely to remain much the same.

A Proposed Resolution of the Conundrum: Revitalize Schooling for a Democratic Society

As a way out of this conundrum, it may be useful to borrow a metaphor from a different domain: economics. There are supply-side and demand-side issues to be reconciled. On the supply side, the UC system must be continuously pressured to find ways to ensure that URM students who are now better prepared to walk in through the front gates, have dorm rooms and seats in classrooms when they arrive. UC must not only continue but also expand its commitment to public schools that do not have the resources necessary to assist underrepresented minority students. Traditional outreach techniques, which include information about necessary college-prep courses, exams, and financial aid possibilities, need to be intensified; classroom space must keep pace with an expanded, well-prepared student population.

When addressing issues on the demand side, it may be useful to revisit the meaning and purpose of public education. We think it would be beneficial to inject a revitalized democratic conception into the practice of public education. Because university admissions policies have considerable power in shaping the curriculum of K–12 schools, UC faculty is in a position to influence what is taught, how it is taught, and what is rewarded when students apply to our campuses. Therefore, individual campuses and the university as a whole can contribute in significant ways to a reorientation that will reduce the tension between parents seeking to protect their privilege and parents seeking to gain access to precious educational resources.

The rhetoric legitimating public education from its inception in colonial times has framed the provision of schooling for all as grounded in a concern for the public good. In the early decades of the republic, the nation's commitment to a democratic form of government was recognized as fragile and in need of constant vigilance. Political and educational leaders such as Thomas Jefferson, Horace Mann, and John Dewey maintained that a well-educated citizenry was crucial for the maintenance and development of representative democracy. A democratic society "must have a type of education which gives individuals a personal interest in social relationships and control, and the habits of mind which secure social change without introducing disorder" (Dewey 1916: 115). Public education was proposed as the institution to serve this democracy-preserving purpose (Cremin 1951; Tyack 1974).

The public-good argument continued throughout much of the twentieth century: Society as a whole benefits if all children are better educated. Public safety is enhanced if people are employed or in school, not in prisons. The economy improves when the workforce is better educated. To help ensure that access is equalized, all citizens—even those who do not have school-aged children—are expected to contribute to the cost of the educational enterprise, through taxation.

Representing the value of public education in terms of preserving democracy and enhancing public tranquility sustained the common school movement of the nineteenth century and continued through the Progressive Era. As the United States became more and more industrialized, however, the purpose of education was reconceptualized. Instead of preparing thoughtful citizens, the function of education is increasingly represented as preparing youth for their proper place in the workforce. This sentiment has been roundly criticized as undemocratic and dysfunctional (e.g., see Bowles and Gintis 1976; Oakes et al. 1999). However, this technical function of public schooling was recognized and advocated by early educational administrators, including Ellwood Cubberley, who later became dean at Stanford:

Our schools are, in a sense, factories, in which raw products (children) are to be shaped and fashioned into products to meet the demands of life. The specifications for manufacturing came from the demands of 20th century civilization, and it is the business of the school to build its pupils according to the specifications laid down. (Cubberley 1916: 338)

With some regularity in US history, policy makers, educators, and government officials demand an overhaul of the educational system (Tyack and Cuban 1995). In the name of school improvement, we have witnessed calls for segregating college-bound students from vocationally oriented students, integrating black and white students, rearranging the order in which high school science courses are taught, reorganizing small schools into comprehensive ones, restructuring those same large high schools into more personalized ones, and many other innovations. The current "standards and accountability" reform effort has dominated the conversation about the organization of education since 1984, when the report *A Nation at Risk* flailed public schools for "committing an act of unthinking educational disarmament" and producing a "rising tide of mediocrity" in public schools (NCEE 1983: 595).

The legislation that emerged from the conclusions reached in *A Nation at Risk* (No Child Left Behind, in particular) was supposed to give states the ability to identify educational problems and address them in measurable ways. Instead, current efforts to reform public education are ironically diminishing its quality and producing mechanistic thinkers rather than complete citizens capable of thinking for themselves (Nichols and Berliner 2006; Nusbaum 2010; Ravitch 2010a).

Many contemporary educational commentators have become convinced that a business or market orientation will save public education (Freidman 1963; Chubb and Moe 1990). Hence we see business rhetoric injected into the policies and practices of public schools, creating a representation of education as a commodity to be bought and sold instead of as a public good. Expressions such as "customers," "consumer choice," "competition," "accountability," "responding to market forces," and "chief education officers" (instead of school directors or principals) have invaded the discourse about public schooling.

The emphasis on standardized testing as the preferred method of measuring students' academic performance reinforces the business-oriented discourse. Increasingly, we are confronted with a school culture in which instruction is reduced to preparing for standardized tests and teachers are blamed for any student failure (McNeil 1998). Market-based policies and practices are degrading our ability to offer a quality education to our youth because the federal formulas defining failing schools under No Child Left Behind and Race to the Top require schools to increase their test scores in order to continue to operate. Defining school success using only standardized test scores does not capture the complexity of the challenges confronting schools that enroll large numbers of low-income students, new immigrants, and non-English-speaking students.

The alternative to the reduction of public education to a commodity is a revitalized conception of education as the cornerstone of democratic society. This means cultivating curiosity through active learning, not rote learning, and instantiating a curriculum that helps shape character, develop sound minds in healthy bodies, and form citizens able to participate in our democracy (Ravitch 2010a). Furthermore, a revitalized democratic education means abandoning passivity and inert receptivity in favor of opportunities for students to have aesthetic, not just cognitive, encounters with engrossing historical narratives, problems in the natural sciences and mathematics, captivating stories, and poetry (Dewey 1916).

Taking Dewey's (1916) injunctions about the relationship between democracy and education seriously, proponents of democratic education want to expose students to the open flow of ideas and faith in the collective and individual capacity of people to create possibilities for resolving problems; concern for the welfare of others and the common good; and concern for the dignity and rights of individuals and minorities. This is a conception of education for democracy as "a way of life"—putting into practice an idealized set of values (Beane and Apple 1995: 6–7).

A school created to offer students democratic experiences incorporates project-based learning; critical reflection and analysis to evaluate ideas, problems, and policies; performance-based assessment; and a commitment to connecting the curriculum to real-world experiences (Sizer 1984, 1992; Meier 1995; Ayers, Quinn, and Stovall 2009). Space is made in the curriculum to study large-scale and local social problems, such as global warming; the consequences of the population explosion; inequality among races, classes, genders; and analysis of news that does or does not appear in newspapers or on TV and the perspective from which it is presented (Ayers, Quinn, and Stovall 2009).

Preuss teachers instantiate a version of a democratic education by linking students' mastery of the academic knowledge demanded by state standards and valorized in elite colleges (and society in general) with the development of critical thinking skills. Preuss students learn to ask challenging questions, including those that enable them to better understand social structures that generate inequality, and to develop a critical consciousness about institutions that position low-income students of color and their ethnic class communities at or near the bottom of the social hierarchy. Critical inquiry continues with students being taught how to gather evidence that enables them to assess the truth value of claims, make a persuasive argument, and present these ideas in writing and in person (Gabay 2011; Kovacic 2011).

Lincoln High School's Center for Social Justice (see Chapter 4) offers courses in which students learn to develop a critical awareness of injustices as they acquire strong academic skills. When appropriate, students are encouraged to take action based on their critical analysis. In one instance, students organized a march from their school to the district's education center to protest proposed teacher layoffs. On another occasion, students distraught over the district's plan to place an ROTC-sanctioned rifle range on their campus were encouraged by their social justice teachers to transform their concern into action. They wrote letters to the school board, challenging the plan. Board members responded by canceling the rifle range. Lincoln students also led a drive to convince the school board to limit the number and types of campus visits by military recruiters.

Fostering critical thinking skills can energize young learners, but teachers face challenges in simultaneously helping their students develop academic skills. This tension surfaced dramatically during the debate over the proposed Lincoln High School rifle range. A school board member—himself a former teacher at Lincoln—returned the students' letters opposing the rifle range with each spelling and grammatical error corrected in red ink.

Encouraging students to critically analyze issues raises the possibility that they may challenge dominant interpretations and call received wisdom into question (Beane and Apple 1995). Neither is popular with those who see the function of education as the unquestioned transmission of knowledge from generation to generation and the socialization of youth into existing forms of society. As recent political decisions in Arizona attest, fostering students' critical thinking skills can prompt backlash. It is now illegal in Arizona for high schools to teach courses that "advocate the overthrow of the US government," "promote resentment toward a race," are "primarily for one race," or "advocate ethnic solidarity instead of individuality" (Arizona HB 2281). That state's attorney general thinks ethnic studies courses in Tucson violate the law because they teach Latinos that they are being victimized and reveal ways in which privilege is associated with whites in positions of power (Lacey 2011). Still, the effort to cultivate active engagement, a critical consciousness, and reflexive self-examination among our students is worth the struggle, because the result can be sophisticated thinkers and hence more thoughtful citizens.

The reformulation of curriculum and instruction we envision also requires a different theory of assessment—one that relies not on a single measure of rote learning but rather on a portfolio of assessments that capture a wide range of cognitive skills and aesthetic sensibilities. The Coalition of Essential Schools (Sizer 1984, 1992; Meier 1995) and schools influenced by Theodore Sizer (Alvarez and Mehan 2006; Rosenstock 2009) use portfolios extensively to measure students' progress. Standardized test results are included in these portfolios, but students' essays, three-dimensional demonstrations or exhibitions of scientific principles, artwork, and musical compositions or musical performances are prominent. In addition, several influential educational and civil rights groups (including the Civil Rights Project, the New York Performance Standards Consortium, the Coalition for Authentic Reform in Massachusetts, the American Evaluation Association, and the American Educational Research Association) recommend the use of a portfolio of measures to judge students' progress. The American Evaluation Association (2002: 1) advocates this approach because "high-stakes testing leads to under-serving or mis-serving all students, especially the most needy and vulnerable, thereby violating the principle of "do no harm." The American Educational Research Association (2000: 1) based its position on the 1999 *Standards for Educational and Psychological Testing*: "Decisions that affect individual students' life chances or educational opportunities should not be made on the basis of test scores alone."

What is the role of the university in this reformulation of public education? It can alter admissions policies to encourage schools to ensure that in grades K–12, students encounter schooling that embodies these principles of learning and assessment. The university should not simply dictate these new terms, of course. It will be more productive to engage K–12 decision makers and community college leaders in constructive dialog about ways to refigure schools for democracy, including making changes in the forms of instruction and methods of assessment.

Improving Schools, Improving Neighborhoods

A number of thoughtful critics have challenged the premise that we might be able to improve the life chances of low-income students of color by improving schooling for the underserved (see, for example, Berliner 2005; Rothstein 2004). It is unfair and misguided to place all the blame for the poor academic performance of students from low-income families on schools, they assert. Likewise, it is unrealistic to expect schools, by themselves, to solve the deep-seated and vexing problem of educational inequality. The "influence of social class characteristics is probably so powerful that schools cannot overcome it no matter how well-trained are their teachers and no matter how well-designed are their instructional plans and climates" (Rothstein 2004: 5).

Low-income families are subject to a number of social and economic conditions that constrain the ability of their children to attain academic success. These conditions are often outside the control of schools. Low-income students are more likely than their middle-class counterparts to have such health conditions as poor vision, asthma, limited hearing, and poor oral health, and they are more likely to have been exposed to lead. Each of these conditions can influence students' performance because they may miss school, pay less attention in class, or be distracted by pain. To make matters worse, low-income families are less likely to receive regular health care, which means that poor health conditions go untreated; this, in turn, can increase school absences and cause children to contract other illnesses.

Low-income families have fewer employment prospects. Not only does underemployment depress the economic resources available to families, but it contributes to lower aspirations among the children, because they do not have role models who raise their expectations for success. Depressed employment is linked to poor housing. Low-income families move often, which in turn means that children change schools often. Some urban schools report a 100 percent mobility rate within a given school year (Rothstein 2004: 46). Transience contributes to students' poor academic performance because they do not experience coherence and continuity in instruction.

The assertion that the conditions of poverty tend to overwhelm even the most earnest school improvement efforts has sparked intense debate. One set of commentators has cautioned against concentrating on the negative conditions in low-income neighborhoods. Taking students' impoverished socioeconomic conditions into account in the classroom will give educators reasons to lower expectations and simplify instruction. They exhort teachers not to make excuses for students based on their home life; instead they should concentrate on providing a demanding curriculum for all students, regardless of their socioeconomic circumstances (or their race, ethnicity, and language capabilities) (Thernstrom and Thernstrom 2003).

Asking teachers to treat students the same regardless of their socioeconomic status, race, gender, or disabling conditions is certainly appealing on the surface. And this suggestion seems consistent with calls for educational equity. However, it may very well be too much to ask teachers to serve as social workers, health practitioners, and safety monitors in addition to the already daunting responsibilities associated with teaching math, natural sciences, and literacy. Recognizing that the "no excuses" ideology places an overwhelming burden on teachers, other educators encourage a more comprehensive approach to address the problem of educational inequity.

With a coordinated system of early-childhood programs, family support services, neighborhood improvement efforts, health care providers, and job counselors deployed in support of educators in schools, the Harlem Children's Zone (HCZ) is touted as an exemplar of a comprehensive community-based approach to academic improvement (Tough 2008). Students at Promise Academy I and II, the HCZ's two charter elementary schools serving mostly low-income underrepresented minority youth, have improved performance on statewide tests. In 2009 HCZ reported that 100 percent of the third-graders at HCZ Promise Academy II scored at or above grade level in statewide math tests; and 100 percent of the Promise Academy I third-graders were at or above grade level (downloaded from www.hcz.org/our-results/accomplishments on September 26, 2010).

While some investigators and political leaders celebrate the success of the Harlem Children Zone's comprehensive approach (Tough 2008; Obama 2008), others remain unconvinced. Grover Whitehurst and Michelle Croft (2010) acknowledge that HCZ charter schools have raised test scores substantially, but these authors claim the two charters have not improved students' academic performance as much as nearby charter schools that operate without a coordinated system of community support. They conclude that the HCZ community-based approach is not successful because standardized test scores have not improved more at the Promise Academies than those at comparison schools. From our point of view, this criticism of HCZ rests on an overly narrow measure of improvement and confuses short-term with long-term goals and the means to achieve them.

If, rather than standardized test scores, improvements in job opportunities, personal health, and neighborhood safety are used as measures of success, then a more robust view of the community-based approach emerges. Consistent with David Berliner's (2005) findings, interdisciplinary university-based research groups in several communities are beginning to forge collaborations with groups from their local communities to develop comprehensive models for promoting community improvements. Similar in many respects to the Harlem Children's Zone, but different in that university faculty are intimately involved in the enterprise, are community-university partnerships in San Diego; Somerville, Massachusetts; Hartford, Connecticut; Austin, Texas; Tucson, Arizona; and Los Angeles and Berkeley, California. These organizations focus on improving economic possibilities, neighborhood safety, and personal health as goals in themselves and as factors contributing to improved educational possibilities (Schensul 2010). The importance of a healthy life and of neighborhood well-being—and the relation of both to improved educational opportunity—are often overlooked in the frenzy to improve test scores.

Collaborative relationships between university and community groups typically distinguish near-term educational outcomes from near-term and long-term health, neighborhood safety, and economic outcomes. When near-term educational outcomes (e.g., high school completion, enrollment in college) are the primary goal, the effects that changes in neighborhood safety, economic, and health services have on children's *absence* from school or *behavior* in school that may be ameliorated by these interventions are measured.

When long-term communication, health, economic improvements, or greater neighborhood safety (e.g., prolonging life, reducing unemployment, reducing crime), are the primary goals, the effectiveness of efforts designed to treat conditions that shorten the number of years an educated student will be productive in society and the workplace are calibrated. For example, when commonplace communication tools, such as cell phones or Facebook, are harnessed to enhance communication within a community, collaborative research teams study their effectiveness as an end in itself and in relation to students' achievement. In the domain of health, when services designed to target problems such as obesity, diabetes, and cardiovascular diseases are introduced, changes in onset rates are tabulated. In the domain of neighborhood safety, when services aimed at reducing injury, suicide, and gang violence are begun, incident rates are collected and compared through time.

Educational, economic, neighborhood safety, and health goals need to be itemized and clearly defined, and specific programs must be designed around those goals. This delineation will improve researchers' chances of determining whether a community-based intervention has added measurable benefits in targeted arenas and has contributed to educational improvements. The availability of detailed empirical data should help resolve the debate between advocates of community-based improvement efforts (Schensul 2010; Tough 2008) and their critics (Whitehurst and Croft 2010).

POLICY INTO PRACTICE IN THE LOCAL CONTEXT

The process of school change we have described and evaluated in this book is informed by and also itself informs the co-construction perspective on public policy (see Appendix 2). Our efforts to simultaneously engage in and study the possibility of institutional change aimed at enhancing the opportunities of low-income students of color to walk in the front door of colleges and universities show that public policy is a contingent process, negotiated in locally organized social contexts.

Conducting design research with colleagues from two charter schools and a more traditional high school has given us firsthand knowledge about how educators on the ground respond to a dizzying array of federal, state, district, and university policies that impose constraints on public schools. As with so many other urban schools, Gompers and Lincoln are further burdened by the impoverished economic conditions in the surrounding neighborhoods (Rothstein 2004; Berliner 2005). But these social and economic constraints did not entirely limit the actions of the activists on the ground who, in the face of considerable opposition, established The Preuss School and Gompers Preparatory Academy, and helped restructure Lincoln High School. These actors were not the tractable or passive recipients of directives issued by the district, or the school board, or the state. Instead, they were creative, determined, and persistent. They accepted some directives, modified others, and rejected still others. In every case, the actions they took shaped the manner in which policy was translated into practice.

Adaptation and Improvisation in School Improvement

As the preceding chapters have demonstrated, actions taken at the upper echelons of the system energize actions at the local level. They do not determine them completely, however. For example, the UC Regents' directive to campuses to find innovative ways to address the underrepresentation problem did not anticipate the proposal initiated by a coalition of UCSD faculty and community groups to build a college-prep school for underrepresented minority youth. NCLB demands for failing schools to reconstitute did not determine the partnership between Gompers and UCSD or the re-formation of Lincoln as four small schools.

The final configuration of Preuss, Gompers, and Lincoln was neither dictated from the top nor known at the outset. These configurations emerged in the throes of an often heated give-and-take of negotiations among school district officials, university faculty, and local activists. The (currently) final—albeit unpredicted—outcomes emerging from these negotiations provide tangible evidence for our claim that social policy is a co-constructed process, formed in a web of interrelated conditions and consequences, where the consequences of actions in one context often become the conditions for another (Hall 1995; Hall and McGinty 1997; Datnow, Hubbard, and Mehan 2002; Hubbard et al. 2006; Coburn 2005).

Policy makers situated at the higher levels of a social organization and activists located on the ground and in the streets need one another. Neither school district leaders, nor university faculty, nor street-level activists acting alone could have achieved the creation of Preuss as a model school, the conversion of Gompers Middle School into a charter school, or the reconstitution of Lincoln as a suite of small schools. In the Preuss case, the original proposal for a grades 6–8 charter school was reformulated as a grades 6–12 school attached to a research center after a confluence of activists, Regents, and community leaders countered the resistance originally registered by campus administrators. In the Gompers case, the outgoing SDUSD school superintendent, then opposed by a newly elected school board, needed the activists to formulate a viable academic plan, cement relations with the university and local community groups, and enlist the support of parents in order to secure passage of the charter petitions. The activists needed the initial directions from the superintendent and the former board about NCLB in order to consider alternative ways to organize their school. Both the outgoing superintendent and activists on the ground benefited from the able assistance and insider knowledge of Brian Bennett, who was then in charge of the district's School Choice office. Bennett met often with the GCMS planning group, interpreting arcane laws and foreshadowing district plans. He also put the street-level activists in touch with the California Charter School Association and the Girard Foundation. These organizations in turn provided start-up funds and valuable information about converting a failing traditional school into a viable charter (Bennett 2008). In the Lincoln case, the demands of NCLB and the availability of Gates Foundation funding reinforced the plans of the superintendent and made possible the long-standing and very vocal demands of articulate community members that the school be preserved and revitalized.

The decisions to create the Preuss charter school at UCSD and the Gompers charter school in southeastern San Diego, and to restructure Lincoln High School, were not direct responses to objectively formulated problems—the lack of diversity on the campus in the Preuss case; the lack of challenging educational environments in the Gompers and Lincoln cases. Instead, the plans that were ultimately approved, and the rhetoric surrounding those plans, promoted a particular interpretation of the "underrepresentation problem" on the UCSD campus and the "lack of quality education problem" in southeastern San Diego. On the one hand, attention was directed toward some factors that influence the numbers of underrepresented students graduating from urban schools and entering college (students' lack of academic preparation, poorly equipped schools in low-income neighborhoods) and diverted from other factors (race and class privilege, power, the ambivalent climate of the UCSD campus, limited economic opportunity, racism). On the other hand, the way in which CREATE, educators, and community groups in southeastern San Diego interpreted the academic preparation problem has reintroduced questions of culture and power into the conversation about academic inequality. For example, these groups problematized teachers', parents', and students' beliefs about students' ability to learn. They also assisted schools with building their capacity to offer rigorous college-prep classes and the academic scaffolds to support them. These acts of reinterpretation illustrate that definitions of equality and inequality are not static, but are continually constructed, re-constructed, and negotiated in relation to changing national, state, and local contexts, and in light of shifting institutional interests and configurations of political power.

There Are No Carbon Copies in School Improvement

The co-construction model of organizational change also challenges the conventional wisdom concerning how successful models of school improvement are brought to scale. The standard view is that school improvement involves replication. Replication commences with the building of a model at a local site, such as a school. Then copies of that original are exported to new settings. Replication implies that extensions of an original prototype will look like—and should copy exactly—the original. By contrast, the co-construction model recognizes that exact replicas of even the most successful of models are neither possible nor desirable. Instead of attempting a perfect replication, the co-construction approach to scaling-up successful models recommends adapting design principles to new circumstances.

The original academic plans of Preuss, Gompers, and Lincoln were thoughtfully designed—influenced by social theory, educators' past experiences, parents' values, and empirical evidence. For example, Gompers educators, like Preuss educators, extended learning time. But instead of adding days to the school year as Preuss educators did, Gompers educators added extra time to each school day. This approach, they felt, would work better at their site because parents in their neighborhood would be more likely to accept longer school days than they would be to accept having their children start school in late August and continue into late June. Gompers educators also recognized the benefits of incorporating teacher professional development activities into the school day rather than offering them after school or during the summer. But, unlike Preuss, where professional development delays the start of school on Fridays, Gompers educators chose to start school late on Wednesday mornings because that would provide students with a rejuvenating break in the middle of the demanding school week. Lincoln educators, like those at Preuss and Gompers, seek to provide families in southeastern San Diego with a range of educational choices for their children. Preuss offers parents from low-income backgrounds an opportunity to send their children to a college-prep school on a university campus, and Gompers offers a similar course of study nearby, in a neighborhood school. Lincoln educators, by contrast, have adopted a structural approach to school choice, whereby parents (in conjunction with their children) select among four different small schools, each with its own distinct academic theme, but all located on the same campus.

The modifications of the original academic plans to meet unanticipated developments at each of the three schools are classes of actions that demonstrate that social actors improvise, even in difficult social circumstances. In modifying the original design, the Gompers, Lincoln, and Preuss teams made creative and resourceful use of a wide variety of intellectual materials in the moment-to-moment flow of daily life in their schools. That improvisational approach is an ongoing process at Preuss, Gompers, and Lincoln, one that contributes significantly to the invention of new practices, new structures, and new symbols. While these new ways of thinking, acting, and talking are stable for the time being, we predict that they, too, will be subject to additional rounds of improvisational modification when evidence on the ground interacts with constraints imposed from above—such as the need to adapt to the devastating effects of the ongoing fiscal crisis in California.

In sum, the creation of The Preuss School, the conversion of Gompers Middle School to Gompers Charter Middle School (and later to Gompers Preparatory Academy), and the reconstitution of Lincoln High School are not only important examples of positive organizational change. They also represent dramatic examples of how public policy is formulated in real life, as policy makers situated at or near the top of a social organization interact with activists located on the ground and in the streets. The subsequent contested relationship among the schools, the district, and the teachers' union speaks volumes about the transformative possibilities of human agency in the ongoing process of enacting public policy in daily life.

The dynamic manner in which Preuss, Gompers, and Lincoln are energizing their theories of action illustrates how successful models can be modified to meet the unique particulars of local contexts. This is a distinguishing feature of the co-construction perspective on school improvement. Formulating educational reform as a co-constructed process is heuristic, therefore, because it instructs us that organizational change is generated in face-to-face interactions among real people, confronting problems in concrete social settings, such as classrooms, school board meetings, courts of law, and state legislatures. Furthermore, these social interactions exist on different levels or planes within a social system. As a result, agents in the contact zones within and between layers of the system make policy in their everyday actions. Including entities such as government offices and funding agencies in the layered formulation of social policy explicitly calls attention to the political and economic conditions that enable possibilities and impose constraints on organizational change, including school reform.

THE RESPONSIBILITY OF COLLEGES AND UNIVERSITIES TO ENHANCE K–12 EDUCATION

In closing, we draw on the many challenges, triumphs, setbacks, and stalemates we, and other CREATE colleagues, have encountered in our ongoing efforts to provide low-income students of color with equal educational opportunities. These experiences provide the basis for some concrete suggestions we hope will be of use to public universities and large urban school districts throughout the country as these organizations and the communities they represent grapple with the challenges of ensuring educational equity in this century's post–affirmative action context.

Public colleges and universities have well-established and time-honored responsibilities to educate their students to become productive and thoughtful citizens. Because of the educational disparities that exist between K–12 schools in well-to-do neighborhoods and those in urban neighborhoods, we propose that colleges and universities assume an additional civic responsibility: that of assisting K–12 educators in confronting the many-layered problem of underrepresentation in higher education, improving the quality of education in elementary and secondary schools, and bettering the life chances of low-income youth.

We suggest that *educational field stations* (Duster et al. 1990; Lytle 2007) associated with university campuses be considered as a model for addressing these intertwined and vexing problems. Educational field stations have developed in several urban neighborhoods affiliated with many campuses (see Chapter 2). Researchers associated with these educational field stations conduct basic and design research at university-assisted schools and other public schools and make the lessons learned about how to establish and sustain a healthy culture of learning in urban schools available to researchers, educators, and policy makers in the educational field.

The educational field station model can be adapted productively by colleges and universities to create model systems that in turn can guide urban schools to obtain an enhanced level of excellence, especially for underrepresented minority youth. Because educational field stations require considerable effort and substantial commitment of resources, researchers/educators might consider starting one model on or off campus before extending the model to partnership schools in low-income neighborhoods. Further, based on CREATE's experiences with Preuss as a model school, it is our view that the tools of design research can be applied to study the principles inherent in these models and adapt the lessons learned to selected K–12 schools in areas with high URM populations.

Applying the educational field station model to engage K–12 education is consistent with and can enliven the research, teaching, and public service missions of public colleges and universities. In some colleges and universities, the activities associated with these three missions are separated. Faculty members conduct research that is distinct from the courses they teach. If they engage in service, it is often voluntary work in a local school, church, or community center. We have found, though, that research, teaching, and service can be linked productively when university faculty form partnerships with urban schools. University-school partnerships not only benefit K–12 education but also improve the quality of undergraduate and graduate education and enhance faculty research (Campbell and Lassiter 2010).

College and university courses that are specifically designed to join the activities of research, teaching, and service facilitate this process. These "practicum in learning courses" have three components: an on-campus seminar, a field experience in local schools or community centers, and discussion sections. In the seminar, undergraduate students from a wide range of disciplines are introduced to relevant literature on the role of language and culture in education, the social organization of schooling, principles of learning, and information about the socioeconomic and ethnic characteristics of the participating community and/or school sites.

To connect theory with practice, students in practicum courses are placed in a variety of school and community settings, where they serve either as tutors or interns. This field experience portion of practicum courses is analogous to the laboratory courses routinely taught in the natural sciences. Engagement in academically linked, community-based learning activities gives undergraduates unique intellectual and cultural opportunities. Freed from the confines of a university classroom, undergraduates who participate in practicum courses are positioned to create and test disciplinarily derived hypotheses in real-life settings, in much the same way that fledgling natural scientists benefit from conducting hands-on experiments in campus laboratories.

When students serve as tutors, they work with elementary school, middle school, or high school students before, during, and after school. When they serve as interns, they are assigned to work closely with more specialized educators, such as counselors, family services staff, school nurses, or information technology/data analysis specialists. For example, an intern working with the school nurse at a high school may contact parents about upcoming information sessions and tabulate information that would help the nurse design effective family interventions. An intern assigned to a school's IT specialist may help design educational materials for courses or student assemblies. In all cases, students write field notes about their weekly experiences, which are linked to assigned readings in regular classroom discussion sessions. At the end of the quarter or semester, they prepare a term paper on a topic that is relevant to their field of study. They then present the paper to the seminar and to educators and staff at the site where they volunteered. These mini-research projects are intended to develop students' knowledge and also be of assistance to the educators at their practicum site.

An axiom in education comes to life in practicum courses: one of the best ways to learn a subject is to try to teach it to others. Evidence suggests that students who participate in an activity-based form of instruction gain a deeper understanding of both their academic majors and the material assigned in practicum courses, and they learn to recognize the relevance of each for real-world settings. They also are provided an opportunity to develop an appreciation of the complexities of everyday life in diverse socioeconomic and racial/ethnic communities. When students confront these complexities not as a topic in a textbook but as lived experiences in everyday social situations, they are poised for truly transformative learning that goes well beyond the passive uptake of prepackaged information provided by their professors during course lectures or seminars.

Our final observation is a reminder about the power of politics and the relevance of organizational culture in organizational change. Attempts to change any large-scale organization, including colleges, secondary, and elementary schools, must take into account organizational culture and politics. Building an educational field station, requiring high schools to offer more college-prep courses, and converting a traditional public school to a charter school are not only technical matters. They are cultural and political undertakings, as well.

Institutionalizing a policy change is much more complicated than writing new regulations and ensuring that new procedures are translated into practice faithfully. Any change in one dimension of an organization affects other dimensions of that organization (Sarason 1972). The proposed practice of increasing college-prep courses can bump up against teachers' beliefs about whether students of color from low-income backgrounds are capable of undertaking a more rigorous course of study. Introducing elements of a college-going culture of learning involves rearranging class schedules, teachers' routines, and standard operating procedures. Teachers may resist change in course schedules because it disrupts long-established routines or preempts activities in which they are personally invested. Asking them to add an Advanced Placement math or science course, an advisory period, or an extra tutoring session to their calendar may prohibit them from using the last period of the day for an extracurricular activity, such as coaching a sports team or advising the drama program.

So, too, colleges and universities that want to establish educational field stations and build model schools for low-income students of color may face opposition as they attempt to spread an elite practice to underserved members of society. A logical extension of Bourdieu's theory is that such attempts will be challenged.

Faculty members who believe that the mission of the university is basic, not "applied," research, or who do not believe that universities should be directly involved in K–12 education, or who question the commitment of funds to university-school partnerships, especially in light of diminished support for public education, may offer resistance. Political opposition must be absorbed in order to successfully execute a significant modification in traditional practice, such as establishing an educational field station. If faculty members can, in fact, unite the technical, cultural, and political dimensions of organizational change within an educational field station, then their actions will assist universities in fulfilling the promise of public higher education to serve as an engine for socioeconomic advancement and as a catalyst for equality of educational opportunities for all, and they will assist underrepresented minority students in walking in the front door of their colleges and universities.

NOTES

1. The passage of Proposition 209 amended the California Constitution to include a new section [Section 31 of Article I (a)], quoted above.

2. California Basic Educational Data System (CBEDS) data for 2006–2007 show that the enrollment of Hispanics in eleventh grade was 42.3 percent and African American enrollment was 85 percent; statewide continuation school enrollment for the same period was 55 percent Hispanic and 11 percent African American.

Appendix 1

Theoretical Orientation

As Chapter 1 explains, the theory orienting our work proposes that culture, structure, and agency are mutually constitutive properties of social life. In this appendix, we provide a more detailed discussion of our perspective, comparing and contrasting it with other approaches commonly used in analyses of social inequality in general, and educational inequity in particular. We begin with an overview of some of the major theories regarding the causes of and constraints on human action, noting the merits and limitations of these perspectives, before turning to an in-depth look at a range of explanations for the long history of unequal education in the United States. In discussing the strengths and weaknesses of both theoretical work and empirical research on educational inequality, we pay special attention to the extent to which existing studies address the interactive role of culture, structure, and agency in shaping educational opportunities and outcomes. We conclude that to understand not only what causes inequities but also what overcomes them requires recognizing that the reciprocal relations between social structure and social action are shaped by cultural processes, which include the taken-for-granted beliefs, values, and understandings we all use to make sense of ourselves and the world around us.

STRUCTURE, CULTURE, AND AGENCY AS MUTUALLY CONSTITUTIVE COMPONENTS OF SOCIAL SYSTEMS

The relation between the ability to choose a course of action freely and constraints on action by forces outside an individual's control has been a topic of intense debate for centuries. If the competing positions were displayed as a continuum, the "free will" position—the idea that people have the capacity to make choices among alternatives unencumbered by external constraints—would anchor one end of the continuum. At the other end of the continuum would be determinism—the idea that people's actions are determined completely by constraints of one kind or another. These include the biological constraints of gender or race, the physical constraint of imprisonment or banishment, the psychological or emotional constraints imposed by belief in an omnipotent religious deity, and the constraints associated with social-historical forces of a political ideology such as communism or capitalism.

Biological formulations concerning the causes of human behavior provide especially striking examples of determinism. Stephen Gould (1991) thoughtfully traces the long history of faulty ways in which "scientists" have made causal attributions to body shape, head size, and cranial capacity as determinants of criminal behavior and of differences in intelligence across class, gender, and ethnic groups. More recently, presumed biological, that is *racial,* differences between blacks and whites have been said to determine differences in intelligence (Jensen 1969; Herrnstein and Murray 1994; Rushton 1995). These accounts, which often give a polite nod to "environmental factors," are reductionist. They acknowledge neither the fundamentally racist character of US society (Ladson-Billings and Tate 1995) nor the dynamic interaction among social structure, culture, and biology, especially the manner in which social life can cause changes in biological makeup. Indeed, the social and the biological are in a feedback loop, as recent epigenetic studies of evolutionary developmental biology show (Jablonka and Lamb 2005).

In the sociological domain, the debate over free will and constraint is most often phrased in terms of structure and agency. Those theorists who hold that people have the will to act freely emphasize people's agency, while those theorists who assert that people's actions are determined by social forces emphasize the constraining forces of social structures. For the most part, the structural or structuralist position has dominated sociological theorizing. Here, we discuss the structure-agency conundrum in the context of the social science literature on education, with a special emphasis on studies that have attempted to explain the pervasive social fact of educational inequality.

The Reproduction of Inequality by Economic Means

A powerful version of structuralist theorizing appears in economically oriented accounts of educational inequality. Martin Carnoy (1974), Samuel Bowles and Herbert Gintis (1976), and Katherine Wilcox (1982), among others, interpret the social facts of unequal educational opportunities in terms of orthodox Marxism, laced with ideas from structural-functionalism. For these authors, the core of the matter is that, as Marx explained, "the capitalist process of production" does more than create surplus value. It "also produces and reproduces the capitalist relation itself; on the one hand, the capitalist, on the other hand, the wage laborer" (Marx 1867: 724).

This "capitalist relation" is established, Bowles and Gintis (1976) claim, by the correspondence established between the organization of work and the organization of schooling. Schools deliberately offer students a differentiated curriculum in order to achieve the twin goals of preparing the sons and daughters of the elites to ascend to their place at the top of the economic hierarchy and training the sons and daughters of the lower classes to accept their lowly places in that same hierarchy. Students' exposure to this differentiated curriculum is facilitated by neighborhood segregation and by tracking within schools. In most cases, attending schools located in their own neighborhoods automatically separates children of workers' families from those of elite families. And in schools that integrate students from different ethnic or social class backgrounds, students from low-income or ethnic minority backgrounds are more likely to be assigned to low-ability groups within classrooms, vocational tracks, or special-education programs, whereas students from more well-to-do backgrounds or white (and, increasingly, Asian) students are more likely to be placed in high-ability groups, college-prep classes, or gifted-and-talented programs (Cicourel and Mehan 1985; Lucas 1999; Oakes 2005).

Invidiously inherent in the differential exposure to material resources afforded by tracking systems is the recapitulation of the relations of authority that exist between manager and worker in the relations of authority between teacher and students (Wilcox 1982). Students in schools in working-class neighborhoods, low-ability groups, or vocational tracks are taught to be docile, to follow rules unquestioningly, and to obey external authority. Allotted fewer educational materials and taught by poorly prepared teachers, these students receive shallow and superficial instruction. Individuality and creativity are suppressed in favor of conformance to drill-and-practice rhythms and routines. The latter provide the limited skills needed in the majority of occupations in American society that require a passive and compliant labor force to perform jobs that lack autonomy and require little individual responsibility. By contrast, students in schools in well-to-do neighborhoods or college-prep tracks are taught to work at their own pace, to make intelligent choices among alternatives, and to internalize and even generate norms rather than follow externally constraining ones. With high-quality educational materials and better-prepared teachers, these students receive challenging and rigorous instruction. The problem-solving and higher-order thinking skills they develop prepare them for jobs as professionals or for positions at or near the top of businesses.

This line of research diminishes the role of the students', parents', and teachers' agency. It dismisses the potentially transformative influence of schooling (Chapter 5) in favor of the argument that schools mystify people by convincing them that their success—or their failure—is a matter of their own doing. The legitimatization of the capitalist order requires that the population be convinced that the people in power deserve the positions they hold; likewise, people in less exalted positions have reason to accept their fate. To make sense of students or schools labeled as "failing," we need "successful" students and schools to serve as a point of contrast. Or, as Harve Varenne and Raymond McDermott (1998: 109) put it, "Legitimately identified success is made on the ground against which failure stands out as 'the problem'" (see also Fine 1991). To legitimate a meritocracy, students are taught that people achieve success and earn rewards by trying hard and expending effort; so, too, they are taught that people bring on failure by not trying hard and expending effort.

The "economic reproduction" account of educational inequality does have some merit. It is helpful to the extent that it calls our attention to the powerful influence of capitalist formations on constructions of inequality. Furthermore, it has led to a persuasive literature on the importance of social class as a determinant of social mobility—or the lack of it (Lareau and Conley 2008; Weis 2008). A problem with structural or structuralist arguments such as these, however, is that they tend to assume a far too rigid causal determinism in social life. In a classic formulation, developed extensively by Emile Durkheim (1982) and carried forward into much of contemporary social theory, social structures are conceived to be independent of social action and impervious to its effects. This conception reifies structures and treats them as primary, immutable, and constraining on social action. Social processes tend to be seen as secondary and superficial. Human actions cannot modify structures. Perhaps to hasten sociology's acceptance as a science, Durkheim (1982) implored sociologists to treat social facts (such as suicide rates) as if they were things—that is, as impervious to human actions—and to tabulate aggregate configurations of these facts.

Determinism is not limited to the sociological classics. It appears in influential contemporary theory as well, notably Michel Foucault's (1977, 1980) theory of discourse. He claims that language has power. Few students of discourse today would disagree that the way in which we use language shapes our thoughts and guides our actions. This is especially the case when agents of the state control the apparatus for disseminating information. But Foucault pushes this formulation to the extreme, asserting that any and all language use is power laden. Even declarations that language is not infused with power are, themselves, statements inflected with power.

This totalizing conception of discourse not only minimizes the possibility of variation in point of view within public political discourse; it also can lead to nihilism, because it leaves little or no room for the possibility of political action that challenges, disrupts, or resists those currently in positions of power. In short, structuralist accounts minimize the efficacy of human action. William Sewell (1992: 2) sums up the problem this way: "Structures tend to appear in social scientific discourse as impervious to human agency, to exist apart from, but nevertheless to determine the shape of, the strivings and motivated transactions that constitute the experienced surface of social life."

Structuring Social Structure

Social scientists have offered a corrective to this rigid causal determinism in social life by asking the constitutive question, If social structures are external to human action, yet constraining on them, how are these social structures assembled? How do they come about as external and constraining? (Pollner 1987). Studies of the "social construction of social facts" such as gender, mental illness, deviance, ethnicity, race, and social inequality have led to a more nuanced conception of the relation between agency and structure. In these more subtle accounts, structure, as a stable entity, always implies "structuring"—an embodied practice that produces a mutually constitutive process. "Whatever aspect of social life we designate as structure is posited as 'structuring' some other aspect of social existence—whether it is class that structures politics, gender that structures employment opportunities, rhetorical conventions that structure texts or utterances, or modes of production that structure social formation" (Sewell 1992: 2). This conception recognizes that agents are empowered to act with and against structures. With knowledge of the processes that inform social life and with some access to material and symbolic resources, social actors have the ability to apply this knowledge and assorted resources to specific contexts and thereby modify them (Sewell 1992).

The mutually constitutive position on the relation between structure and agency also helps social scientists avoid what is known as "radical subjectivism" or the "constitutive fallacy" (Mehan and Wood 1975: 199–207). That idea, unfortunately associated with conversation analysis and certain interpretations of ethnomethodology, claims social life is constructed anew on each and every occasion of social interaction. Social actors cannot make up meanings in any old way, however: "Men make their own history, but they do not make it as they please; they do not make it under self-selected circumstances, but under circumstances already given, given and transmitted from the past" (Marx 1852: 1). The construction of meanings is constrained by the structure of language, historical precedents, social conventions, and institutional histories. The mutually constitutive position we employ facilitates studies of the situated artful practices of social actors and the ways in which these are employed to create an objectified everyday world within the institutionalized, cultural, and historical dimensions of social context.

Social structure shapes social action that in turn is shaped by social structure—a process that is often simultaneous as well as reciprocal. Pierre Bourdieu calls this modification of a strict structuralist position either "ethnomethodological constructivism" (Bourdieu and Passeron 1990: viii) or "constructivist structuralism" (Bourdieu and Waquant 1992). Anthony Giddens's (1979: 5) expression, "structuration," captures this position more elegantly: "Structure is both medium and outcome of the reproduction of practices and 'exists' in the generating moments of this constitution." Structures shape people's practices, but it is also people's practices that constitute (and reproduce) structures (Sewell 1992: 4). Human agency and structure presuppose each other; that is, they mutually constitute each other.

This formulation opens up the possibility of social change. Social actors are capable of putting their knowledge into action in creative and innovative ways. This means their actions may have the consequence of transforming the very structures that gave them the capacity to act in the first place (Sewell 1992: 4).

CULTURE, STRUCTURE, AND AGENCY
IN EDUCATIONAL STUDIES

The idea of "the structuring of social structures" (Mehan 1978) or "structuration" (Giddens 1979) provides a perspective on social relations that is an improvement over formulations that bifurcate social structures and social actions. In the recursive formulation we have adopted, social structures and social actions are reflexively related. In other words, while social structure shapes social action by structuring the conditions in which people live and work, it is through situated processes of social action that social structures come into being and people make sense of them.

Race is a central structure in US society, but it is often overlooked by educators—and researchers—in the United States (Pollock 2005). Some recent research highlights those aspects of society, schools, and classrooms that concentrate on the meanings, causes, and consequences of educational inequality based on race. This work avoids treating race as either an ideological construct or as an objective condition. Treated as an ideological construct, race implies a constellation of beliefs and values that people hold about racial groups, such as the deficit belief that African American parents do not care about the education of their children, or that Latinos do not subscribe to the American work ethic. Treated as an objective condition, race devolves into false generalizations and stereotypes based on skin color, such as that black men are hypersexual or that Asian men are slender and effeminate. To counter these kinds of misconceptions, researchers confront the stratifying practices that construct the racialized nature of US society, in which race (and gender) are used to discriminate and stratify, thus contributing significantly to educational inequality (Omi and Winant 1994; Solórzano 1998; Yoso 2006; Ladson-Billings and Tate 1995).

A lingering problem in sociology is that culture tends to be subsumed or minimized in the structure-agency dynamic. The economic reproduction account of social inequality outlined above, for example, exaggerates the degree of integration between the demands of capitalist elites and the organization of schooling (Apple 1982; Giroux 1988; MacLeod 1995; McLaren 1997). It reduces to the same kind of functionalist argument it presumably replaced (Karabel and Halsey 1977: 40n). It does not examine the processes and practices of schooling and other cultural arrangements that reproduce inequalities (Mehan 1992). It reduces human actors—students, teachers, parents, workers, and employers—to passive role-players shaped exclusively by the demands of capital (MacLeod 1995; Mehan 2009).

We argue that the cultural sphere is critically important and should be treated as an object of critical inquiry in its own right. As the site of social differences and power struggles, culture profoundly impacts both structure and agency. The reflexive analytic approach we adopt recognizes that relations between social structure and social practices or actions are shaped by cultural processes, including taken-for-granted beliefs, values, and understandings. Our perspective draws on the work of Bourdieu (1977, 1985) and colleagues (Bourdieu and Passeron 1990; Bourdieu and Waquant 1992), who have provided a more subtle account of inequality by proposing that cultural elements are reflexively related to economic structures, schooling, and educational outcomes.

As we explained in Chapter 1, Bourdieu argues that families of each social class develop distinctive cultural knowledge ("cultural capital"). Children of the elite classes inherit substantially different cultural knowledge, skills, manners, norms, dress, style of interaction, and linguistic facility than do the sons and daughters of families in the lower classes. These family-shaped characteristics form an individual's *habitus,* a system of lasting transposable dispositions that guides individuals' actions in social space (Bourdieu 1977). Students from elite classes, by virtue of a certain linguistic and cultural competence acquired through family socialization, are provided the means of appropriating success in school. Children who read "good books," visit museums, attend symphonies, and go to the theater acquire an ease and familiarity with the dominant culture that the educational system implicitly requires of its students in order for them to be academically successful. Knowledge of and familiarity with dominant uses of language, types of writing, and cultural and literary allusion transmitted through the family are required to gain and maintain access to and mastery of the curriculum.

Furthermore, the sons and daughters of the elite benefit from their families' connections to important and productive social relationships, or what Bourdieu (1985) calls "social capital" (see also Bourdieu and Passeron 1990). Social capital is understood by analogy to economic capital. In the same way that money can be exchanged for valued goods and services, a social relationship can be converted into valued outcomes, such as getting into college or acquiring employment. Participation in highly valued cultural activities also connects elite parents and their sons and daughters with each other, which, in turn, strengthens their ties to privileged social networks. Thus, social capital, like economic capital, can produce profits or benefits in the social world, can be converted into other forms of capital, can accumulate, and can reproduce itself in identical or in expanded form (Bourdieu 1985).

In order for students to progress through the educational system and exercise control over their lives and their futures, they need to gain access to networks that are rich in social capital. Such networks are characterized by the presence of institutionally well-placed adults who can, either directly or indirectly, provide youths with institutional resources and opportunities. These "institutional agents" (Stanton-Salazar 2000; Stanton-Salazar, Vásquez, and Mehan 2000) can be located in or between formal bureaucratic organizations (e.g., schools, government agencies, federally sponsored programs, colleges and universities, churches), but they also appear in voluntary civic and political associations and in small-scale, neighborhood institutions. Due to their privileged positions in social networks, institutional agents have the power to give or withhold knowledge about resources and opportunities under the control of their own institution or under the control of neighboring institutions (Stanton-Salazar, Vásquez, and Mehan 2000). Thus, the power of institutional agents is derived from their ability to situate youth within resource-rich social networks by actively manipulating the social and institutional forces that determine who shall "make it" and who shall not.

The lack of success members of the working class typically experience in the occupational structure occurs because they lack material and economic resources, certainly. But they also do not have the appropriate cultural capital and social connections to climb the occupational ladder. Without these types of capital, students are limited in their chances to learn from educational material and interact profitably with teachers. This in turn limits their opportunities in the world of work. From the point of view of the student, then, gaining access to educational opportunities and expanded life choices entails having the right kind of cultural capital and being able to gain access to resource-rich social networks.

In sum, Bourdieu claims that schools contribute to the reproduction of inequality by rewarding the cultural capital of the elite classes and systematically devaluing that of the lower classes. Cultural processes, including schooling, mediate social structure and human agency. These processes are not always overt. They often work behind the backs and against the will of stakeholders in the school system (e.g., teachers, students, their parents) to "ensure the transmission of cultural capital across generations and to stamp pre-existing differences in inherited cultural capital with a meritocratic seal of academic consecration by virtue of the special symbolic potency of the credential" (Bourdieu and Passeron 1990: ix–x).

This more nuanced view overcomes the economic determinism in Bowles and Gintis's (1976) position. Still, problems remain. Bourdieu has been criticized for minimizing the possibility of movement between social classes (Mehan 1992; Sewell 1992) and for minimizing the possibility of alterations or modifications of an individual's habitus (Horvat and Davis 2010). People's dispositions, aspirations, and expectations are theorized as firmly established by the early socialization experienced in family life. Bourdieu also does not show us in concrete social situations how the school devalues the cultural capital of the lower classes and valorizes the cultural capital of the upper classes. Furthermore, he treats students as passive bearers of cultural capital provided by their parents and teachers. Fortunately, recent ethnographic work—some specifically influenced by Bourdieu's theoretical orientation—and other work not directly influenced by it—gives us insight into how cultural capital works in specific contexts to provide opportunities to learn for some classes of students but not others.

Students' Contributions to Unequal Educational Possibilities

A series of articulate ethnographies has begun to establish a balance between structural determinants, cultural processes, and social agency in explaining educational inequality. While acknowledging that structural constraints inhibit students' opportunities to excel, these studies examine students' own contributions to their difficulties as well as the cultural institutions that constitute structure and agency. Work by Paul Willis (1977), Linda Valli (1986), Jay Macleod (1995), Michael Apple and Lois Weis (1983), Lois Weis (2008), and Douglas Foley (2010) focuses on the experiences of working-class youth in Britain and the United States who developed deep insights into the economic condition of their social class under capitalism. Valli (1986) describes how gender expectations shape high school girls' decisions to select courses of study that prepare them for low-paying clerical jobs rather than more professional careers. Willis (1977) describes the "ear'oles," a group of working class youth who adhered to the achievement ideology, studied hard, and conformed to the rules and regulations of the school and the "lads" who rejected achievement ideology, subverted teacher and administrator authority, and disrupted classes. MacLeod (1995) describes a group of white working class youth, "the Hallway Hangers," who, like the lads, reject schooling as a means of social mobility, and the "Brothers," a group of black working-class youth who accept schooling as a way out of the ghetto.

John Ogbu (1974, 1987, 2003) studied "involuntary immigrants" (African American, Latino, and Native American students) who equate the achievement ideology with "acting white." Eschewing identification with the conformity associated with doing well academically, the students Ogbu focuses on disengage from the rhythms and rituals of schooling, oppose school rules, reject respect for external rewards and orderly work habits, and disdain the subordination associated with the achievement ideology. Tragically, their resistance contributes to their low status, first in the academic and later in the economic realm.

Although thoughtful critics have cautioned against homogenizing the experiences of working-class and underrepresented minority youth (Carter 2006a, 2006b; Horvat and O'Conner 2006; Foster 2008), the agency attributed to struggling students in these ethnographic accounts certainly distinguishes them from the abstract theorizing and determinism of both Bowles and Gintis (1976) and Bourdieu and Passeron (1990). Unlike the students in Bowles and Gintis's rendition, who passively internalize mainstream values of individual achievement, and the students in Bourdieu's original theory, who simply carry cultural capital on their backs or in their heads, the working-class and students of color in the ethnographies cited above make real choices in their everyday lives. At first glance, the working-class students' rebellious behavior and their low academic achievement and high dropout rate seem to stem from lack of self-discipline, or from dullness, laziness, or an inability to envision their own success in the future. In reality, the causes of their behavior are quite different. The students' unwillingness to participate comes from their assessment of the costs and benefits of playing the game. It is not that schooling does not propel students up the ladder of success; it is that their own chances for achieving this upward mobility are too slim to warrant the attempt. Given this logic, the oppositional behavior of Macleod's Hallway Hangers, Foley's *vatos*, and Willis's lads is a form of resistance to an institution that cannot deliver on its promise of equal educational opportunity for all students.

Incorporating Cultural Processes in a Theory of Educational Inequality

Adding the notion of "students' resistance" to the lexicon employed to understand educational inequality, then, reveals the contributions social actors make to their own plight. This line of research shows us, as Ogbu (1974, 2003) phrases it, how victims contribute to their own victimization. A second step in building a comprehensive sociological theory that explains educational inequality involves incorporating the cultural processes that reflexively relate structural constraints and social agency. The actions of peer groups, parents, and students' perceptions are three such influential cultural processes.

Dorothy Holland and Margaret Eisenhart (1990) found that actions within the college peer group activated a crucial cultural process in the construction of the traditional female identity that suppresses the academic identity offered by college.

Talented women at two universities scaled back their aspirations for business and professional careers even though throughout their lives they had expressed high aspirations. The intervening cultural mechanism of the college peer group (which, at the sites under investigation, embraced a cultural meaning system arranged around romantic love), enticed academically oriented women and reinforced the orientation of those who saw college only in instrumental terms—as a way to get a job or a husband.

Holland and Eisenhart found that the culture of romance promotes options with sad consequences. College-going women who utilize sexual attractiveness to escape dreary lives and/or to avoid bumping up against the glass ceiling do not acquire the credentials that college has to offer. They end up untrained for any good job and thus are assured of economic dependence on men. Ironically, then, women's immersion in romance embeds them more deeply in the culture of male domination and female submission and in doubled work: waged and unwaged (Holland and Eisenhart, 1990: 50; see also Valli 1986).

MacLeod (1995) asserts that peer-group affiliation coupled with parents' actions shaped the differential responses the Brothers and the Hallway Hangers made to similar socioeconomic circumstances. The Brothers thought that the civil rights movement had curbed racial inequality and improved educational opportunity. Based on those perceptions, they conformed to school norms and pursued the achievement ideology. Family life also mediated. The parents of the Brothers wanted their children to have professional careers. Toward that goal, they exercised control over their sons, setting a relatively early curfew and expecting them to perform to a certain level at school; violations of academic expectations were punished by restrictions, and the punishments were enforced. Members of the Brothers' peer group reinforced the home-based rules and expectations. The parents of the Hallway Hangers did not take steps like these. They gave their sons free rein and did not monitor schoolwork. Peer-group members reinforced parents' actions by not discouraging one another's resistance.

Annette Lareau (1989, 2003) and colleagues (Lareau and Horvat 1999) have compared parent-school relations in working-class neighborhoods with those in upper middle-class neighborhoods. This work provides us with a detailed understanding of the way parents shape students' academic careers and their opportunities to learn while in school. Lareau and other researchers (especially Delgado-Gaitan 1990; Fine 1991, 1993; Reese et al. 1995; Valdez 1996; Valenzuela 1999; Epstein 2001; Cooper 2011) find that teachers in most schools value and encourage parent involvement, seeing it as a reflection of the concerns parents have for their children. But not all parents are able to respond fully or consistently to school expectations for parent involvement. The quantity and quality of parental involvement is linked to the social and cultural resources, including disposable time and income, available to parents in different social class positions. Working-class parents struggle to put food on the table, arrange for housing, and negotiate often unsafe neighborhoods. These very basic concerns necessarily take precedence over responding to teachers' requests to volunteer in the classroom, attend back-to-school nights, or participate in school governance. Middle-income parents, with their occupational skills, social status, and near-autonomous control over their use of time, have the resources to manage child care, transportation, and work schedules. Thus, they are able to meet with teachers, monitor homework, hire tutors if their children are struggling academically, and participate in school-sanctioned activities.

Accompanying this access to resources is a different cultural logic of raising children (Lareau 2003). Middle-income parents enroll their children in a wide array of out-of-school activities that are organized and controlled by parents and other adults. Activities such as ballet, soccer, music lessons, and gymnastics dominate the lives of middle-class children—and their parents. By ensuring that their children take part in these and other cultural experiences, middle-class parents exert a concerted effort in cultivating their children's development. Working-class and poor parents, by contrast, do not consider the concerted development of their children to be an essential part of good parenting. They see child development as the unfolding of a natural process.

The enactment of these cultural logics entails different consequences. Although both working-class and middle-class parents want their children to succeed in school and in life, their different social class locations lead them to deploy different strategies to achieve those goals. The strategies working-class parents deploy—trusting teachers to educate their children, setting clear boundaries between adults and children, allowing children to control their own leisure activities—does not enhance their children's opportunities for learning how to engage institutional agents (e.g., teachers, health care professionals, government officials) with confidence. The strategies deployed by middle-income parents—concerted cultivation of their children and assorted opportunities for participating in culturally valued activities—do enhance their children's exposure to adults, such as teachers, in important social institutions, such as schools. And even though middle-income parents seem stressed by their often-frantic devotion to their children's extracurricular activities (Lareau 2003), it must be acknowledged that these children develop a sense of confidence, ease, and familiarity with the dominant culture's norms, manners, and ways of speaking. These are precisely the skills that Bourdieu says promote students' social and cultural capital and, in turn, enhance their opportunities to learn and advance through the educational and economic systems.

The careful ethnographies discussed above draw our attention toward everyday life and away from abstract theorizing. In doing so, they forcefully inform us that externally constraining forces, such as those dominating the theories of Bowles and Gintis and Bourdieu and Passeron, when taken alone do not account adequately for the actions of people. Culturally grounded resources help people interpret patriarchal and socioeconomic constraints. Furthermore, comparisons of people's actions in different cultural formations demonstrate quite clearly that individuals and groups respond to structures of domination in diverse and sometimes unpredictable ways.

As insightful as these studies are about the contribution of culture to educational inequality, it is ironic that they do not actually observe face-to-face interaction inside schools. Fortunately, another set of studies, discussed below, has opened the black box of schooling to expose some of the stratifying practices that shape the educational possibilities of students.

Stratifying Practices Shape Educational Possibilities

Most Americans, including educators, hold strong beliefs about meritocracy, hard work, and family background as determinants of academic success. These culturally grounded values and beliefs inform school sorting practices such as ability grouping and tracking, which in turn enable or constrain students' opportunity to gain access to educational resources such as college-prep classes (Oakes, Gamoran, and Page 1992; Mehan et al. 1996; Gamoran et al. 1995; Lucas 1999; Oakes 2005).

Historically, educators in the United States have responded to differences among individuals and groups by separating students and exposing them to different curricula. Since the 1920s, most high schools have offered a "tracked" curriculum—sequences of academic classes that range from slow-paced remedial courses to rigorous academic ones. Today, tracking starts as early as elementary school, where students who are perceived to have similar skills are placed in small groups, often called "ability groups," for the purposes of instruction. Students who have less measured ability are placed in low-ability groups. Students with greater amounts of measured ability are placed in high-ability groups. The curriculum in low-ability groups is reduced in scope, content, and pace, relative to what is offered in high-ability groups. Often an informal arrangement in elementary school, tracking becomes institutionalized in middle schools and high schools. Students who have been assigned to the college-prep track receive a distinct curriculum and are separated from students who have been assigned to the vocational track.

Tracking was justified at the height of industrialization because it supported an emerging belief in the United States and Great Britain that a crucial function of schools was to prepare students for jobs (Cubberley 1916). Industrial leaders who adopted a factory model of production divided labor into jobs and occupations that required different kinds of skills. As a result, workers who had different kinds of knowledge were needed to fill those different kinds of jobs. The school was to serve as a rational sorting device as well as a provider of training, matching students' talents to the demands of the workplace (Turner 1960). Thus, rigorous academic classes could prepare students heading for jobs that required high-level thinking and decisionmaking skills, whereas vocational programs could prepare students for less-skilled jobs or for technical training after high school.

Tracking students to prepare them for different work lives was viewed as both functional and democratic. Tracking was functional because it matched students to the appropriate slots in the workforce, thereby providing the nation with the range of workers it needed. Tracking was democratic because schools presumably sorted students based on their talent, effort, and hard work, thereby providing students with the education that best met their abilities (Davis and Moore 1945; Parsons 1959; Turner 1960).

Critiques of Stratifying Practices

Research and public commentary have shown that the practice of tracking in schools does not fulfill either of its promised benefits. It neither provides students with equal educational opportunities nor serves the needs of employers for a well-educated albeit compliant workforce. Students from low-income and ethnic or linguistic minority backgrounds are disproportionately represented in low-track classes, and they seldom move up to high-track ones. Students placed in low-track classes seldom receive the educational resources equivalent to those made available to students placed in high-track classes. Students in low-track classes often suffer the stigmatizing consequences of negative labeling. And, they are not prepared well for the workplace. Based on a meta-analysis of three hundred tracking studies, John Hattie (2009) finds the practice has minimal effects for students at all levels of schooling and produces negative effects on equity. "No one profits," Hattie (2009: 90) concludes, "because tracking limits students' scholarly opportunities, achievements, and life chances."

Accounts of the *differential distribution* of students to ability groups and tracks have been summarized comprehensively (Oakes, Gamoran, and Page 1992; Lucas 1999; Oakes 2005). The distribution of students to high-, middle-, and low-ability groups or to academic and general tracks seems to be related to ethnicity and socioeconomic status. Children from low-income or one-parent households, or from families with an unemployed worker, or from linguistic and ethnic minority groups, are more likely to be assigned to low-ability groups or tracks. Furthermore, ethnic and linguistic minority students are consistently underrepresented in programs for the "gifted and talented."

Schools serving predominantly poor and minority students offer fewer advanced and more remedial courses in academic subjects than schools serving more affluent and majority students. Even in comprehensive high schools that bring students from different backgrounds together under one roof, researchers have found a strong relationship between educational opportunity and both socioeconomic background and ethnicity. In each case, the relationship is simple and direct: the greater the percentage of minorities, the larger the low-track program; the poorer the students, the less rigorous the college-prep program. Moreover, as college aspirations increase, the college track itself is increasingly subdivided into multiple tracks—with the most advantaged students typically found in tracks consisting of Advanced Placement classes and honors sections of college preparatory classes (Oakes, Gamoran, and Page 1992; Lucas 1999; Oakes 2005).

Researchers also report *differential treatment* of students once they have been placed in different tracks (Cicourel and Mehan 1985). Within elementary school classrooms, ability groups are taught by the same teacher, but students in different groups do not receive the same type or amount of instruction. For example, low-ability groups are taught less frequently and are subjected to more control by the teacher. High-ability groups progress further in the curriculum over the course of a school year, and this advantage accumulates over time. As a result, students with a sustained membership in high-ability groups are likely to have covered considerably more material by the end of elementary school.

Differential treatment of students in different tracks continues in secondary schools: low-track classes consistently offer less exposure to academic topics, and the topics that are covered are less demanding than those covered in high-track classes, where the material typically is more complex. Lower-track students take fewer math and science courses, and the courses they take in these areas are less demanding. Higher-track students take three to five times more advanced courses in math and science than their lower-track peers (Haycock 2006) and more honors and advanced courses. Students in nonacademic tracks take more courses in the arts and vocational subjects because they have more room in their schedule for elective courses. College-bound students take significantly fewer vocational courses than non-college-bound students (Oakes, Gamoran, and Page 1992).

In addition to being subjected to differential access to curriculum and instruction, students in different tracks get different kinds of teachers. Some schools and school districts allow teachers to choose their teaching assignments based on seniority, whereas other schools and districts rotate the teaching of low- and high-ability classes among teachers. In either case, it is not uncommon for class assignments to be used as a reward for teachers judged to be more powerful or successful and as a sanction against teachers judged to be weaker or undeserving. Many teachers covet high-track classes because they find students in these classes more willing to participate in academic work and they pose fewer disciplinary problems. Whether schools assign teachers or teachers choose their assignments, students in low-income and minority neighborhoods are more likely to get less-experienced teachers than students in more affluent neighborhoods. For example, teachers of low-track classes at the secondary level in math and science are consistently less experienced, are less likely to be certified in math or science, hold fewer degrees in these subjects, have less training in the use of computers, and are less likely to think of themselves as master teachers (Haycock 2006). A vicious cycle for the low-tracked is the result. Repeated assignment to the bottom of the school's status hierarchy may demoralize teachers, reducing their competency, which in turn may mean that students who have the greatest need for the best teachers end up instead with the least-qualified teachers.

Perhaps the most severe criticism of tracking is that it takes on a caste-like character. Once students are placed into low-ability groups, they seldom are promoted to high groups. Students placed in low-ability groups in elementary school are more likely to be placed in general and vocational tracks in high school, whereas students placed in high-ability groups in elementary school are more likely to be placed in college-prep tracks in high school. Placement in vocational and nonacademic classes can trap ethnic and linguistic minority students despite their achievements in school. Tracking has distorted Horace Mann's vision for the "common school"—an institution that was intended to educate students from all sectors of society—rich and poor students, children of new immigrants, and children of established families.

Classroom Discourse Shapes Educational Possibilities

Close analysis of the social organization of classroom discourse adds yet another dimension to our understanding of how culture, structure, and agency are linked. Studies of language use in homes and schools (e.g., Mehan 1979; Philips 1982; Erickson and Mohatt 1982; Heath 1983; Cazden 1988; Tharp and Gallimore 1988; McCarty et al. 1991; Gutiérrez, Rymes, and Larson 1995; Gutiérrez,

Baquedano-López, and Tejada 1999; Lee 2001; Erickson 2004) have suggested that recitation-type school lessons may be compatible with the discourse patterns in middle- and upper-income white families but may be incompatible with the discourse patterns of certain low-income and language-minority group families. Typical public school classrooms demand individualized performance, emphasize competition among students, dispense praise and criticism in public, employ an interrogative format using "known information questions," and expect students to label objects and discuss them out of context. Whereas these discourse patterns are prevalent in the homes of middle- and upper-income families, they are not as prevalent in the homes of lower-income families. These discontinuities, in turn, may contribute to the lower achievement and higher dropout rates among certain language-minority students.

Although not cast in terms of Bourdieu's theory, these comparisons of discourse patterns and language use at home and at school show the interactional operation of certain aspects of cultural capital to produce opportunities to learn for members of some social classes and not others. Because the language use of middle-income parents matches the often implicit and tacit demands of the classroom, middle-income children are being equipped, through interactions in their own homes, with the very skills and techniques that are rewarded in the classroom. Likewise, because the language use of low-income parents does not match the discourse of the classroom, low-income children are not accumulating at home the type of cultural capital that is so highly valued in the classroom.

SUMMARY

In sum, cultural processes within peer groups and families, structural constraints, and students' decisions to act in conformity with or to resist the expectations and demands of schooling mutually constitute each other. The fact that different groups of students and their parents react differently to objectively similar socioeconomic circumstances reveals that some reproduction theories are overly deterministic and underplay the role of cultural processes. The reaction of Willis's lads, Macleod's Hallway Hangers, and the women Holland and Eisenhart found to have been seduced by the culture of romance vindicate Bourdieu's theory. Confronting a closed opportunity structure, these individuals lowered their aspirations and openly resisted the educational institution and its achievement ideology. But neither Bowles and Gintis nor Bourdieu and Passeron do as well in explaining the actions of working-class youth, or women, and new immigrants with high academic aspirations. The ear'oles (Willis 1977) and the Brothers (MacLeod 1995) experienced the same habitus and were exposed to the same hidden curriculum of the school as were the lads and the Hallway Hangers, but the ear'oles and the Brothers responded to it by eagerly adopting the achievement ideology and maintaining high aspirations for success.

The mutually constitutive conception that emerges from this work does not reduce social life either to individuals' actions or to unavoidable social forces. Instead, cultural forms and practices shed their status as passive reflections of structural forces and play active roles in human action and social structure. Our mutually constitutive conception recognizes that agents are empowered to act with and against structures. With some access to cultural resources, both material and symbolic, social actors have the ability to apply these resources in social contexts and thereby modify social structures.

Appendix 2

Contributions to a Theory of Social Policy

Appendix 1 suggests that a co-construction perspective is heuristic for the study of educational inequality. By depicting culture, structure, and agency as equal participants in a reflexive system of social action, we gain better insight into the processes that structure inequality. In this appendix, we explore the utility of the co-construction perspective for a theory of social policy. We begin by comparing the features of the technical-rational and co-construction perspectives and suggest that the latter approach provides more nuanced analyses and findings than the former models that dominated the field previously. We then discuss how the co-construction perspective informs the processes by which public policy is put into daily practice in our local San Diego context.

THE TECHNICAL-RATIONAL AND CO-CONSTRUCTION PERSPECTIVES ON PUBLIC POLICY

From the late 1960s through the early 1980s, public policy studies concentrated in large part on large-scale governmental efforts such as Lyndon Johnson's Great Society and its component programs (e.g., Project Follow Through, Headstart, special education, and bilingual education). The social policy research of the time tended to take Weberian notions of technical rationality seriously—probably too seriously. The technical-rational perspective on public policy incorporates principles from classical management theory. These principles place a premium on planning, organization, command, coordination, and control, on the presumption that "authority and responsibility should flow in a clear unbroken line from the highest executive to the lowest operative" (Smith and Keith 1971: 241).

The technical-rational approach envisions the development and enactment of policy as involving two groups: designers and implementers. Program designers (sometimes called "the design team") are situated at the top of bureaucracies. They make the plans. Implementers are positioned down the chain of command; they work at the local level of bureaucracies. These "street level bureaucrats" (Lipsky 1982) carry out the plans; that is, they complete the predetermined goals and objectives of the design team. In this grammar of implementation, the causal arrow of change travels in one direction—from active, thoughtful designers to passive, pragmatic implementers. As the authors of one of the seminal works on implementation of a government policy succinctly defined it, "Implementation is the ability to forge subsequent links in the causal chain so as to obtain the desired results" (Pressman and Wildavsky 1973: xv). If things go wrong, the people on the ground may be blamed for circumventing or openly subverting well-intended reforms by acting irrationally, protecting their own interests, or not following directions.

By contrast, the co-construction position regards policy as an ongoing process of constructing and negotiating meaning in real-life settings. In these settings, policy actions both shape and are shaped by organizational norms, routines, and standard operating procedures. Politically, policy is a mechanism for powerful actors to manage contested perceptions by focusing attention on some conditions rather than on others and by promoting a particular interpretation of those conditions. Policy is also a means for powerful actors to legitimate particular meanings by granting them the authority derived from these actors' official status. Finally, policy works to shore up institutional authority by communicating an institution's commitment to particular values and ideas (Rosen and Mehan 2003).

The co-construction perspective contributes to public policy theory by reinforcing the idea that public policy is both a process and a product of constitutive human activity (Hall and McGinty 1997; Levinson and Sutton 2001; Rosen 2001; Datnow, Hubbard, and Mehan 2002; Rosen and Mehan 2003). As a *process,* policy is a means by which statements of value and definitions of reality are constructed, asserted, validated, and negotiated. As *products,* policies are the material residues of these actions. They are cultural objects and artifacts that "embody the authority to define goals and command means" (Levinson and Sutton 2001: 5), legitimize and reinforce particular views of reality, and grant those definitions some form of "official" (i.e., institutionalized or publicly recognized) status. From this constitutive point of view, solutions to a political problem and the language used to legitimate the solutions are so intertwined that they are hard to separate.

The co-construction perspective, furthermore, depicts social action within the public policy process as dynamic. Street-level bureaucrats are not represented as either necessarily compliant or passive actors. Likewise, actors in positions of power are not necessarily seen as rationally and intentionally calculating courses of action and then directing their underlings to implement these plans. Instead, those at the top as well as those at the bottom of bureaucracies are understood to be making organizational choices in situations that involve uncertainty.

The co-construction perspective also recognizes, first, that agents at *all* levels of the system contribute to the policymaking process; and second, that that process is characterized by continuous interaction among social actors within and between levels of organizational systems. Therefore, proponents of the co-construction approach focus on social life as it is generated in face-to-face interactions among real people who are confronting real problems, in concrete social settings. In educational encounters, social actors may respond to policy directives in a variety of ways—initiating alternatives, advancing or sustaining directives, resisting or actively subverting them. Most important, the agency of and interaction between participants in the educational policymaking process is perceived as being part of a complex dynamic, one that *shapes* and *is shaped by* the structural and cultural features of school and society.

Interactional Encounters Embedded in Nested Contexts

The interactional encounters in which policy is made unfold within various successively contextualized layers of organizations—such as the personal, interpersonal, community, and state levels of interaction. Some actions, such as the University of California Regents' decision to ban affirmative action, Congress's decision to pass No Child Left Behind, and the federal government's decision to implement Race to the Top, take place at a distance from our everyday lives and local circumstances. We have less control over actions undertaken at a distance ("distal circumstances") than we do over those that take place near at hand ("proximal circumstances"), in our local space (Latour and Woolgar 1979).

Distal and proximal circumstances are not necessarily separate and distinct, however. The distal is often embodied in the proximal, and vice versa. Put another way: face-to-face interactions contain within them vestiges of system properties. So, for example, when, as happened at Gompers, the governor comes to town to celebrate the opening of a school, we have a situation in which an actor who usually operates from afar suddenly appears in our midst. His presence influences us; and, presumably, our presence influences him. Likewise, when one of our CREATE staff members accompanies the UCSD chancellor to Sacramento and interacts with state legislators, the proximal is brought into contact with the distal.

These layered sites of interaction also can be expressed as *nested contexts*. In educational settings, a classroom often is depicted as the center, surrounded by other layers or levels of the context. Michael Cole (1999) cites Urie Bronfenbrenner's (1979) formulation of human development as a prime example of this *nested* conception of context. Bronfenbrenner conceives of social life as starting with the microsystem at the core and proceeding outward through mesosystems and exosystems to the macrosystem. In educational research, the nested sense of context appears in Michael Fullan's (1991: 49) description of the classroom, school, district, state, and nation "levels" of the implementation system; in Barbara Rogoff's (2003) and Katherine Wilcox's (1982) descriptions of classroom socialization as shaped by organizational and community constraints; and in Milbrae McLaughlin and Joan Talbert's (1993) analysis, in which the classroom is positioned in the center of school, community, higher education institutions, professional, and environmental levels of contexts.

The nested sense of context is important because it calls our attention to the fact that social life is generated in face-to-face interaction, and then acknowledges that face-to-face interaction occurs within wider dimensions of social life—the organizational, the institutional, the structural. Its value is limited, however, whenever one site, and only one site, is placed at the center, thereby pushing other sites to the periphery. The nested sense of context also can leave the (incorrect) impression that social life is unidirectional; forces emanating from higher levels of context appear to cause or determine action at lower levels. Although actions initiated at some distance away from local events may indeed constrain or shape actions, they do not totally determine them. Similarly, actions initiated in local situations can generate or construct conditions or structures that affect events in settings far removed.

For example, constraints originating at a distance from the classroom influence teacher-student interaction. Instruction generally takes place in confined physical spaces and circumscribed time segments. Teachers typically organize instruction and call upon students to demonstrate their knowledge. Classroom interaction varies, but usually only within these narrow parameters; it is not easy to escape the constraints imposed upon the teaching-learning setting. Schools are a part of formal education in industrialized societies. This means teachers develop their particular recipes for teaching within limits that are beyond their control. The state establishes standards for the length of the school day and school year, and the number of students per class; imposes an age-graded system; and requires the availability of certain teaching materials. Public expectations (e.g., that students can read by the end of first grade, meet college entrance requirements by the end of high school, etc.) reinforce these state-organized constraints.

High school teachers in France, Japan, Germany, South Korea, and many other countries operate within a highly competitive system that uses a high-stakes exam as a gatekeeping encounter. This arrangement, in turn, exerts pressure on teachers at the elementary level to make judgments about passing or retaining individual students at the end of each academic year. Likewise, US high school teachers instruct students with the knowledge that the provisions of federal policy (such as No Child Left Behind) and the requirements of colleges and universities (to say nothing of well-to-do parents) demand coverage of a certain amount of literature, mathematics, and science. These requirements and expectations discourage innovation, including the use of instructional systems that are built on cooperative learning, project-based learning, and portfolio assessment. Instead of encouraging creativity, constraints created in situations far from the immediate teaching environment prompt the repeated appearance of similar features in the formal teaching-learning situations we call classrooms.

Of course, it is important to recognize that although actions emanating at a distance may constrain local actions, influence is multidirectional: local actions can change and shape structural features of the system. For example, teachers often vary considerably in how they interpret the conventions of the school and the dictates of the state. Differences in the organization of classroom interaction have been found in some cultures (Erickson and Mohatt 1982; Au 1980; Au and Jordan 1981; Tharp and Gallimore 1988; McCarty 1991), once again reminding us of the reality of cross-cultural variation in the face of social, political, and economic constraints. More fundamentally, we must remember that in order for an event we call the lesson to occur, the teacher and students must engage in "lesson making" (Mehan 1979; Cazden 1986; Varenne and McDermott 1998): "Without forgetting for a moment that the power relations among participants are often unequal, it is no less important when using the nested-contexts approach to take into account the fact that context creation is an actively achieved, two sided process" (Cole 1999: 134).

Conditional Processes in Policy Formation

Peter Hall's concept of the "conditional matrix" (or "conditional process") helps us avoid the traps of structural determinism and unidirectionality that potentially plague the nested sense of context in policy studies.[1] Hall depicts social policy as a web of interrelated conditions and consequences, where the consequences of actions in one context may become the conditions for the next (Hall 1995; Hall and McGinty 1997). That is, interactions in one policy context generate "outcomes," which often take the form of written documents such as policy statements and new or revised rules or procedures; these outcomes in turn potentially condition the interactions of other actors in other contexts in the policy chain.

Whereas the embedded sense of context can be interpreted to mean that events at higher levels of the context occur first and are more important analytically, the conditional process does not automatically assign an a priori importance to any one context. Events certainly occur in the chronological past, present, or future, and near to or far away from us. And we can use these temporal divisions to clarify our statements about events. But we must also recognize the mutual influence of one context upon the other when accounting for social policy in general, and the implementation of educational reforms in particular.

Take, for example, the classic sociological topic of occupational advancement. A person may, at age twenty-one, make $18,000 a year in a computer-programming job. She may at age thirty-five make $300,000 as president of a computer company. If she anticipates at twenty-one that in the future she will gain upward mobility by the time she is thirty-five, then the $18,000 a year salary will hold a different meaning for her than if she expects to remain in the same job forever. As Alfred Schutz (1962) noted, very few future events involving human actors turn out exactly as expected because at the very least, the person has grown older, a state that cannot be experienced ahead of time. Similarly, after our hypothetical programmer becomes company president, her former position takes on a different meaning for her (it was "preparation," "learning the work ethic," "hard knocks") than it would have if she had not become president. In the latter case, the computer-programming job might be seen as a "treadmill," a "dead end." There are *chronological* pasts, presents, and futures in this scenario, but as George Herbert Mead (1954) and Schutz (1962) observed, their *social* influence upon one another transforms the purely physical metric into a social one as the course of events unfolds.

Emergence, Power, and Perspective in Organizational Change

What Mead (1954) called *emergence* exists because the past influences the symbolic definition of the present, the definition of the present is influenced by inferences about the future, and the events of the future will reconstruct our definition of the past. Or, as Schutz (1962), and later the ethnomethodologists (e.g., Garfinkel 1967; Cicourel 1973) phrased it, events have a retrospective and a prospective sense of occurrence. What is not actually perceived is filled in from the standpoint of the present, while unclear information is allowed to pass, with the expectation that later information will provide clarity. Applying these ideas to the policy context, Hall (1995: 408) says,

> The social organization of the policy process as a network of relations across space and time can be viewed prospectively, retrospectively and in the present. Prospectively, it is a means to produce desired behavior at a future time in distant locations. Retrospectively, it emerges out of historical pasts and embeds structural contexts. In the present it has to be constituted through collective activity that dialectically relates past and future, "structure" and intention.

Organizational change unfolds in unpredictable and nonlinear ways through the interaction of individuals in different settings under conditions of uncertainty, diversity, and instability. In our examination of school change in San Diego, we presented evidence for the emergent nonlinear, nondeterministic characteristics of the process. In addition, we attempted to increase understanding of the dynamics of change by highlighting the role of power and perspective. A person's location in social institutions and cultural arrangements can influence her interpretation of events (Thomas and Thomas 1928). Gender, ethnicity, and social class are particularly powerful realities that shape differences in meaning. These power relations are constituted on the terrain of everyday discourse in social institutions, including schools, and influence the perceptions that participants have on social events and objects, such as educational reform efforts.

All perspectives are not equal, however. W. I. Thomas and Dorothy Swain Thomas (1928) were correct when they said that people define situations as real and these definitions are real in their consequences. Because of institutional arrangements, however, some positions accrue material and symbolic resources that enable incumbents of those positions to impose meanings upon other individuals or groups. Psychiatrists, for example, have the power to hospitalize patients against their will, and even if the patients think they are healthy. Judges can confine people in prisons even if the accused think they are innocent. And educators (such as counselors and testers) have the power to alter the course of students' educational careers by assigning them to different courses of study or educational tracks (Erickson and Shultz 1982; Mehan et al. 1986; Sjöström 1997). Power is a central feature of the educational policy process, both in development and in implementation (Berliner and Biddle 1995; Hargreaves and Fullan 1998).

As a result of the institutional distribution and application of power, the meaning of a policy, a reform effort, or certain aspects of a reform effort may not necessarily be shared by all stakeholders; there can be disagreement or conflict over the meaning of actions, events, even the reform itself. If there is consensus, it is not the automatic result of a shared culture. Consensus is not given. It is achieved through negotiation, and often strife. Thus, it is fragile, subject to revision and change.

NOTE

1. We prefer the expression *conditional process* to *conditional matrix* because a *matrix* implies, to us at least, the rectangular arrangement of elements into columns and rows. Such imagery is too static, too angular; it is not in keeping with the fluidity of the rest of Hall's thinking. We feel that substituting *process* for matrix better captures the reality of the development and enactment of public policy.

References

Alim, H. Samy. 2011. "Hip-Hop and the Politics of Ill-literacy." Pp. 232–246 in Bradley A. U. Levinson and Mica Pollock (eds.), *A Companion to the Anthropology of Education*. Malden, MA: John Wulkey and Sons.

Alpert, Dede. 2006. Remarks before the San Diego Unified School District Board of Education. February 6.

Alpert, Emily. 2007. "When Charters Close, Public Schools Foot the Bill." *Voice of San Diego*. December 10. www.voiceof sandiego.org/articles.

Alvarez, Doris, and Hugh Mehan. 2006. "Whole School Detracking: A Strategy for Equity and Excellence." *Theory into Practice* 45 (1): 82–89.

American Educational Research Association. 2000. "AERA Position on High Stakes Testing." www.aera.net/about/policy/stakes.htm.

American Evaluation Association. 2002. "American Evaluation Association Position Statement on High Stakes Testing in Pre K–12 Education." www.eval.org/hst3.htm.

Amrein, A. L., and David C. Berliner. 2002. "High-Stakes Testing, Uncertainty, and Student Learning." *Education Policy Analysis Archives* 10 (18). http://epaa.asu.edu/epaa/v10n18/.

Angrist, Joshua D., Susan M. Dynarski, and Thomas J. Kane. 2010. *Who Benefits from KIPP?* Cambridge, MA: National Bureau of Economic Research.

Apple, Michael W. 1982. *Education and Power*. Boston: Routledge and Kegan Paul.

Apple, Michael W., and Lois Weis. 1983. *Ideology and Practice in Education: A Political and Conceptual Introduction*. Philadelphia: Temple University Press.

Argyris, Chris, and Donald Schön. 1978. *Organizational Learning: A Theory of Action Perspective*. Reading, MA: Addison Wesley.

Arizona House Bill 2281. www.azleg.gov/legtext/49leg/2r/bills/hb2281s.pdf.

Au, Kathryn HuPei. 1980. "Participation Structures in a Reading Lesson with Hawaiian Children." *Anthropology and Education Quarterly* 11 (2): 91–115.

Au, Kathryn HuPei, and Cathy Jordan. 1981. "Teaching Reading to Hawaiian Children: Finding a Culturally Appropriate Solution." Pp. 139–152 in Henry T. Trueba, Grace P. Guthrie, and Kathryn HuPei Au (eds.), *Culture and the Bilingual Classroom*. Rowley, MA: Newberry House.

Ayers, William, Therese Quinn, and David Stovall (eds.). 2009. *Handbook of Social Justice in Education*. New York: Routledge.

Banks, James A., and Cherry A. McGee Banks (eds.). 2002. *Handbook of Research on Multicultural Education*, 2nd ed. New York: MacMillan.

Beane, James A., and Michael Apple. 1995. *Schooling for Democracy*. New York: ASCD.

Bennett, Brian. 2008. Unpublished Remarks. Presented to California Charter Schools Association Conference. January 12.

Berliner, David. 2005. "Our Impoverished View of Educational Reform." *Teachers College Record.* www.tcrecord.org/content.asp?contentid=12106.

Berliner, David, and Bruce Biddle. 1995. *The Manufactured Crisis in Education: Myths, Fraud, and the Attack on America's Public Schools.* Reading, MA: Addison Wesley.

Betts, Julian, and Paul T. Hill. 2006. *Key Issues in Studying Charter Schools and Achievement: A Review and Suggestions for National Guidelines.* Seattle: Center for Reinventing Public Education.

Betts, Julian, Kim S. Rueben, and Anne Danenberg. 2000. *Equal Resources, Equal Outcomes? The Distribution of School Resources and Student Achievement in California.* San Francisco: Public Policy Institute of California.

Bohren, Aislinn, and Larry McClure. 2009. *The Preuss School UCSD: School Characteristics and Students' Achievement.* La Jolla: UCSD CREATE. http://create.ucsd.edu.

Bourdieu, Pierre. 1977. *Outline of a Theory of Practice.* Cambridge: Cambridge University Press.

———. 1985. "The Forms of Capital." Pp. 241–258 in J. G. Richardson (ed.), *Handbook of Theory and Research for the Sociology of Education.* New York: Greenwood.

Bourdieu, Pierre, and Jean Passeron. 1990. *Reproduction in Education, Society, and Culture,* 2nd ed. London: Sage.

Bourdieu, Pierre, and Luc Waquant. 1992. *An Invitation to a Reflexive Sociology.* Chicago: University of Chicago Press.

Bowles, Samuel, and Herbert Gintis. 1976. *Schooling in Capitalist America.* New York: Basic.

Bronfenbrenner, Urie. 1979. *The Ecology of Human Development.* Cambridge, MA: Harvard University Press.

Brown, Michael T., Mark Rashid, and David Stern. 2010. "The Effect of California Standards Tests as Alternatives to the SAT in Predicting Freshman Grades." Pp. 155–172 in Eric Grodsky and Michal Kurlaender (eds.), *Equal Opportunity in Higher Education.* Cambridge, MA: Harvard Education Press.

Bruner, Jerome. 1986. *Actual Minds, Possible Worlds.* Cambridge, MA: Harvard University Press.

Bryk, Anthony, and Barbara Schneider. 2003. *Trust in Schools: A Core Resource for Improvement.* New York: Russell Sage Foundation.

Brzezinski, Zbigniew. 2007. "Remarks before the Senate Foreign Relations Committee," February 1. Reprinted in *Harpers Magazine,* April 2007, 19–23.

Buchanan, Gregory, Christina Perkins, and Robert Mannie. 2007. *UCSD Preuss Charter School Grades Investigation.* UCSD: Audit and Management Advisory Services.

Burawoy, Michael. 2005. "For Public Sociology." *American Sociological Review* 70 (1): 4–28.

Burawoy, Michael, William Gamson, Charlotte Ryan, et al. 2004. "Public Sociologies." *Social Problems* 51 (1): 103–130.

Burris, Carol C., Ed Wiley, Kevin G. Welner, et al. 2008. "Accountability, Rigor, and Detracking: Achievement Effects of Embracing a Challenging Curriculum as a Universal Good for All Students." *Teachers College Record* 110 (3): 571–608.

Burris, Carol C., Kevin G. Welner, and Jennifer Bezoza. 2009. *Universal Access to a Quality Education: Research and Recommendations for the Elimination of Curricular Stratification.* Boulder, CO: University of Colorado Education Policy Research Unit.

California Charter Schools Association. 2011. "Operating a Charter School." Downloaded from www.calcharters.org/operating/ on January 27, 2011.

California Round Table on Educational Opportunity. 1981. "Statement of Purpose and Initial Agenda." Sacramento: California Roundtable.

Campbell, Elizabeth, and Luke Eric Lassiter. 2010. "From Collaborative Ethnography to Collaborative Pedagogy: Reflections on the Other Side of Middletown Project and Community-University Research Partnerships." *Anthropology and Education Quarterly* 41 (4): 370–385.

Carnoy, Martin. 1974. *Education as Cultural Imperialism.* New York: David McKay.

Carnoy, Martin, Rebecca Jacobsen, Lawrence Mishel, et al. 2005. *The Charter School Dust-Up: Examining the Evidence on Enrollment and Achievement.* New York: Teachers College Press Economic Policy Institute.

Carter, Prudence L. 2006a. *Keeping It Real: School Success Beyond Black and White.* New York: Oxford University Press.

———. 2006b. "Straddling Boundaries: Identity Culture and School." *Sociology of Education* 79: 304–328.

Casey, Katherine. 2006. *Literacy Coaching: The Essentials.* Portsmouth, NH: Heinemann.

Cazden, Courtney B. 1988. *Classroom Discourse.* Portsmouth, NH: Heinemann.

CER (Center for Educational Reform). 2004. "Charter School Evaluation Reported by the New York Times Fails to Meet Professional Standards." Paid advertisement. *New York Times.* August 25.

Chang, Gordon C., and Hugh Mehan. 2006. "Discourse in a Religious Mode." *Pragmatics* 16 (1): 1–23.

———. 2008. "Why We Must Attack Iraq: Bush's Reasoning Practices and Argumentation System." *Discourse and Society* 19 (4): 449–478.

Chubb, John E., and Terry M. Moe. 1990. *Politics, Markets, and America's Schools.* Washington, DC: Brookings Institute.

Cicourel, Aaron V. 1964. *Method and Measurement in Sociology.* New York: Free Press.

———. 1973. *Cognitive Sociology.* New York: MacMillan.

Cicourel, Aaron V., and Hugh Mehan. 1985. "Universal Development, Stratifying Practices, and Status Attainment." *Research in Social Stratification and Mobility* 4: 3–27.

Coburn, Cynthia. 2004. "Beyond the Decoupling: Rethinking the Relationship between the Institutional Environment and the Classroom." *Sociology of Education* 77: 211–244.

Cohn, Carl. 2006a. "The Superintendent, Peacemaker." *Voice of San Diego.* June 26. www.voiceofsandiego.org.

———. 2006b. E-mail to Cecil Steppe, Chair, GCMS Board of Directors. March 6.

———. 2007. E-mail to Marc Santos. January 10.

Cole, Michael. 1999. *Cultural Psychology: A Once and Future Discipline.* Cambridge, MA: Harvard Education Press.

Coleman, James S., Ernest Q. Campbell, Carol J. Hobson, et al. 1966. *Equality of Educational Opportunity.* Washington, DC: US Office of Education.

College Board. 2010. *Trends in Higher Education.* New York: College Entrance Examination Board.

Collins, Randall. 1979. *The Credential Society: An Historical Sociology of Education and Stratification.* New York: Academic Press.

Conchas, Gilbert Q., and Louie F. Rodriguez. 2006. *Small Schools and Urban Youth.* Los Angeles: Sage.

Cookson, Peter W. Jr., and Caroline Hodges Persell. 1985. *Preparing for Power: America's Elite Boarding Schools.* New York: Basic.

Cooper, Catherine R. 2011. *Bridging Multiple Worlds: Cultures, Identities, and Pathways to College.* New York: Oxford University Press.

CPEC. 2009. Student Data. Sacramento: California Postsecondary Education Commission.

CREDO. 2009. *Multiple Choice: Charter School Performance in 16 States*. Stanford, CA: CREDO.

Cremin, Lawrence A. 1951. *The American Common School*. New York: Teachers College Press.

Cuban, Larry. 1992. "What Happens to Reforms That Last? The Case of the Junior High School." *American Educational Research Journal* 29 (2): 227–251.

———. 1998. "How Schools Change Reforms: Redefining Reform Success and Failure." *Teachers College Record* 99 (3): 153–177.

Cubberley, Edward Patterson. 1916. *Public School Administration*. Cambridge, MA: Riverside.

Darling-Hammond, Linda. 1997. *The Right to Learn: A Blueprint for Creating Schools That Work*. San Francisco: Jossey-Bass.

———. 2010. *The Flat World and Education: How America's Commitment to Equity Will Determine Our Future*. New York: Teachers College Press.

Datnow, Amanda, Lea Hubbard, and Hugh Mehan. 2002. *Extending Educational Reform: From One School to Many*. New York: Routledge Falmer.

Datnow, Amanda, Geoffrey Borman, and Sam Stringfield. 2000. "School Reform Through a Highly Specified Curriculum: A Study of the Implementation and Effects of the Core Knowledge Sequence." *Elementary School Journal* 101 (2): 167–191.

Davis, Kingsley, and Wilbert E. Moore. 1945. "Some Principles of Stratification." *American Sociological Review* 10: 242–249.

Deal, Terrence, and Guilbert C. Hentschke. 2004. *Adventures of Charter School Creators: Leading from the Ground Up*. Lanham, MD: Scarecrow Education.

deBeck, John. 2005. Remarks before the Board of Trustees, San Diego Unified School District. March 1.

Delgado-Gaitan, Concha. 1990. *Literacy for Empowerment: Role of Parents in Their Children's Education*. London: Falmer.

Delpit, Lisa. 2006. *Other People's Children: Cultural Conflict in the Classroom*. New York: W. W. Norton.

de Velasco, Jorge Ruiz, Greg Austin, Don Dixon, et al. 2008. *Alternative Education Options: A Descriptive Study of California Continuation High Schools*. Los Angeles: West Ed.

Dewey, John. 1900. *The School and Society*. Chicago: University of Chicago Press.

———. (1916) 1997. *Democracy and Education: An Introduction to the Philosophy of Education*. New York: Free Press.

Douglass, John A. 2000. *The California Idea and American Higher Education*. Palo Alto, CA: Stanford University Press.

Duncan, Arne. 2010. Question and Answer Session with the Secretary of Education. November 19. YouTube.com/witch?v=A. December 1.

Duncan-Andrade, Jeffrey. 2009. "Youth and Social Justice in Education." Pp. 449–454 in William Ayers, Therese Quinn, and David Stovall (eds.), *Handbook of Social Justice in Education*. New York: Routledge.

Durkheim, Emile. 1982. *The Rules of Sociological Method*. New York: Free Press.

Duster, Troy, Aaron V. Cicourel, Eugene H. Cota Robles, et al. 1990. *Making the Future Different: Report of the Task Force on Black Student Eligibility*. Oakland: Office of the President of the University of California.

Dutro, Elizabeth. 2011. "Review: Waiting for Superman." Boulder, CO: NEPC. Downloaded from http://nepc.colorado.edu//thinktank/review-waiting-superman on January 26, 2011.

Education Trust. 2003a. *Latino Achievement in America*. Washington, DC: Education Trust. Downloaded from www.edtrust.org.

———. 2003b. *African American Achievement in America*. Washington, DC: Education Trust. Downloaded from www.edtrust.org.

Epstein, Joyce. 2001. *School, Family, and Community Partnerships: Preparing Educators and Improving Schools*. Boulder, CO: Westview.

Erickson, Frederick E. 1996. "On the Evolution of Qualitative Approaches to Education Research: From Adam's Task to Eve's." *Australian Educational Researcher* 23 (2): 1–5.

———. 2004. *Talk and Social Theory*. London: Polity.

Erickson, Frederick E., and Gerry Mohatt. 1982. "Participant Structures in Two Communities." Pp. 132–175 in George D. Spindler (ed.), *Doing the Ethnography of Schooling*. New York: Holt, Rinehart, and Winston.

Erickson, Frederick E., and Jeffrey Shultz. 1982. *The Counselor as Gatekeeper*. New York: Academic Press.

Evans, Michelle. 2005a. Remarks before the Board of Trustees, San Diego Unified School District. March 1.

———. 2005b. Interview with Shannon Bradley. Subsequently shown on UCSD Impact Show, "Charter Schools," on UCSD TV.

ExEd. 2011. State of California Budget Information. San Diego: Excellent Education.

Fine, Michelle. 1991. *Framing Dropouts: Notes on the Politics of an Urban Public High School*. Albany: SUNY Press.

———. 1993. "[Ap]parent Involvement: Reflections on Parents, Power, and Urban Public Schools." *Teachers College Record* 94: 682–719.

Flanagan, Kerry. 2008. *Survey of Charter Schools in San Diego*. Los Angeles: California Charter Schools Association.

Flynn, Pat. 2011. "UCSD Policy Limits Community College Students." Downloaded from www.signonsandiego.com/news/2011/mar/18/ucsds-new-transfer-standard-roils -community/ on March 21, 2011.

Foley, Douglas E. 2010. *Learning Capitalist Culture: Deep in the Heart of Tejas*, 2nd ed. Philadelphia: University of Pennsylvania Press.

Foley, Douglas, and Angela Valenzuela. 2006. "Critical Ethnography: The Politics of Collaboration." Pp. 217–234 in Norman K. Denzin and Yvonna S. Lincoln (eds.), *The Sage Handbook of Qualitative Research*, 3rd ed. Los Angeles: Sage.

Foster, Kevin. 2008. "Forward Looking Criticisms: Critiques and Enhancements for the Next Generation of the Cultural-Ecological Model." Pp. 577–592 in John U. Ogbu (ed.), *Minority Status, Oppositional Culture, and Schooling*. New York: Routledge.

Foucault, Michel. 1977. *Language, Countermemory, Practice*. Ithaca, NY: Cornell University Press.

———. 1980. *Power/Knowledge*. New York: Pantheon.

Fox, Marye Ann. 2005. Letter to the Board of Trustees, San Diego Unified School District. La Jolla: UCSD. February 17.

Fox, Marye Anne, and Paul Drake. 2007. Letter to UC San Diego Campus Community. December 12.

Frankenberg, Erica, and Genevieve Siegel-Hawley. 2009. *Equity Overlooked: Charter Schools and Civil Rights Policy*. Los Angeles: Civil Rights Project/*Proyecto Derechos Civiles* at UCLA.

Frankenberg, Erica, Genevieve Siegel-Hawley, and Jia Wang. 2010. *Choice Without Equity: Charter School Segregation and the Needs for Civil Rights Standards*. Los Angeles: Civil Rights Project/*Proyecto Derechos Civiles* at UCLA.

Freidman, Milton. 1963. *Capitalism and Freedom.* Chicago: University of Chicago Press.

Fry, Wendy. 2009. "News Report." San Diego News Network. July 1.

Fullan, Michael G. 1991. *The New Meaning of Educational Change,* 2nd ed. New York: Teachers College Press.

Gabay, Jan. 2011. Interview with Hugh Mehan. March 9.

Galligani, Dennis. 2000. Communication with Hugh Mehan at the meeting of UCOP Outreach and CREATE Staff. La Jolla: UCSD. April.

Gamoran, Adam, Martin Nystrand, Mark Berends, et al. 1995. "An Organizational Analysis of the Effects of Ability Grouping." *AERJ* 32 (4): 687–715.

Gao, Helen. 2005a. "Popular Gompers Principal Loses Post: Reassigned Leader Has Backed Charter Efforts." *San Diego Union Tribune.* February 10: A1.

———. 2005b. "Moving of Gompers Principal Protested." *San Diego Union Tribune.* February 11: B1 and B10.

———. 2005c. "Schools Await Charter Decision: San Diego Board Is Expected to Vote on Achievement Plans." *San Diego Union Tribune.* February 28: A1.

———. 2005d. "4 Schools Win Charter Status: Low Achievers Hope to Turn Things Around." *San Diego Union Tribune.* March 2: A1.

———. 2007. "17 Charter Schools Offered Space at District Campuses." http://webblog .signonsandiego.com/news/education/20070212-99999-1m14charter.html.

Garcia, Eugene E., Ricard Duran, Troy Duster, et al. 1993. *Latino Student Eligibility and Participation in the University of California.* UC Santa Cruz: Latino Eligibility Task Force.

Garfinkel, Harold. 1967. *Studies in Ethnomethodology.* Englewood Cliffs, NJ: Prentice Hall.

———. 2002. *Ethnomethodology's Program: Working Out Durkheim's Aphorism.* Lanham, MD: Rowman and Littlefield.

GCMS. 2001. Presentation before the Board of Trustees, San Diego Unified School District. March 1.

Gibson, Margaret. 1988. *Accommodation without Assimilation: Sikh Immigrants in an American High School.* New York: Cornell University Press.

Gibson, Margaret (ed.). 1991. "Ethnicity and School Performance: Complicating the Immigrant/Involuntary Minority Typology." *Anthropology and Education Quarterly* 28: 3.

Giddens, Anthony. 1979. *Central Problems in Social Theory.* Berkeley: University of California Press.

———. 1984. *The Constitution of Society.* Berkeley: University of California Press.

———. 1993. *New Rules of Sociological Method.* Cambridge, MA: Polity.

Giroux, Henry A. 1988. *Schooling and the Struggle for Public Life: Critical Pedagogy in the Modern Age.* Minneapolis: University of Minnesota Press.

Gleason, Phillip, Melissa Clark, and Emily Dwoyer. 2010. *The Evaluation of Charter School Impacts.* Princeton, NJ: Mathematica Policy Research.

Goffman, Erving. 1961. *Asylums.* Garden City, NY: Anchor.

Goldman, Shelly. 2010. Personal communication. November 20.

Gonzáles, Jose. 2005. Letter to Vincent Riveroll, Director GCMS. SDUSD: Office of the General Counsel. October 7.

González, Norma. 2004. "Disciplining the Discipline: Anthropology and the Pursuit of Quality Education." *Educational Researcher* 33 (5): 17–25.

González, Norma, Luis C. Moll, and Cathy Amanti (eds.). 2004. *Theorizing Practices: Funds of Knowledge in Households and Classrooms.* Cresskill, NJ: Hampton.

Gould, Stephen J. 1991. *The Mismeasure of Man.* New York: W. W. Norton.

Gouldner, Alvin W. 1970. *The Coming Crisis of Western Sociology*. New York: Basic.

Green, Victor H. (1955) 1964. *The Negro Motorist Green Book—An International Travel Guide*. Pamphlet. Washington, DC: Smithsonian Institution.

Grodsky, Eric, and Michal Kurlaender. 2010. "The Demography of Higher Education in the Wake of Affirmative Action." Pp. 33–58 in Eric Grodsky and Michal Kurlaender (eds.), *Equal Opportunity in Higher Education*. Cambridge, MA: Harvard Education Press.

Grubb, Norman, and Laura Goe. 2002. *The Unending Search for Equity: California Policy, the "New" School Finance, and the Williams Case*. www.decentschools.org.

Guggenheim, Davis. 2010. *Waiting for Superman*. Paramount Vantage (film).

Gumperz, John J. 1982. *Discourse Strategies*. Cambridge: Cambridge University Press.

Gusfield, Joseph R. 1966. *Contested Meanings: The Construction of Alcohol Problems*. Madison: University of Wisconsin Press.

———. 1981. *The Culture of Public Problems: Drinking, Driving, and the Symbolic Order*. Chicago: University of Chicago Press.

Gutiérrez, Kris D., Patricia O. Baquedano-López, and Carlos Tejada. 1999. "Rethinking Diversity: Hybridity and Hybrid Language Practices in the Third Space." *Mind, Culture, and Activity* 6 (4): 286–303.

Gutiérrez, Kris D., Betsy Rymes, and Joanne Larson. 1995. "Script, Counterscript, and Underlife in the Classroom: James Brown vs. Brown vs. Board of Education." *Harvard Educational Review* 65 (3): 445–471.

Hall, Peter M. 1995. "The Consequences of Qualitative Analysis for Sociological Theory: Beyond the Microlevel." *Sociological Quarterly* 36 (2): 397–423.

———. 1997. "Meta-power, Social Organization, and the Shaping of Social Action." *Symbolic Interaction* 20 (4): 397–418.

Hall, Peter M., and Patrick J. W. McGinty. 1997. "Policy as the Transformation of Intentions: Producing Programs from Statutes." *Sociological Quarterly* 38 (3): 439–467.

Haney, Walter. 2000. "The Myth of the Texas Miracle in Education." *Education Policy Analysis Archives*. http://epaa.asu.edu/epaa/v8n4.

Hanushek, Eric A., and Margaret E. Raymond. 2004. "Does School Accountability Lead to Improved Student Performance?" Working Paper 10591. National Bureau of Economic Research.

Hargreaves, Andy, and Michael Fullan. 1998. *What's Worth Fighting for Out There?* New York: Teachers College Press.

Hart, Gary, and Sharon Burr. 1996. "The Story of California's Charter School Legislation." *Phi Delta Kappan* 78: 37–40.

Harvey, William B. 2002. *Minorities in Higher Education*. Washington, DC: American Council on Education.

Hassel, Bryan C., and Godard M. Terrell. 2006. *Charter School Achievement: What We Know*. Washington, DC: National Alliance for Public Charter Schools.

Hattie, John. 2009. *Visible Learning: A Synthesis of Over 800 Meta-analyses Relating to Achievement*. New York: Routledge.

Haycock, Kati. 2006. *Promise Abandoned*. Washington, DC: Education Trust.

Haycock, Kati, and Susan Navarro. 1997. *The Achievement Gap in American Education*. Washington, DC: Education Trust.

Heath, Shirley Brice. 1983. *Ways with Words*. New York: Cambridge University Press.

Herrnstein, Richard J., and Charles Murray. 1994. *The Bell Curve: Intelligence and Class Structure in American Life*. New York: Free Press.

Hinchey, Patricia H. 2010. *Getting Teacher Assessment Right: What Policymakers Can Learn from Research*. Boulder, CO: National Education Policy Center.

Holland, Dorothy, and Margaret Eisenhart. 1990. *Educated in Romance*. Albany: SUNY Press.

Holquist, Michael. 1984. "The Politics of Representation." *Quarterly Newsletter of the Laboratory of Comparative Human Cognition* 5: 2–9.

Horvat, Erin McNamera, and Cathy O'Conner. 2006. *Beyond Acting White: Reframing the Debate on Black Student Achievement*. Lanham, MD: Rowman and Littlefield.

Horvat, Erin McNamera, and James Earl Davis. 2010. "Schools as Sites for Transformation: Exploring the Contribution of Habitus." *Youth and Society* 20 (10): 1–29.

Hubbard, Lea, and Rucheeta Kulkarni. 2009. "Charter Schools: Learning from the Past, Planning for the Future." *Journal of Educational Change* 10 (2–3): 173–189.

Hubbard, Lea, Hugh Mehan, and Mary Kay Stein. 2006. *Reform as Learning: School Reform, Organizational Culture, and Community Politics in San Diego*. New York: Routledge Falmer.

Hurtado, Sylvia. 1994. "The Institutional Climate for Talented Latino Students." *Research in Higher Education* 35 (1): 21–41.

Hutchins, Edwin. 1995. *Cognition in the Wild*. Cambridge, MA: MIT Press.

Hymes, Dell H. (ed.). 1972. *Reinventing Anthropology*. New York: Pantheon.

Jablonka, Eva, and Marion J. Lamb. 2005. *Evolution in Four Dimensions*. Cambridge, MA: MIT Press.

Jacob, Brian A., and Stephen D. Levitt. 2003. "Rotten Apples: An Investigation of the Prevalence and Predictors of Teacher Cheating." NBER Working Paper No. w9413. Cambridge, MA: National Bureau of Economic Research.

Jacob-Almeida, Raquel. 2012. "A Boy Crisis? The Politics of Representing Boys as Academically Disadvantaged." Unpublished PhD dissertation. La Jolla: UC San Diego.

Jacobs, Jane. 1961. *The Death and Life of Great American Cities*. New York: Random House.

Jencks, Christopher S., Michael Smith, Henry Acland, et al. 1972. *Inequality: A Reassessment of the Effect of Family and Schooling in America*. New York: Basic.

Jencks, Christopher S., Susan Bartlett, Mary Corcoran, et al. 1978. *Who Gets Ahead? The Determinants of Economic Success in America*. New York: Basic.

Jencks, Christopher S., and Meredith Phillips (eds.). 1998. *The Black-White Test Score Gap*. Washington, DC: Brookings Institution.

Jensen, Arthur. 1969. "How Much Can We Boost IQ and Scholastic Achievement?" *Harvard Educational Review* 39 (1): 1–123.

Jones, Makeba, and Susan Yonezawa. 2008. "Student Inquiry in Racially Mixed Classrooms." Pp. 212–216 in Mica Pollock (ed.), *Everyday Antiracism: Concrete Ways to Successfully Navigate the Relevance of Race in School*. New York: New Press.

———. 2008/2009. "Student-Driven Research." *Educational Leadership* 66 (4): 65–69.

Jones, Makeba, Susan Yonezawa, Elizabeth Ballesteros, and Hugh Mehan. 2002. "Shaping Pathways to Higher Education." *Educational Researcher* 3: 3–17.

Kadumu, Walter. 1997. Testimony before the UCSD Outreach Task Force. July 23.

Karabel, Jerome. 2005. *The Chosen: The Hidden History of Admission and Exclusion at Harvard, Yale, and Princeton*. Boston: Houghton Mifflin.

Karabel, Jerome, and A. H. Halsey (eds.). 1977. *Power and Ideology in Education*. Oxford: Oxford University Press.

Kenda, Allison. 2008. Interview with Gordon C. Chang. November 13.

Kohn, Alfie. 1998. "Only for My Kid: How Privileged Parents Undermine School Reform." *Phi Delta Kappan* (April): 569–577.

———. 2002. *Education Inc.: Turning Learning into a Business*. Portsmouth, NH: Heinemann.

Kovacic, Kelly. 2011. Interview with Hugh Mehan. March 10.

Lacey, Marc. 2011. "Citing 'Brainwashing,' Arizona Declares a Latino Class Illegal." *New York Times*. January 8: A1, A12.

Ladson-Billings, Gloria, and William F. Tate. 1995. "Towards a Critical Race Theory of Education." *Teachers College Record* 97: 47–68.

Lake, Robin J., and Paul T. Hill. 2005. *Hopes, Fears, and Reality: A Balanced Look at American Charter Schools in 2005*. Seattle: Center on Reinventing Public Education.

Lakoff, George. 2004. *Don't Think of an Elephant: Know Your Values and Frame the Debate*. White River Junction, VT: Chelsea Green.

Lareau, Annette. 1989. *Home Advantage: Social Class and Parental Intervention in Elementary Education*. London: Falmer.

———. 2003. *Unequal Childhoods: Class, Race, and Family Life*. Berkeley: UC Press.

Lareau, Annette, and Erin McNamera Horvat. 1999. "Moments of Inclusion, Class, Cultural Capital in Family-School Relationships." *Sociology of Education* 72: 37–53.

Lareau, Annette, and Dalton Conley (eds.). 2008. *Social Class: How Does It Work?* New York: Russell Sage Foundation.

Latour, Bruno, and Steve Woolgar. 1979. *Laboratory Life: The Social Construction of Scientific Facts*. Beverly Hills, CA: Sage.

Lee, Carol D. 2001. "Is October Brown Chinese: A Cultural Modeling Activity System for Underachieving Students." *American Educational Research Journal* 38 (1): 97–142.

Lee, Sue. 2009. "Saturday Academy: An Intervention for At-Risk and English Language Learners." Unpublished Master of Arts paper. Providence, RI: Brown University.

Levinson, Bradley A. U., and Margaret Sutton. 2001. *Policy as Practice: A Sociocultural Approach to the Study of Educational Policy*. Westport, CT: Ablex.

Levinson, Bradley A. U., Douglas E. Foley, and Dorothy C. Holland (eds.). 1996. *The Cultural Production of the Educated Person: Critical Ethnographies of Schooling and Local Practice*. Albany: SUNY Press.

Lewis, Catherine C. 2002. *Lesson Study: A Handbook of Teacher-Led Instructional Improvement*. Philadelphia: Research for Better Schools.

Linn, Robert L. 2000. "Assessments and Accountability." *Educational Researcher* 29 (2): 4–15.

Lipsitz, George. 1998. *The Possessive Investment in Whiteness*. Philadelphia: Temple University Press.

Lipsky, Michael. 1982. *Street Level Bureaucracy: The Dilemmas of the Individual in Public Services*. New York: Russell Sage Foundation.

Lucas, Samuel R. 1999. *Tracking Inequality: Stratification and Mobility in American High Schools*. New York: Teachers' College Press.

———. 2001. "Effectively Maintained Inequality." *American Journal of Sociology* 106 (6): 1642–1690.

Lynch, Maie, and Jennifer Engle. 2010a. "Big Gaps Small Gaps: Some Colleges and Universities Do Better than Others in Graduating African American Students." Washington, DC: Education Trust.

———. 2010b. "Big Gaps Small Gaps: Some Colleges and Universities Do Better than Others in Graduating Hispanic Students." Washington, DC: Education Trust.

Lytle, Cecil. 2007. *The Burden of Excellence*. La Jolla, CA: RELS.

MacLeod, Jay. 1995. *Ain't No Makin' It: Leveled Aspirations in a Low-Income Neighborhood*, 2nd ed. Boulder, CO: Westview.

Magee, Maureen. 2006. "Charter School Fight at District's Door." *San Diego Union Tribune.* March 15.

———. 2009. "Schools Battle Over Shared Space." *San Diego Union Tribune.* July 4. Available at www3.signonsandiego.com/stories/2009/jul04.

Mahar, Dora. 2005. "Interview with Shannon Bradley." Subsequently shown on UCSD Impact show "Charter Schools," on UCSD TV.

Malen, Betty, and Martin Knapp. 1997. "Rethinking the Multiple Perspectives Approach to Education Policy Analysis: Implications for Policy-Practice Connections." *Journal of Educational Policy* 12 (5): 419–445.

Malinowski, Branislow. 1922. *Argonauts of the Western Pacific: An Account of Native Enterprise and Adventure in the Archipelagoes of Melanesian New Guinea.* London: G. Routledge and Sons.

March, James G. 1988. *Decisions and Organizations.* Oxford: Blackwell.

Marx, Karl. (1852) 1964. *The 18th Brumaire of Louis Bonaparte.* New York: International Publishers.

———. (1867) 1976. *Capital.* London: Penguin.

Mathews, Jay. 2009. *Work Hard, Be Nice: How Two Inspired Teachers Created the Most Promising Schools in America.* Chapel Hill, NC: Algonquin.

McCarty, Teresa L., Regina Hadley Lynch, Stephen Wallace, et al. 1991. "Classroom Inquiry and Navajo Learning Styles: A Call for Reassessment." *Anthropology and Education Quarterly* 22: 42–59.

McClure, Larry. 2011. *Preliminary Analysis of Proposal to Change Criteria for the UCSD Transfer Admissions Guarantee Program (TAG).* UCSD: CREATE. http://create.ucsd.edu.

McClure, Larry, Raquel Jacob-Almeida, Betsy Strick, et al. 2005. *The Preuss School UCSD: School Characteristics and Students' Achievement.* La Jolla: UCSD CREATE. http://create.ucsd.edu/Research_Evaluation/Preuss Report December2005.pdf.

McClure, Larry, and J. César Morales. 2004. *The Preuss School at UCSD: School Characteristics and Students Achievement.* UCSD: CREATE.

McDonough, Patricia. 1997. *Choosing Colleges: How Social Class and Schools Structure Opportunity.* Albany: SUNY Press.

McEntree, Jennifer. 2007. "Cohn Emerges from Predecessor's Shadow." *Voice of San Diego.* Available at www.voiceofsandiego.org/articles/2007/03/20/news/01cohn032007.txt.

McLaren, Peter. 1997. *Revolutionary Multiculturalism: Pedagogies of Dissent for the New Millennium.* Boulder, CO: Westview.

McLaughlin, Milbrae, and Joan E. Talbert. 1993. *Contexts that Matter for Teaching and Learning.* Stanford, CA: Stanford University Center for Research on the Context of Secondary School Teaching.

McNeil, Linda. 1998. *Contradictions of Reform.* New York: Routledge.

Mead, George Herbert. 1954. *The Philosophy of the Present.* Chicago: Open Court.

Medina, Jennifer. 2010. "Students' Passing Rates Plummet in New York." *New York Times.* July 29: A21.

Mediratta, Kavitha, Seema Shaw, Sara McAlister, et al. 2008. *Organized Communities, Stronger Schools: A Preview of Research Findings.* Providence, RI: Annenberg Institute of School Reform at Brown University.

Mehan, Hugh. 1978. "Structuring School Structure." *Harvard Education Review* 48 (1): 32–64.

———. 1979. *Learning Lessons.* Cambridge, MA: Harvard University Press.

———. 1992. "Understanding Inequality in Schools: The Contribution of Interpretive Studies." *Sociology of Education* 65 (1): 1–20.

———. 1997. "The Discourse of the Immigration Debate: A Case Study in the Politics of Representation." *Discourse and Society* 8 (2): 249–270.

———. 2009. "A Sociological Perspective on Opportunity to Learn and Assessment." Pp. 42–75 in Pamela A. Moss, Diana C. Pullin, James Paul Gee, Edward Haertel, and Lauren Jones Young (eds.), *Assessment, Equity, and Opportunity to Learn.* New York: Cambridge University Press.

Mehan, Hugh, and Gordon Chang. 2010. "Is It Wrong for Us to Want Good Things? The Origins of Gompers Charter Middle School." *Journal of Educational Change* 12: 47–70.

Mehan, Hugh, and Houston Wood. 1975. *The Reality of Ethnomethodology.* New York: Wiley Interscience.

Mehan, Hugh, Julian R. Betts, and Peter Gourevitch. 2008. *Grade Discrepancies at the Preuss School: A Case Study in the Politics of Representation.* www.create.ucsd.edu.

Mehan, Hugh, Lea Hubbard, and Mary Kay Stein. 2005. "When Reforms Travel: The Sequel." *Journal of Educational Change* 5: 1–33.

Mehan, Hugh, Nadia Khalil, and Jose César Morales. 2010. "Going the Distance: The Challenges of Traversing Cultural and Geographic Space Between Home and School." Pp. 23–48 in Guadalupe López-Bonilla and Karen Englander (eds.), *Discourses and Identities in Contexts of Educational Change.* New York: Peter Lang.

Mehan, Hugh, Jane Mercer, and Robert Rueda. 2002. "Special Education." *The Encyclopedia of Education and Sociology.* New York: Garland.

Mehan, Hugh, Charles E. Nathanson, and James M. Skelly. 1990. "Nuclear Discourse in the 1980s: The Unraveling Conventions of the Cold War." *Discourse and Society* 1 (2): 133–165.

Mehan, Hugh, Alma Hertweck, J. Lee Meihls, et al. 1986. *Handicapping the Handicapped.* Stanford, CA: Stanford University Press.

Mehan Hugh, Lea Hubbard, Angela Lintz, et al. 1996. *Constructing School Success: The Consequences of Untracking Low Achieving Students.* Cambridge: Cambridge University Press.

Mehan, Hugh, Gail Kauffman, Cecil Lytle, et al. 2010. "Using Educational Field Stations to Increase Diversity and Access in Higher Education." Pp. 173–194 in Eric Grodsky and Michal Kurlaender (eds.), *Equal Opportunity in Higher Education: The Past and Future of Proposition 209.* Cambridge, MA: Harvard Education Press.

Meier, Deborah. 1995. *The Power of Their Ideas: Lessons for America from a Small School in Harlem.* Boston: Beacon.

Mesdaq, Najib. 2008. Interview with Gordon C. Chang. November 10.

Michels, Robert. 1915. *Political Parties: A Sociological Study of the Oligarchical Tendencies of Modern Democracy.* Tr. Eden Paul and Ceder Paul. New York: Free Press.

Mills, C. Wright. 1940. "Situated Action and the Vocabulary of Motives." *American Sociological Review* 5: 904–913.

———. 1959. *The Sociological Imagination.* New York: Oxford University Press.

Miron, Gary, and Christopher Nelson. 2002. *What's Public about Charter Schools?: Lessons Learned about Choice and Accountability.* Thousand Oaks, CA: Corwin.

Miron, Gary, Jessica L. Urschel, William J. Mathis, et al. 2010. *Schools without Diversity: Education Management Organizations, Charter Schools, and the Demographic Stratification of the American School System.* Boulder, CO: Education and the Public Interest Center and Education Policy Research Unit. http://epicpolicy.org/publication/schools-without-diversity.

Mussey, Season S. 2008. "Navigating the Transition to College: First-Generation Undergraduates Negotiate Identities and Search for Success in STEM and Non-STEM Fields." Unpublished EdD dissertation. La Jolla: UCSD.

NAEP (National Assessment of Educational Progress). 2005. *The Nation's Report Card. America's Charter Schools: Results from the NAEP 2003 Pilot Study.* Washington, DC: NCES 2005-456.

National Academy of Sciences. 1999. *High Stakes: Testing for Tracking, Promotion, and Graduation.* Washington, DC: National Academy of Sciences.

NCEE (National Commission on Excellence in Education). 1983. *A Nation at Risk: The Imperative for Educational Reform.* Washington, DC: NCEE.

NCES (National Center for Educational Statistics). 2001. *Digest of Educational Statistics 2001,* table 143. Washington, DC: NCES.

NCLB. 2001. No Child Left Behind Act of 2001. PL 107–110. 115 Stat. 1425.

Nelson, F. Howard, Bella Rosenberg, and Nancy Van Meter. 2004. *Charter School Achievement on the 2003 National Assessment of Educational Progress.* Washington, DC: American Federation of Teachers.

Newman, Denis, Peg Griffin, and Michael Cole. 1989. *The Construction Zone.* New York: Cambridge University Press.

Nichols, Sharon L., and David C. Berliner. 2006. *Collateral Damage: How High-Stakes Testing Corrupts America's Schools.* Cambridge, MA: Harvard Education Press.

Noddings, Nell. 1984. *Caring: A Feminine Approach to Ethics and Moral Education.* Berkeley: University of California Press.

Nusbaum, Martha 2010. *Not for Profit: Why Democracy Needs the Humanities.* Princeton, NJ: Princeton University Press.

Oakes, Jeannie. 1992. "Can Tracking Research Inform Practice? Technical, Normative, and Political Considerations." *Educational Researcher* 21 (4): 12–21.

———. 2003. *Critical Conditions for Excellence and Equity.* UCLA: UC ACCORD.

———. 2005. *Keeping Track: How Schools Structure Inequality,* 2nd ed. New Haven, CT: Yale University Press.

Oakes, Jeannie, Adam Gamoran, and Reba N. Page. 1992. "Curriculum Differentiation: Opportunities, Outcomes, and Meanings." Pp. 570–608 in Phillip Jackson (ed.), *Handbook of Research on Curriculum.* New York: Macmillan.

Oakes, Jeannie, John Rogers, Patricia McDonough, et al. 2000. *Remedying Unequal Opportunities for Successful Participation in Advanced Placement Courses in California High Schools. A Proposed Action Plan Submitted to the ACLU.* UCLA: UC ACCORD.

Oakes, Jeannie, Karen Hunter Quartz, Steven Ryan, et al. 1999. *Becoming Good American Schools: The Struggle for Civic Virtue in Educational Reform.* San Francisco: Jossey-Bass.

Oakes, Jeannie, Amy Stuart Wells, Susan Yonezawa, et al. 1997. "Detracking: The Social Construction of Ability, Cultural Politics, and Resistance to Reform." *Teachers College Record* 98 (3): 482–510.

Obama, Barack H. 2008. "Harlem Children's Zone Speech." YouTube, January 11, 2011.

Ogbu, John U. 1974. *The Next Generation: An Ethnography of Education in an Urban Neighborhood.* New York: Academic Press.

———. 1987. "Variability in Minority School Performance: A Problem in Search of an Explanation." *Anthropology and Education Quarterly* 18: 312–334.

———. 2003. "Black American Students in an Affluent Suburb: A Study of Academic Disengagement." Manwah, NJ: Erlbaum.

Omi, Michael, and Howard Winant. 1994. *Racial Formation in the United States*. New York: Routledge.

Ong-Dean, Colin. 2009. *Distinguishing Disability: Parents, Privilege, and Special Education*. Chicago: University of Chicago Press.

Orfield, Gary, and Edward Miller (eds.). 1998. *Chilling Admissions: The Affirmative Action Crisis and the Search for Alternatives*. Cambridge, MA: Harvard University Civil Rights Project.

Parsons, Talcott. 1959. "The School Classroom as a Social System." *Harvard Educational Review* 29: 297–318.

Payne, Charles, and Tim Knowles. 2009. "Promise and Peril: Charter Schools, Urban School Reform, and the Obama Administration." *Harvard Educational Review* 79 (2): 227–239.

Pedulla, Joseph, and George F. Madaus. 2004. *Perceived Effects of State-Mandated Testing Programs on Teaching and Learning: Findings from a National Survey of Teachers*. Chestnut Hill, MA: Center for the Study of Testing, Evaluation, and Educational Policy, Boston College.

Peshkin, Alan. 1991. *The Color of Strangers, the Color of Friends*. Chicago: University of Chicago Press.

Petersons College Profiles. 2009. www.petersons.com/collegeprofiles.

Pew Research Center. 2009. "College Enrollment Hits All-Time High." Washington, DC: Pew Research Center.

Philips, Susan U. 1982. *The Invisible Culture: Communication in Classroom and Community on the Warm Springs Reservation*. New York: Longman.

Pister, Karl. 2000. Retirement speech, UCOP Outreach Leaders Retreat. Rancho Santa Fe, CA. June 15.

Pogash, Carol. 2010. "Charter Extension Denied to Low-Scoring Stanford School." http://nytimes.com/2010/04/16/education/16sfcharter.html?emc=eta1&pagewanted=print.

Pollner, Melvin. 1987. *Mundane Reason: Reality in Everyday and Sociological Discourse*. New York: Cambridge University Press.

Pollock, Mica. 2005. *ColorMute*. Princeton, NJ: Princeton University Press.

Powers, Jeanne M. 2004. "High-Stakes Accountability and Equity: Using Evidence from California's Public Schools Accountability Act to Address the Issues in *Williams v. State of California*." *American Educational Research Journal* 41 (4): 763–796.

Pressman, Jeffrey L., and Aaron Wildavsky. 1973. *Implementation*. Berkeley: University of California Press.

Price, Hugh B. 2002. *Achievement Matters*. New York: Kensington.

Ravitch, Diane. 2010a. *The Death and Life of the Great American School System*. New York: Basic.

———. 2010b. "The Myth of Charter Schools." *New York Review of Books* 62 (17): 22–24.

Reese, Leslie, Steven Balzano, Ronald Gallimore, et al. 1995. "The Concept of *Educación*: Latino Family Values and American Schooling." *International Journal of Educational Research* 23 (1): 57–81.

Regents of the University of California v. Bakke, 438 U. S. 265 1978.

Renzulli, Linda A., and Vincent J. Roscigno. 2007. "Charter Schools and the Public Good." *Contexts* 6 (1): 31–66.

Richardson, Sharletta. 2005. Remarks before the Board of Trustees, San Diego Unified School District. March 1.

Riveroll, Vincent. 2008. Remarks made to SDUSD Charter Renewal Team. April 29.

Rogoff, Barbara. 2003. *The Cultural Nature of Human Development*. New York: Oxford University Press.

Rosebery, Ann S., Beth Warren, and Faith R. Conant. 1992. *Appropriating Scientific Discourse: Findings from Language Minority Classrooms.* Cambridge, MA: Technical Educational Research Center.

Rosen, Lisa. 2001. "Myth Making and Moral Order in a Debate on Mathematics Education Policy." Pp. 295–316 in Margaret Sutton and Bradley A. U. Levinson (eds.), *Policy as Practice: Toward a Comparative Sociocultural Analysis of Educational Policy.* Westport, CT: Ablex.

Rosen, Lisa, and Hugh Mehan. 2003. "Reconstructing Equality on New Political Ground: The Politics of Representation in the Charter School Debate at UCSD." *American Educational Research Journal* 40 (3): 655–682.

Rosenbaum, Michael D., et al. 2000a. First Amended Complaint. Papers filed with the Superior Court of the State of California. *Williams v. California* Web site, www.decentschools.org.

———. 2000b. Plaintiffs' Liability Disclosure Statement. Papers filed with the Superior Court of the State of California. *Williams v. California* Web site, www.decentschools.org.

Rosenstock, Larry. 2009. "Project-Based Learning at High Tech High." http://newlearninginstitute.org/21stcenturyeducation/student-centered-learning/project-based-learning-at-high-tech-high.html.

Rothman, David. 1980. *Conscience and Convenience.* Boston: Little Brown.

Rothstein, Richard. 2004. *Class and Schools: Using Social, Economic, and Educational Reform to Close the Black-White Achievement Gap.* New York: Economic Policy Institute.

Rubin, Beth (ed.). 2006. "Detracking and Heterogeneous Grouping." *Theory into Practice* 45 (1).

Rumbaut, Ruben, and Kenji Ima. 1988. *The Adaptation of Southeast Asian Refugee Youth: A Comparative Study.* San Diego: San Diego State University.

Rushton, J. Philippe. 1995. *Race, Evolution, and Behavior.* New Brunswick, NJ: Transaction.

Sadler, Philip M., Gerhard Sonnert, Robert H. Tai, et al. 2010. *AP: A Critical Examination of the Advanced Placement Program.* Cambridge, MA: Harvard Education Press.

Sanchez, Lionel. 2007. "Helix High Students Mistakenly Given As to 36 Students." *San Diego Union Tribune.* December 15.

Sanday, Peggy R. 1976. *Anthropology and the Public Interest: Fieldwork and Theory.* New York: Academic Press.

San Diego Unified School District (SDUSD). 2006a. Consideration of Requests for Facilities from Charter Schools for the 2006–2007 School Year. SDUSD: District Staff Report, submitted to the Board of Education. February 28.

———. 2006b. Facility Requirements for 2006–2007 School Year for Charter Schools Recommended for Facilities Allocation. Attachment B to SDUSD Board Agenda, March 28.

———. 2007. Deliberation and Action on Final Offers in Response to Requests for Allocation of Facilities for Charter Schools under Proposition 39 (Education Code Section 47614) for the 2007/08 School Year. SDUSD: Office of the Deputy Superintendent. Attachment to SDUSD Board Minutes, March 27.

———. 2008. MAP Proposal, Millennial Tech Middle School. April.

San Diego Union Tribune. 2005. "Union in Control, City School Board Takes Distressing Turn." February 13.

———. 2006. Editorial. March 5.

Sarason, Seymour. 1972. *The Creation of Settings and the Future of Societies.* San Francisco: Jossey-Bass.

———. 1997. "Revising the Creation of Settings." *Mind, Culture, and Activity* 4 (3): 175–182.

Schensul, Jean J. 2010. "Engaged Universities, Community-Based Research Organizations, and Third-Sector Science in a Global System." *Human Organization* 69 (4): 307–320.

Schultheis, Franz. 2010. "Passer, Classer, Placer: l'Ecole au Centre de la Sociologie Bourdieusienne." Colloque Bourdieu. Friborg Suisse. 9 Septembre.

Schutz, Alfred. 1962. *Collected Papers, Volume 1: The Problem of Social Order*. The Hague: Nijhoff.

Schwarzenegger, Arnold. 2009. "Governor's Open Letter to All State Employees Regarding Proposed Spending Cuts." www.dpa.ca.gov/news/news/2008/20081106-01.htm.

Sejnowski, Terrence, Aaron V. Cicourel, Gary Cottrell, et al. 2008. "Why UCSD Should Correct the Deeply Flawed Audit of The Preuss School." Public letter, January 8. *San Diego Union Tribune.* January 15.

Selznick, Phillip. 1949. *TVA and the Grassroots.* Berkeley: University of California Press.

Senge, Peter. 1990. *The Fifth Discipline.* New York: Doubleday.

Sewell, William H. 1992. "A Theory of Structure: Duality, Agency, and Transformation." *American Journal of Sociology* 98 (1): 1–29.

Shapiro, Michael. 1988. *The Politics of Representation.* Madison: University of Wisconsin Press.

Shweder, Richard A. 2006. *Why Do Men Barbeque? Recipes for Cultural Psychology.* Cambridge, MA: Harvard University Press.

Sizer, Theodore R. 1984. *Horace's Compromise: The Dilemma of the American High School.* New York: Houghton Mifflin.

———. 1992. *Horace's School: Redesigning the American High School.* New York: Houghton Mifflin.

Sjöström, Stefan. 1997. *Party or Patient? Discursive Practices Relating to Coercion in Psychiatric and Legal Settings.* Umea: Borea Bokförlag.

Smith, Louis, and Paul Keith. 1971. *Anatomy of an Educational Innovation.* New York: John Wiley.

Solórzano, Daniel. 1998. "Critical Race Theory, Racial and Gender Microaggressions, and the Experiences of Chicana and Chicano Scholars." *International Journal of Qualitative Studies in Education* 11 (1): 121–136.

Soodai, Maryam. 2005. Comments before the SDUSD School Board. March 1.

Spearman, Charles. 1927. *The Abilities of Man: Their Nature and Measurement.* New York: Macmillan.

Spector, Malcolm, and John I. Kitsuse. 1987. *Constructing Social Problems.* Hawthorne, NY: Aldine de Gruyter.

Stanton-Salazar, Ricardo. 2000. *Manufacturing Hope and Despair: The School and Kin Support Networks of US-Mexican Youth.* New York: Teachers College Press.

Stanton-Salazar, Ricardo, Olga Vásquez, and Hugh Mehan. 2000. "Engineering Success through Institutional Support." Pp. 213–247 in Sheila Gregory (ed.), *Academic Achievement of Minority Students' Perspectives, Practices, and Prescriptions.* Lanham, MD: University Press of America.

Steele, Claude M. 1997. "A Threat in the Air: How Stereotypes Shape the Intellectual Identities and Performance of Women and African-Americans." *American Psychologist* 52: 613–629.

Steppe, Cecil. 2005. Remarks before the Board of Trustees, San Diego Unified School District. March 1.

———. 2006. Letter to Sandra Robles. San Diego: GCMS.

Stevens, Mitchell. 2007. *Creating a Class: College Admissions and the Education of Elites.* Cambridge, MA: Harvard University Press.

Strick, Betsy. 2009. *College Enrollment and Persistence of Preuss and Comparison Students in the Classes of 2005 and 2006.* La Jolla: UCSD CREATE. http://create.ucsd.edu.

Stuit, David A., and Thomas M. Smith. 2009. "Teacher Turnover in Charter Schools." Paper presented at the 2009 Annual Meeting of the American Educational Research Association (AERA). San Diego, CA. April 12.

Suárez-Orozco, Carola, and Marcelo M. Suárez-Orozco. 1997. *Transformations: Immigration, Family Life, and Achievement Motivation among Latino Students.* Stanford, CA: Stanford University Press.

Sutton, Marsha. 2005. "Note to School Board: Take the Next Step—Give Riveroll Back to Gompers." *Voice of San Diego.* March 10. www.voiceofsandiego.org/education/.

———. 2006a. "Understanding Charter Schools—and Why We Should Care." www.sdranchcoastnews.com/sdrcn%20pages/m37.html. March 18.

———. 2006b. "District Assaults Charters with 'Kind Regards,' Part I." *Voice of San Diego.* March 6.

———. 2006c. "District Assaults Charters with 'Kind Regards,' Part II." *Voice of San Diego.* March 7.

———. 2009a. "Cheating Scandal Exposes District Problem." *San Diego News Network.* May 26. www.sdnn.com/Sandiego.

———. 2009b. "Gompers' Protest over District's Latest Scheme." www.sdnn.com/SanDiego/2009-06-29. July 3.

Tharp, Roland, and Ronald Gallimore. 1988. *Rousing Minds to Life.* New York: Cambridge University Press.

Thernstrom, Abigail, and Stephen Thernstrom. 2003. *No Excuses: Closing the Racial Achievement Gap.* New York: Simon and Schuster.

Therriault, Susan Bowles, Allison Gruner Gandhi, et al. 2010. *Out of the Debate and Into the Schools: Comparing Practices and Strategies in Traditional, Pilot, and Charters in the City of Boston.* Boston: Boston Foundation.

Thomas, William Isaac, and Dorothy Swain Thomas. 1928. *The Unadjusted Girl.* New York: Harpers.

Tough, Paul. 2008. *Whatever It Takes: Geoffrey Canada's Quest to Change Harlem and America.* New York: Houghton Mifflin.

Tucker, Mark S., and Judy B. Codding. 1998. *Standards for Our Schools.* San Francisco: Jossey-Bass.

Turner, Ralph H. 1960. "Sponsored and Contest Mobility and the School System." *American Sociological Review* 25: 855–867.

Tuttle, Christina Clark, Bing-ru Teh, Ira Nichols-Barrer, et al. 2010. *Student Characteristics and Achievement in 22 KIPP Middle Schools.* Washington, DC: Mathematica Policy Research.

Tyack, David B. 1974. *The One Best System: A History of American Urban Education.* Cambridge, MA: Harvard University Press.

Tyack, David B., and Larry Cuban. 1995. *Tinkering Toward Utopia: A Century of Public School Reform.* Cambridge, MA: Harvard University Press.

UC Regents. 2001. Resolution RE-28. www.ucop.edu/sas/adguides.html.

UCSD. 1997. Final Report of the Outreach Task Force. La Jolla: UCSD.

UCSD Admissions Committee. 2011. Minutes of February 2 meeting.

University of California Office of the President (UCOP). 2009. *Underrepresented Minorities as a Percentage of California Public High School Graduates and New Freshmen, System-wide, Fall 1989 to Fall 2009.* Oakland: University of California Institutional Research Department.

University of California Outreach Task Force. 1997. *New Directions for Outreach: A Report by the Outreach Task Force for the Board of Regents of the University of California.* July 19.

US Department of Education. 1997. *A Study of Charter Schools: First Year Report.* Washington, DC: Department of Education.

Valdez, Guadalupe. 1996. *Con Respeto: Bridging the Distances between Culturally Diverse Families and Schools.* New York: Teachers College Press.

Valenzuela, Angela. 1999. *Subtractive Schooling: US Mexican Youth and the Politics of Caring.* Albany: SUNY Press.

Valli, Linda. 1986. *Becoming Clerical Workers.* Boston: Routledge and Kegan Paul.

Varenne, Harve, and Raymond P. McDermott. 1998. *Successful Failure: The Schools America Builds.* Boulder, CO: Westview.

Voice of San Diego. 2008. "A Test for Schools." March 3. www.voiceofsandiego.org/hottopic/charters.

Weber, Max. 1958. *The Protestant Ethic and the Spirit of Capitalism.* New York: Free Press.

———. 1994. *Weber: Political Writings: Cambridge Texts in the History of Political Thought.* Cambridge: Cambridge University Press.

Weber, Shirley. 2005. Remarks before the Board of Trustees, San Diego Unified School District. March 1.

Weick, Karl E., and Karlene H. Roberts. 1993. "Collective Mind in Organizations: Heedful Interrelating on Flight Decks." *Administrative Science Quarterly* 38: 357–381.

Weis, Lois (ed.). 2008. *The Way Class Works.* New York: Routledge.

Wells, Amy S. 1998. "Beyond the Rhetoric of Charter School Reform: A Study of Ten California School Districts." Los Angeles: UCLA Charter School Study. www.geies.ucla/docs/charter.PDF.

Wells, Amy S. (ed.). 2002. *Where Charter School Policy Fails: The Problems of Accountability and Equity.* New York: Teachers College Press.

Wheelock, Anne. 1992. *Crossing the Tracks: How "Untracking" Can Save America's Schools.* New York: New Press.

White, Katie Weitz, and James Rosenbaum. 2008. "Inside the Black Box of Accountability." Pp. 97–116 in Alan R. Sadovnik, Jennifer O'Day, George W. Bohrstedt, et al. (eds.), *No Child Left Behind and the Reduction of the Achievement Gap: Sociological Perspectives on Federal Education Policy.* New York: Routledge.

Whitehurst, Grover J., and Michelle Croft. 2010. *The Harlem Children's Zone, Promise Neighborhoods, and the Broader, Bolder Approach to Education.* Washington, DC: Brown Center on Education Policy at Brookings.

Wilcox, Katherine. 1982. "Differential Socialization in the Classroom Implications for Educational Opportunity." Pp. 268–309 in George Spindler and Louise Spindler (eds.), *Doing the Ethnography of Schooling.* New York: Harcourt, Brace, World.

Williams, Joe, and Thomas Toch. 2006. *Extreme Makeover: Two Failing Schools Get New Starts as Charters.* Washington, DC: Education Sector.

Williams, Patricia. 2005. *The Alchemy of Race and Rights: Diary of a Law Professor.* Cambridge, MA: Harvard University Press.

Williamson, Tasha. 2008. Communication with Makeba Jones. July 15.

Willis, Paul. 1977. *Learning to Labor.* New York: Columbia University Press.

Winerip, William. 2010. "Equity of Test Is Debated as Children Compete for Gifted Kindergarten." *New York Times.* July 26: A16.

Wood, Houston. 1999. *Displacing Natives: The Rhetorical Production of Hawai'i.* Boulder, CO: Rowman and Littlefield.

Yang, K. Wayne. 2009. "For and Against the School-Education Dialectic in Social Justice." Pp. 455–464 in William Ayers, Therese Quinn, and David Stovall (eds.), *Handbook of Social Justice in Education.* New York: Routledge.

Yonezawa, Susan, Makeba Jones, and Hugh Mehan. 2001. "Partners for Preparation: Redistributing Social and Cultural Capital." Pp. 145–166 in William J. Tierney and Linda S. Hagedorn (eds.), *Increasing Access to College: Extending the Possibilities for All Students.* Albany: SUNY Press.

Yoso, Tara J. 2006. *Critical Race Counterstories among the Chicana/Chicano Pipeline.* New York: Routledge.

Young, Alford A. Jr. 2010. "New Life for an Old Concept: Frame Analysis and the Reinvigoration of Studies in Culture and Poverty." *Annals of the American Academy of Political and Social Science* 629: 53–74.

Zald, Mayer, and Patricia Denton. 1963. "From Evangelicism to General Service: The Transformation of the YMCA." *Administrative Science Quarterly* 8: 214–234.

Ziebarth, T., M. B. Celio, R. J. Lake, and L. Rainey. 2005. "The Charter Schools Landscape in 2005." In R. J. Lake and P. T. Hill (eds.), *Hopes, Fears, and Reality: A Balanced Look at American Charter Schools in 2005.* Seattle: Center on Reinventing Public Education.

Zimmer, Ron, Brian Gill, Kevin Booker, et al. 2009. *Charter Schools in Eight States: Effects on Achievement, Attainment, Integration, and Competition.* Santa Monica, CA: RAND.

Index

About the Author and Contributors

Hugh Mehan is Professor Emeritus of Sociology and founding director of The Center for Research on Educational Equity, Access, and Teaching Excellence (CREATE) at the University of California–San Diego. He is a member of the National Academy of Education, and is the author of six books. In 2008 he was presented with the Lifetime Achievement Award by the AERA.

Gordon Chang is Assistant Professor of Sociology at Western Illinois University. He was formerly Lecturer at UC Davis's Department of Sociology and Postdoctoral Researcher at UC San Diego's Center for Research on Educational Equity, Assessment, and Teaching Excellence. He has taught courses and done research in the areas of cultural sociology, political sociology, qualitative methods, and the sociology of education. His works on the discourse of war and peace and charter schools have appeared in *Journal of Consumer Culture, Pragmatics, Discourse and Society,* and *Journal of Educational Change.*

Makeba Jones is currently a Project Research Scientist at UC San Diego's Center for Research on Educational Equity, Assessment, and Teaching Excellence. She earned her PhD in Education from UCLA in 2000. Her interests include urban school reform, teacher-leadership, student voice, youth engagement, and the college pipeline for low-income youth. She has several publications on student voice, including "Student-Driven Research" (with Susan Yonezawa) that appeared in the 2008/2009 volume of *Educational Leadership.*

Season Mussey serves as an Assistant Professor at Texas A&M University Central Texas. She received her doctorate in education from the University of California–San Diego in 2009. Her interests include promoting social justice through research on urban education reform, critical race and gender studies, transitions from K–12 to higher education, and teacher preparation. Formerly, she taught biological science in grades 6–12 for eleven years, including a six-year tenure at The Preuss School UCSD.